T0368758

THE GREAT HURRICANE OF 1780

The Story of the Greatest and Deadliest Hurricane of the Caribbean and the Americas

WAYNE NEELY

iUniverse, Inc.
Bloomington

The Great Hurricane of 1780
The Story of the Greatest and Deadliest Hurricane
of the Caribbean and the Americas

iUniverse books may be ordered through booksellers or by contacting:

iUniverse
1663 Liberty Drive
Bloomington, IN 47403
www.iuniverse.com
1-800-Authors (1-800-288-4677)

ISBN: 978-1-4759-4926-1 (sc)
ISBN: 978-1-4759-4927-8 (e)
ISBN: 978-1-4759-4928-5 (dj)

Printed in the United States of America

iUniverse rev. date: 09/16/2012

DEDICATION

This book is dedicated first and foremost to all of the victims of *The Great Hurricane of 1780.'*

To Joshua Taylor, Wesley Rolle and Pleasant McCreary- Thanks for being such great true friends of mine through the good and bad times of my life-I will never forget what each of you did for me and I will always value and cherish each of your friendships.

To the great teachers(Margaret Jeffers, Kathy-Ann Caesar, Horace and Selvin Burton, Nigel Atherly and others) at the Caribbean Meteorological and Hydrology Institute in Barbados who provided me with the basic and in-depth knowledge on the subject of Meteorology which allowed me to write these books on hurricanes.

Booker T. Washington once said, "Success is to be measured not so much by the position that one has reached in life as by the obstacles which he has overcome while trying to succeed."

Nelson Mandela once said, "Always be a part of something bigger than yourself!"

Mahatma Gandhi once said "You must be the change you want to see in the world!" and "My imperfections and failures are as much a blessing from God as my successes and my talents and I lay them both at His feet."

Contents

FOREWORD

Historic records of hurricanes in the Atlantic Basin are fairly well-documented back to about 1850, at least crudely in some tracking books. There has been a great deal of documentation on various damaging hurricanes prior to 1850; interestingly, many intense hurricanes of the past have literally changed the course of history for many locations in the U.S. and other countries impacted by Atlantic, Caribbean, and Gulf of Mexico hurricanes. One of the greatest disasters on record came with the Great Hurricane of 1780, *"Hurricane San Calixto II."* Wayne Neely, author of numerous books on hurricanes, once again hits the mark by providing an outstanding account of this devastating hurricane that to this today remains the deadliest of all in any Atlantic Basin record book. The Great Hurricane of 1780 changed the course of the American Revolution. It ripped through the Caribbean Islands with deadly force at a time when Caribbean island residents and mariners had little understanding of what a hurricane really was, not to mention they had little forewarning and no routine forecasts for these deadly events at that time.

Mr. Neely digs into history unfolding in the late 18th century and provides us with an excellent historical account of the far-reaching impacts from the Great Hurricane of 1780. From the weakness of very slow moving ships to the poorly build structures many people lived in at that time, Mr. Neely elaborates on the sheer devastation of this massive storm disaster. I was drawn into imagining how things could have been very different then if they had the ability to see, track, and forecast hurricanes like we do today. Perhaps the world would be a very different place! Wayne Neely paints a vivid picture of the crude understanding about hurricanes that mariners and residents had back then and how vulnerable entire ship fleets were to the ravages of a hurricane so great that once trapped within its emanating tentacles of huge waves, they were stopped helpless before nature's fury of deadly winds and water surrounding its eye. You cannot afford to miss this glimpse back in time and, like me, imagine how different the outcome of American history would have been if today's weather monitoring and forecasting technology were available at that time. You must read this book!

Dr. Steve Lyons
Hurricane and Wave Expert

Dr. Steve Lyons is one of the world's foremost experts on Hurricanes, Tropical and Marine weather. He obtained his B.S., M.S. and Ph.D. in Meteorology from the University of Hawaii in 1981. Steve's expertise is in Tropical and Marine Meteorology. He has participated in more than 50 national and international conferences and provided World Meteorological Organization training courses in marine meteorology, tropical meteorology and ocean wave forecasting. Each spring Steve is a guest speaker at many hurricane preparedness conferences from Texas to New York and even the Bahamas. Steve is a fellow of the American Meteorological Society; he has published more than 20 papers in scientific journals, and written more than 40 technical reports and articles for the National Weather Service and for the Navy. Prior to joining The Weather Channel in April 1998, Steve managed the Tropical Analysis and Forecast Branch of the Tropical Prediction Center, National Hurricane Center. In 2010 he left The Weather Channel and is now the Meteorologist in Charge at the San Angelo, Texas, National Weather Service Office.

PREFACE

Hurricanes are one of nature's most awesome phenomena and occur in many tropical and subtropical areas across the world every year. From June 1st through November 30th each year, the coastal areas of the North Atlantic come under threat from the ferocious winds and floodwaters of the hurricanes that form in the Atlantic Ocean basin. The majority of these storms happen in the summer and early fall in tropical and subtropical areas where the sea surface temperatures are above 26.5°C and the dynamics of the atmosphere are conducive to the formation of hurricanes. No doubt about it, they are among the most destructive forces in nature. Extreme rainfall, unbelievably high waves, winds of incredible ferocity-nothing can compare to the destructive potential of hurricanes. We are accustomed to reading about hurricanes in the newspapers, on a computer, or even watching film footage of them on the local and international television news stations. There is no question about it, they are tremendously exciting and awe inspiring and it is quite easy to see why. They cut right across the mundane and sometimes too predictable routines of our everyday lives, and they fill us with a renewed wonder at the sensational power of the forces of nature. Then we feel a twinge of guilt at being excited, because we know, as we read about and watch them, that people are losing their homes, their businesses, their belongings, their well-being, their peace of mind and even their lives. In some powerful hurricanes, entire communities are wiped out and then we feel sorry for the disaster victims. Our responses invariably contain this guilty triple-take of excitement, shame and pity, and we feel we have to suppress our sense of exhilaration because of some natural weather phenomenon which we in this region call hurricanes.

Earth is a unique and dynamic planet. It is the only one in the Solar System that has both an atmosphere and oceans of water, and these have created ideal conditions for life to evolve and flourish. Currents in the atmosphere and oceans transport heat and moisture around the globe, so that life can exist almost everywhere on this planet. These currents also create the weather that we are familiar with today. This changes daily, but in predictable patterns. To understand the weather and predict its behavior, we need to know the properties of the atmosphere. These properties includes, the air temperature, atmospheric pressure, wind speed, relative humidity, and cloudiness. The pattern of weather in a particular place over a long period of time is its climate. Simply put, weather is what's going on in the atmosphere in any one location at a particular time. Fortunately, nothing is as simple as that. There are a variety of factors that can influence the weather. Among the most important are the heating of the earth by the sun and differences in atmospheric pressure. Low atmospheric pressure usually means stormy weather; on the other hand, high atmospheric pressure usually means pleasant or good weather. The pressure at the centre of a hurricane is extremely low so there is always stormy weather associated with a hurricane. Although the causes of extreme weather are often well understood, it is still impossible to predict weather more than a few days ahead. This is because the weather is a very complex and dynamic system, where even a small disturbance, such as microscopic raindrop in a cloud, can affect how the weather develops.

Understanding weather allows us to plan our days, our vacations, travels, and our crops. As a matter of fact, weather is a complex and dynamic process driven by the sun; the earth's oceans, rotation, and inclination; and so many other factors that many of its mysteries still remain unexplained even to this day. To say that weather is an important factor in everyone's life is a huge understatement. Being prepared for what the weather brings can be as simple as turning on the TV to catch the latest early morning weather forecast before heading to work or to the beach, or as complicated as examining long-range forecasts to decide which crops to plant, or when and where to evacuate from an approaching storm. Weather constantly affects people in small ways but can also have major consequences when a hurricane threatens our well-being, livelihoods, or even our lives. It seems inconceivable that when looking at great storms, such as this one in 1780, that something so large and deadly could have a beneficial side. But hurricanes are really just huge heat engines that pick up warmth from the oceans in the warmer latitudes and transport it to colder latitudes, helping to restore or balance the earth's warm and cold zones, giving us as humans the ability to live and survive on an otherwise very volatile planet.

Hurricanes are no novelty to the islanders, but the fury of one that occurred in 1780 was definitely memorable. In fact, it was a mega hurricane of gargantuan proportions as you will see later. No one at the time who lived through the howling winds, terror of a sky filled with the flying debris and roofs of the demolished houses never forgot it. Winds were estimated to have reached at least a Category 5 intensity on the Saffir-Scale had it occurred today. Property damages throughout the Caribbean were astounding and at least 22,000[1] persons lost their lives as a direct result of this massive and deadly hurricane. In Barbados, one of the main islands devastated by this storm, the island's sugar crop was entirely lost for that year and was negatively impacted for years to follow, leaving the residents without a valuable source of income. By noon of that day, many houses were either significantly damaged or totally destroyed. By three o'clock in the afternoon, Carlisle Bay in Barbados was devoid of ships for all had broken away from their moorings and some had been driven ashore and wrecked while others were driven out to sea never to be seen again. The entire island was devastated, and its unsheltered inhabitants were reduced to the last extremity of misery and despair. This island was devastated, but this great storm was not done yet, because this storm respected no cultural or political frontiers. It then went onto devastate St. Lucia, the French island of Martinique and the Dutch island of St. Eustatius causing heavy causalities on all of these islands.

This book is about a select sub-group of natural disasters which we call hurricanes, which often have far-reaching consequences and have created many rippled effects across our Caribbean landscape and history. A natural disaster is a climatic or environmental occurrence that either kills or injures people, damages property, or causes significant financial losses. Most are unpredictable, spontaneous calamities called "Acts of God." Some, such as fire, may need human intervention to get started, while others such as hurricanes simply need heat as a catalyst to get them started. All of these disasters were crucial shapers of the world we live in. It is very important to understand why disasters like hurricanes happen. It was all too easy in past centuries to portray hurricanes as chaotic and unforeseeable. People were actively encouraged especially by spiritual and community leaders to think of them as acts of punishment by a vengeful god or the Almighty God. This is a particularly cruel mindset; a family bereaved by a hurricane has to bear the additional grief that some evil god or the Almighty God had deliberately struck their loved ones down and that they must have done something wicked to deserve the punishment. As we shall see, the Great Hurricane of 1780 did something significant to change that.

The eighteenth century brought a great increase in our understanding of the way the world around us works. Nowadays, we have come to accept the fact that hurricanes are foreseeable but some hurricanes such as this great storm in 1780 could not have been foreseen whereby avoiding action could have been taken to reduce loss of lives. However, some hurricanes, like the one in this book is purely natural but some of them are human induced and makes the devastation, such as Jeanne in 2004 in Haiti (2,400 persons died in this storm in Haiti) even worse. The mudslides that happened in Haiti by this storm were produced by the combination of heavy rainfall and layers of loose mountainside debris and rocks' lying on these steep mountain sides, but this disaster was made far worse by people who had misguidedly built settlements on the valley floors and on the severely deforested mountain sides.

Tall tales and truth have been told about the weather for as long as there have been people around to tell them. Sorting the 'tall' from the 'truth' is not so easy because only a few records have been confirmed by reliable meteorological measurements. Systematic observations started only in 1814 when the Radcliffe Observatory in Oxford, England, began recording changes in the weather. However, in the

United States, daily weather records started in 1885 in an observatory founded by Abbott Lawrence Rotch in Milton, Massachusetts. The observatory (the Blue Hill) continues to keep meteorological records and holds the record for the longest continuously operating weather-observing station at the same location within the United States. Extreme weather events such as this great hurricane which occurred in 1780 can only be officially cited as records only if the weather station that recorded them has a long-term set of weather measurements. Just how long weather stations should maintain meteorological data before declaring records remains a matter of debate, but the general consensus is that at least 10 years of measurements are required before an extreme reading is declared to be a record. The accurate records maintained by today's weather stations across the world enable comparisons to be made and extremes of weather to be documented. Together, these extremes reveal the enormous power of the forces that contribute to our weather.

Weather forecasting is today a complex and highly technical scientific process, relying on observations, satellite and radar images and computer simulations. It has come a long way since the days of superstition and sky gods. The modern science of weather is called meteorology. The persons who study the atmosphere are called meteorologists and they prepare their forecasts in two stages. First, they study current weather conditions by examining weather maps, radar and satellite images, and local weather measurements. Next, they use their knowledge of meteorology to predict how the current conditions will change. This science would not have been possible without discovering the behavior of the components-water, heat, and air-that make up the weather. It was approximately 300 years ago that people first began to experiment scientifically with these elements. Through their experiments, they learned about atmospheric pressure, which makes up the air, and why water disappears as it evaporates. These early meteorologists invented a variety of crude measuring instruments that allowed them to test their theories and devise new ones. Two of the most important scientific developments in this field were the thermometer, which is used for measuring temperatures, and the barometer, which measures atmospheric pressure.

Today, using sophisticated equipment; meteorologists can predict the arrival of extreme weather conditions, such as hurricanes with great accuracy. Driven by heat from the sun, and by the planet's rotation, the air around the earth and the water in the seas and oceans are both in constant motion. The effect is like a gigantic 'machine' in which air and water are constantly redistributing heat energy around the planet. We experience this machine as weather-sunshine, rain, wind, fog, snow, and hail. Weather happens in the layer of gases that surround the earth, called the atmosphere. Without the atmosphere there would be no life on earth and we would be burned by the intense heat of the daytime sun or frozen by the icy chill of the night.

Our amazing planet earth provides us with all of our needs. It gives us water to drink, fertile soils in which to plant our crops, winds to fill a sail on a sailboat, and snow to let us race down a mountainside on a ski. But sadly, it also has a dark side. The gentle rains can become a torrential downpour that feeds raging floodwaters and the light winds can become strong and powerful gusts which can destroy even the strongest of structures. The atmosphere is a layer of air that is wrapped around our planet. It protects us from the sun's destructive radiation and helps keep the earth warm and at an ambient temperature to allow life on earth. During the day, the atmosphere prevents us from being burned by the intense heat of the sun and at night, it stops heat from escaping into space. The atmosphere extends upward from the surface to around 620 miles, but the world's weather takes place in the lowest and amazingly the smallest part, called the troposphere, which reaches high into the sky. Within this layer, the air is constantly moving, carrying much needed heat and moisture around the globe. Too much movement can generate giant storms that can cause great devastation in the form of hurricanes.

Hurricanes are the unstable, unreliable creatures of a moment in our planet's natural history. But their brief life ashore can leave scars that never quite heal. Well over two hundred years ago, the Great Hurricane of 1780 roared through the prosperous and sugar rich colonies of the Caribbean. It was such a powerful storm that some modern day meteorologists described it as a very intense hurricane of at least a Category 4 or 5 hurricane intensity on the Saffir-Simpson Scale. Hurricanes will always be with us, and people will always need to try to understand the process that cause them, to monitor them, predict when they might strike next, and try to prevent them from leading to great disasters such as the Great Hurricane of 1780. This book provides a fantastic introduction to this great storm, its effects on the Caribbean and how they coped with a storm of such great magnitude. Hopefully, this book will inspire you to learn more about these awe-inspiring but dangerous storms which we call hurricanes. There will always be more information than we need to know, and as the population of our planets increases and global warming begins to take hold as some scientists predict that it would, an increasing number of hurricanes means that we will definitely need all of the help we can get to deal with these great disasters.

No hurricane in the North Atlantic region has even come close to matching the death toll from this massive storm until 1998's Hurricane Mitch, which struck Central America. That hurricane took the lives of 10,000 to 18,000[2] people, mostly from the countries of Nicaragua and Honduras. However, the Great Hurricane of 1780 still overshoots that devastating statistic. An estimated 22,000 people perished between early to mid October in the eastern Caribbean, mainly in the Lesser Antilles, with the heaviest losses on the islands of Martinique, St. Eustatius and Barbados. Beyond these heavy casualties, it's estimated that thousands of sailors, mostly French and British, who were campaigning in the region for dominancy also perished in the storm when the rough seas and strong winds plowed into their vessels. Although the exact strength of the storm is unknown, anecdotal evidence of its destruction leads modern researchers to conclude that the Great Hurricane of 1780 was a Category 5 storm, possibly with winds in excess of 200 miles per hour.

This storm occurred over two and a half centuries ago and had a great impact on the history and tactics of naval warfare and had a profound effect on the imperial policies of all the major powers battling for supremacy in the Caribbean and the Americas. The definite objective proposed in this book is an examination of the general history of Europe and the Americas and the Caribbean with particular reference of this storm's impact on the course of history in these nations. Historians generally have been unfamiliar with the conditions of this hurricane and its great impact on the outcomes on the many wars fought between these nations until this powerful storm changed that perception about hurricanes in general. This is particularly true of the general devastation created with such storms before this hurricane. This hurricane is often considered a turning point storm, because it changed the outcome of the major wars fought for the control of these Caribbean islands and the future continental United States. Prior to this storm, it was easy to say in a general way that the destructive hurricanes were only considered just a minor setback to the islands they devastated, but after this devastating and life altering storm it forced the residents of this region to look at storms including this one in a different way.

INTRODUCTION

Over the last 22 years of my existence as a professional Bahamian meteorologist, hurricanes and their impact on my country of the Bahamas and the region as a whole has led me to write seven books on hurricanes. These books have allowed me to procure some of the best meteorologists in the business to write the foreword for me, from Bryan Norcross, Herbert Saffir, Dr. Phil Klotzbach, and Professor William Gray and in this book Dr. Steve Lyons. This was done to not only add credibility to these books but to also show the importance of hurricanes and their great impact on the lives of people of all walks of life here in the Caribbean and the Americas. The weather affects everyone whether we like it or not. It is our constant companion-as tranquil, as turbulent, as phenomenal, and sometimes as unpredictable as life itself.

An appreciation of nature's beauty has always been one of the privileges of humanity, but only in this century has science succeeded in explaining many of the weather's complex and diverse mysteries. Hopefully, this book will help you to observe and understand the multifaceted workings of hurricanes as revealed by the powerful and sophisticated tools of the twentieth-century meteorology. Weather forecasting is one of those rare activities that bind nations in a common goal from which people worldwide benefit daily. Through weather satellites and the combined efforts of the more than 180 member countries of the World Meteorological Organization, we can track the forces of nature, such as devastating hurricanes, that control our weather and forecast their behavior up to a week or more ahead of time. Meteorology is one of the oldest sciences and also one of the most diverse and challenging. As the world begins to come to grips with global environmental issues ranging from global warming and El Niño to acid rain, meteorology is assuming an important new role in reinforcing the development of policies aimed at securing the long-term survival of the planet.

The word "Meteorology" comes from the Greek words: μετέωρον, *metéōron,* meaning "high in the sky"; and λόγος, *lógos,* meaning "knowledge." Meteorology is the interdisciplinary scientific study of the atmosphere that focuses on weather processes and forecasting it for the benefit of mankind. Meteorologists do two main jobs. They collect data and process the information about the weather from day to day. Then they use this information to help them forecast future weather patterns and trends. Meteorologists collect information from weather stations scattered all over the world to assist them with forecasting the weather on a daily basis. Weather is the day-to-day condition of the atmosphere in terms of temperature, pressure, cloud cover, precipitation, wind, and moisture at a particular time over a particular place. These are the elements of which the weather is made and occurs because the atmosphere is constantly changing. Where the atmosphere thins to near vacuum, high above the earth's surface, there is no weather. But near the surface of the earth, where the atmosphere is dense and heavy, you see the ever-changing, dramatic, and often violent weather show with spectacular extreme weather events such as hurricanes. But it takes more than air to make the weather function. If the earth's atmosphere was never heated, mixed, or moved about, there would be no weather or more appropriately, there would be no changes in the weather. There would be no winds, no changes in air pressure or temperature, no storms, rain, or snow. Because of this constant motion within the earth's atmosphere and the earth's rotation around the sun, makes the weather patterns on earth very unpredictable.

The air around us obeys the strict laws of physics. Its movement in its basic form is determined by a simple temperature principal which is, warm air rises and cold air sinks. Wind is the movement of the air around the earth. The movement of the wind around our planet is driven by the uneven heating of the earth's surface by the sun, which creates regions of warmer and cooler air. These differences in temperature set the air moving. These convection movements, which are linked to the earth's rotation, are the cause of winds. Winds are affected by a great many factors (such as the proximity of an ocean or mountains, or the tilt of the earth), sometimes leading to violent events such as, gales, thunderstorms, tornadoes and hurricanes. Heat is the catalyst that mixes the atmosphere together to make the weather work on a daily basis. The weather acts as a type of safety valve for the earth, preventing any one area of the world from getting too hot or too cold. It works by shifting hot air to cold regions of the earth and cold air to hot regions. The warmest part of the world is the tropical region on both sides of the equator. This region produces a huge amount of hot and moist air, which rises and then flows toward the North and South Poles, where the air is coldest. This movement of air restores the balance of heat in the atmosphere and the end result is life here on earth as we know today.

All weather changes are brought about by temperature and pressure changes in different parts of the atmosphere. Different parts of the world receive different amounts of heat from the sun. As a result, they have different weather patterns throughout the year. These ever-changing weather patterns within the earth's atmosphere over a long period of time is called 'climate' and it is the historical record and description of average daily and seasonal weather events that help describe a region. Statistics are generally drawn over several decades. The word climate is derived from the Greek word 'Klima' meaning inclination, and reflects the importance early scholars attributed to the sun's influence on the earth. The planet's climate is therefore ultimately determined by the behavior of the weather systems of the various geographic regions around the world. A 'weatherperson' will try to provide you with a forecast for tomorrow's picnic or fishing trip. Whereas a climatologist will get back to you next week or month with his or her estimate of what changes in atmospheric carbon dioxide might do to the temperature trends in this region over the next 300 years. Climate results from the accumulated impact over a long period of time of the weather day after day. In this region near the equator, the climate is hot all year round providing the perfect conditions for hurricanes to form. These constantly changing, ever moving bodies of powerful whirlwinds called hurricanes are all natural phenomena that have swept the earth for eons, bringing destruction and anguish to mankind whenever they encounter man's ever expanding society.

The world's great North Atlantic hurricanes are apocalyptic machines that move across, feed off and push water from oceans to varied shores across the region and out of large lakes, and makes water a powerful weapon of destruction. But surprisingly, they start out as swirling dusts in the arid heart of the Sahara, one of the driest places on earth. Sadly, no one sees their origin. Demonstrating the complex relationships that drive the earth's weather events, many of the big storms that have plagued the Caribbean and the Americas were spawned in Africa. Most historic North Atlantic hurricanes originated in 'easterly waves,' disturbances in barometric pressure and wind speed caused when extreme heat from the Sahara Desert in North Africa butts up against cooler temperatures along the Gulf of Guinea on the West African coast. In fact, the northwest part of Africa, jutting into the Atlantic like the handle of a jug, is home to the Sahara, the world's largest desert, nearly equal in size to the continental United States of America.

These temperatures here are so hot that they can push 110°F or more, and the world's record of 132°F is found there. It is this stark contrast in temperature that is responsible for the making of a fledgling Atlantic storm. Some 2,500 miles to the east of the Atlantic coast, rising as a physical barrier between the desert and the rich Nile River deltas of Egypt and Sudan, are the Tibesti Mountains in Chad. Cooler wind crossing these mountains makes its way toward the Sahara. In the desert, vapours rises off the ground. The hot vapours, and warm air coming in from where the 'jug handle' (the southern shore on the Gulf of Guinea), slams into the cooler mountain winds and form clouds and thunderstorms. In one summer, as many as one hundred of these perturbations in the normal wind flow pattern called 'tropical waves' make their way west across the continent toward the Atlantic Ocean. In a 500 mile track of land area between the desert and the western shore lies the Sahel, an Arabic word for shore. The seeming contradiction of great storms growing from a dry desert has not been lost on weather researchers. In fact, one renowned Professor

William Gray from Colorado State University has concluded that in years of great drought over Sahara, there have been more powerful storms.

As the summer beats through July and August, all eyes are focused on Africa and the tropics. The sun bears down on the stretch of ocean and land between the equator and the Tropic of Cancer, and land, air and water get hotter and hotter. Once a storm has left the African coast and is over the waves, warm water exacerbates it like gasoline poured on a flame. The storm moves off the African coast near the Cape Verde Islands-hence the name 'Cape Verde Type Hurricanes.' People all along the Atlantic coasts have come to know these Cape Verde type storms because these are often the deadliest and most powerful storms of all the four types of hurricanes occurring within this region. As an easterly wave moves west across the Atlantic, it develops into a hurricane in a four-part process. The wave, which meteorologists call a tropical disturbance, becomes a tropical depression when its winds reach speeds of up to 38 mph and began to rotate around a central vortex. The depression becomes a tropical storm when wind speeds increase to 39 to 73 mph and the central vortex becomes more delineated and the easily recognizable eye feature of the storm starts to become noticeable. The final stage is the hurricane and this is reached when winds exceed 74 mph, and the easily recognizable eye feature of the storm starts to become very distinct in a mature hurricane.

An attempt has been made to produce in this book, in a clear and precise discussion, with all of the essential facts and theories regarding the Great Hurricane of 1780 and its deadly and extremely destructive track across the Caribbean. This book has been specifically designed so that the reader will be well versed and empowered about hurricanes in general and most importantly, about the nature and impact of the Great Hurricane of 1780 on the entire Caribbean. In addition, the reader will get the inside story of the 'Greatest Storm' this region has ever seen in the last 600 years even surpassing, Hurricanes Katrina, Gilbert, David, Andrew, Mitch, the Great Galveston Hurricane of 1900, the Great Miami Hurricane of 1926 and many other historic hurricanes. It was only since 1780, and the Great Hurricane of 1780, that persons within this region have been shocked and amazed into recognizing the fact that these vast storms can and do arise within our coastal regions and can create unbelievable destruction and death. As a matter of fact, in 1780 people learned it several times over because of at least three very destructive hurricanes which struck the Caribbean that year.

The Lesser and Greater Antilles and other areas of the Caribbean sustained the greater portion of deaths and destruction from this storm. This was a very unusual storm based on its magnitude, formation, location and the time of year it formed. From all indications and historical records, this was an extremely powerful, destructive and deadly hurricane and when it was finished with this region, thousands of persons were dead. The remaining people on the various Windward and Leeward Islands who were fortunate enough to have survived this powerful storm were rendered homeless and starving for many months after the storm. After the storm, many persons died of starvation-due to lack of food or drinkable water.

Thankfully, this storm is often regarded as a 'once in a lifetime storm' because of the massive record death toll, so it might not be possible to see such a hurricane of this magnitude within this region ever again. However, as a meteorologist I have learned that you can never really say 'never' with nature because sometimes she always seems to make it a habit to break 'unbreakable' records or repeat herself with even greater fury. Planet earth is such an astonishing and remarkable place to live because there are so many physical processes in action, such as devastating hurricanes and the Great Hurricane of 1780 always seems to be always on the top of the list for both strength and death toll. To understand and appreciate life in 1780, you will be required to go back to a time when life was not so easy for the residents of the Caribbean and wars between countries within this region and around the world were quite regular as they were constantly fighting for dominancy and supremacy of the Caribbean, North America, Europe and the rest of the world.

The fury that nature releases on the tropics during hurricane season cannot be avoided and throughout history the Caribbean has experienced its share. From broken homes and lost loved ones, history has shown just what devastation nature can leave in its' wake through devastating hurricanes. Hurricanes, cyclones, typhoons are all different names for the same type of storm that are regarded as the biggest storms on earth. Every year there are numerous hurricane type storms that occur throughout the world. Most are minor hurricanes that take place out at sea and rarely touch any landmass. But occasionally a much more powerful hurricane strikes a populated landmass, unleashing the equivalent energy of several nuclear bombs. When a major hurricane happens close to densely populated areas, they can cause catastrophic damage like this one did in 1780. In writing this book, I did an extensive amount of research and used various research materials such as, newspaper articles, Governor's reports, ship captains' logs, numerous old and new books, personal reports of prominent historical persons who experienced this storm, notes and manuscripts. In addition, I had additional access to notes and writings from various other sources such as, the Library of Congress, the National Hurricane Center and NOAA (National Oceanic Atmospheric Administration), the Barbados and Martinique National Archives and Museums, the Caribbean Institute of Meteorology and Hydrology and several other noted schools, public and private colleges and university libraries and archives from various islands in the Caribbean, the Bahamas and the United States.

CHAPTER ONE
PRELUDE TO A 'GREAT' HURRICANE

The year of 1780 was a very destructive year for hurricanes in the North Atlantic. While adequate data is not available for every storm that occurred, some parts of the coastline were populated enough to give data for the significant hurricane occurrences. The hurricane season of 1780 was one of the worst in recorded history. At least eight destructive storms struck the American and Caribbean shores that year. In October, three storms in three successive weeks caused unparalleled economic and military destruction. The most destructive hurricanes of this year all occurred in October and caused at least 1,000 deaths each; this event has never been repeated and only in the 1893 and 2005 seasons were there two such hurricanes. Surprisingly, these storms came at intervals of about 110 years. The period of years from 1780 to 1893 is 113 years, and the period from 1893 to 2006 is 113 years and the greatest storm of them all was the Great Hurricane of 1780. An estimated 22,000 people perished between October 10 and October 18 in the eastern Caribbean, mainly in the Lesser Antilles, with the heaviest losses occurring on the islands of Martinique, St. Eustatius and Barbados. Beyond these casualties, it's estimated that thousands of sailors, mostly French and British, who were campaigning in the region also perished in the storm when the dramatic weather plowed into their vessels. Although the exact strength of the storm is unknown, anecdotal evidence of its destruction leads modern researchers to conclude that the Great

Hurricane of 1780 was a Category 5 storm, possibly with winds in excess of 200 miles per hour.

This storm was born sometime in the early fall of 1780, somewhere in the tropical waters of the North Atlantic Ocean and sadly, no one saw, tracked or even followed it by satellite. At that time weather satellites did not exist, and no ship happened to be near the young but strengthening storm as it neared the Caribbean. Unseen and unknown, it began its long journey into the islands of the Lesser and Greater Antilles in the southern Caribbean. These islands at the time were the commerce ports and melting pots for merchants, pirates, and military men flying many flags from various countries throughout the Caribbean, the Americas and Europe. These islands were a rich and interesting place to be at that time, full of life and intrigue. As it travelled, the storm fed on warm, moist air. It grew into a huge mass of dark clouds. Winds nudged and shoved the storm northwestward across the Atlantic and into the Caribbean Sea. Within the clouds, lightning crackled, thunder crashed, and strong winds howled. Sheets of torrential rain fell. Still unseen as it approached the southern Caribbean; this powerful storm was whirling toward the Caribbean with great intensity. By the time it drew near, it was already a full-fledged hurricane, carrying winds of at least 155 miles per hour according to some historians. By the time the storm had arrived, it had taken many of the Caribbean residents and sailors by complete surprise resulting in massive causalities both on land and at sea.

The second of three storms in the month of October to strike the Caribbean in 1780, was known simply as the Great Hurricane of 1780 and it was the single deadliest storm to ever have affected the Western Hemisphere. Between October 10 and 18, this catastrophic hurricane carved a path of destruction from Barbados to Bermuda. In Barbados, nearly every building on the island was totally demolished by the storm, and production of sugar and rum-two commodities so vital to the local economy were drastically curtailed, and did not recover for at least four years. The Barbados Mercury would later report that *"in most plantations all of the buildings, the sugar mills excepted, are laid level with the earth, and that there is not a single estate on the island which entirely escaped the violence of the tempest."* More than 4,326 inhabitants died on this island, and the survivors were

2

so traumatized that six months later a British newcomer reported, *"The melancholy appearance of every person and thing, struck me with a degree of terror not easily to be described."*[1] Many settlers abandoned their plantations and estates and returned to England, leaving the island's economy even further depressed.

The Great Hurricane of 1780 struck a nearly fatal blow to the economy of the Caribbean. It was so devastating to the British fleet in the region that their presence throughout the Caribbean and especially North America were thereafter significantly reduced. Although not meteorologically unusual for hurricanes to occur in that location, the hurricane's path took it directly over several of the most populated islands of the region in that locale and that in itself added greatly to the significant death toll. However, what made this storm so unique were the location, the time of year it occurred, and the massive death toll it racked up on these islands. Not for more than two hundred years would the death toll of a North Atlantic hurricane again exceed 10,000 and that was Hurricane Mitch of 1998. The Great Hurricane of 1780 was in many ways the worst hurricane in this region's hurricane history. News of this powerful and deadly hurricane travelled far and wide and sealed the reputation of the Caribbean as a dangerous place for trade and habitation. The year of 1780 was a turning point in the history of the Caribbean, marking the end of a long period of prosperity and the beginning of an episode of economic, social and cultural decline.

Hurricanes are among the most destructive forces on planet earth. Winds from these powerful storms can gusts up to 200 miles per hour. While other storms such as tornadoes can create even stronger winds, they rarely last for more than a few minutes; by contrast, hurricanes can last for days or even weeks. The destructive effects of hurricanes have been chronicled for thousands of years, and entire fleets have been sunk and cities destroyed by vicious winds and mountainous seas. The Japanese term *Kami-kazi*, meaning 'Divine Wind' referred to the hurricane-like storms that sank the fleets of the Mongol emperor Kublai Khan in 1274 and 1281 as they prepared to attack Japan. Damages caused by hurricanes ranges from complete and utter devastation to relatively minor inconveniences. The greatest destruction is usually from water damage resulting from a storm surge that causes a rise in ocean level as the hurricane approaches a land area. The height of and the potential damage from the storm surge depends upon the slope of the ocean floor along the coast and other contributing factors. As hurricanes move inland from the coast or over colder waters, they become low-pressure systems, extra-tropical storms or simply rain depressions. These often bring heavy rainfall to inland areas and cause widespread flooding.

Great whirling storms roar out of the oceans in many parts of the world. They are called by several names-hurricanes, typhoons, and cyclones are the three most familiar ones. But no matter what they are called, they are all the same sort of storms. They are born in the same way, in tropical waters throughout the world. They develop in the same way, feeding on warm, moist air, and they do the same kind of damage, both ashore and at sea. Other storms may cover a bigger area or have higher winds, but none can match both the size and the fury of hurricanes. They have over the many centuries, earned the reputation as the earth's mightiest storms. Like all storms, they take place in the atmosphere, the envelope of air that surrounds the earth and presses on its surface. No one knows exactly what happens to trigger the birth of these storms. But when conditions are right, warm, moist air is set in motion. It begins to rise rapidly from the surface of the ocean in a low pressure area, and the end result is a powerful and destructive hurricane.

We are all like fish swimming at the bottom of a giant ocean of air, an atmosphere that both sustains life and sometimes takes it away. The atmosphere is an endless source of curious, beautiful, mysterious, and sometimes deadly phenomena. Nature is often said to be tamed, but natural disasters kill about a million people around the world every decade, and leave millions more homeless. There is nothing tamed or tamable about hurricanes. Drawing on energy from the sun and of the earth's residual heat, these titanic forces landscape the planet according to their random nature or design. There is no refuge or protection against them except to get out of their way. Hurricanes cause devastation all over the world, but they are all born in the same latitudes-the tropics. This is where the main ingredients of a hurricane reside: warm oceans of at least 26.5°C or more, warm air, light winds at the surface and in the upper atmosphere (weak wind shear), and moisture in the atmosphere. Yet while all of these ingredients exist for much of the summer in tropical climates, they do not always result in deadly storms. The catalyst needed for these conditions to become a hurricane is an atmospheric disturbance.

As a result of its great size and intensity, the hurricane when fully developed, is the most destructive of all storms. Winds of tornadoes may blow with greater fury but they are compact storms and are confined to a narrow path, 1,000 feet in average width, whereas it is not unusual for the violent winds of the hurricane to cover thousands of square miles and affect many islands and countries in this region. Mountainous storm surges accompany intense hurricanes at sea; their destructive forces are revealed in the appalling records of ships sunk or cast ashore. They cause high surges that inundate low coastal areas. Storm waves break on the shore, in some situations like a wall of water or a series of great waves. Cities and towns have been wiped out, never to be rebuilt. Though born in the tropics, some of these storms move long distances and occasionally devastate sections far remote from their place of origin. In some of the most severe hurricanes, losses of human lives have been estimated in the hundreds and even thousands and property damage in the millions of dollars.

From the earliest antiquity, mankind has searched for a way to explain the mysterious and terrifying natural event we call hurricanes. Ancient legends throughout history believed that hurricanes were the work of evil gods. The Maya Indians of Central America believed that hurricanes were caused by the evil god Huracán who inflicted great punishment on its subjects when he was displeased or angry. Today, meteorologists have a greater understanding of hurricanes. Despite modern advancements in meteorology, meteorologists still realize that they are still notoriously difficult to predict their formation and movement with some degree of pin point accuracy. Hurricanes are the most dramatic, most dangerous, and most feared of all weather phenomena that exists within the restless atmosphere called earth. Yet these hurricanes are an integral part of the life and dynamics of our planet by inducing exchanges of heat and cold on a vast global scale from the equator to the poles, from the upper to lower atmosphere, and by the continual releasing of energy. Hurricanes act as safety valves and essential balancers of the earth's climate. They bring both life-giving rain and destruction, and in one form or another, these storms frequent nearly every section of the globe.

The atmosphere has persistently protected all living creatures on earth by forming a gaseous shield against destructive radiation and waves of solar and cosmic energy. With powerful winds, raging storm surges and torrential rains, more than 80 of these hurricanes rise from the tropical seas each year and rotate in large curved paths across oceans and lands. Most of these hurricanes are minor storms and some of them rarely touch land. However, a powerful storm may make landfall unleashing the equivalent energy of several nuclear bombs. When major hurricanes strike a land area, or pass over or close to densely populated areas, they can cause catastrophic damage, destroying whole cities, killing thousands of people, and leaving many more people homeless. Towering up to 50,000 feet high and covering ten thousands of square miles, these hurricanes rotate around its relatively calm central eye like a giant top, bringing death and destruction whenever it encounters segments of man's ever expanding population. In an average year, more than 100 disturbances with hurricane potential are observed in the North Atlantic; on average, only ten of these reach the tropical storm stage, and only about six mature into hurricanes. On average, two of these hurricanes strike the United States, where they are apt to kill 50-100 people, from Texas to Maine, and cause hundreds of millions of dollars in property damage. In a worse than average year, the same storms cause several hundred deaths, and property damage totaling billions of dollars. Given that the hurricane, as an engine, is inefficient, and difficult to start, sustain, and most tropical storms never reach the hurricane stage, however, some tropical storms still do. A certain number every season will manage to accumulate the complex combination of natural forces required. When one does, it is an awesome natural event indeed.

Natural hazards come from above the earth's surface in the form of weather. From a heavy snowfall that can start an avalanche to a ferocious hurricane striking a coastal town, scientists have come to learn that the world's weather is governed by three simple elements and they are:-water, air, and heat. The heat of the sun evaporates water from the oceans, turning it into invisible water vapour. Warm air rises, so the water vapour is carried up into the atmosphere. Eventually, it reaches a colder region of air, where it turns into tiny droplets that form clouds. But just as warm air rises, cold air sinks. These forces moving in opposite directions produce winds and air currents. The winds and the clouds produce all types of extreme weather conditions across the world, including severe thunderstorms, tornadoes and hurricanes. Hurricanes often bring torrential rainfall, severe floods and powerful winds which can all devastate huge areas of land. Although scientists do not yet completely understand the complex conditions within the atmosphere, by keeping close tabs on developing tropical storms and using advanced computer models, they have made remarkable strides in forecasting hurricanes in recent years.

Communities, nations and especially their ships have been ravaged by hurricanes from time immemorial. The ancient Mayan Indians of Central America, who named their storm god 'Huracán' wisely, built their cities inland from the hurricane prone coasts out of the great respect which they had for hurricanes. The first Europeans on record to encounter a hurricane were Christopher Columbus and his crew on their journeys to the New World. In 1495, during one of his later voyages to the New World, the fleet of Christopher Columbus weathered a hurricane while docked at the island of Hispaniola in the Caribbean Sea, forcing him to declare in his journal that *'Nothing but the service of God and the extension of the monarchy would induce him to expose himself to such dangers from hurricanes ever again.'*[2] The early Spanish colonial explorers learned that a hurricane respects no one, including the Conquistadors who built a Spanish empire in the New World. Today's treasure hunters still pluck gold coins and jewels from the bottom of the ocean in the Florida Keys, the Bahamas, and along the Atlantic Coast where hurricanes sunk Spanish treasure fleets in the sixteenth, seventeenth, and eighteenth centuries. Yet beyond scattered accounts from early colonists and mariners who lived through these storms which they described as whirlwinds and ancient images from the Caribbean and Central American civilizations whose iconic depictions of these storm gods featured anti-clockwise spirals. Hurricanes remained almost entirely mysterious and rarely understood up through the eighteenth century. However, by the early nineteenth century some colonists began to gradually realize that hurricanes were seasonal and were likely to strike during summer months when temperatures were at their maximum.

Hurricanes are seasonal threats in the Caribbean and the rest of the North Atlantic region. Most storms develop in the eastern Atlantic Ocean off the African Coast, although some arise within the Caribbean Basin itself. In both cases, these storms originate in the region where the northeasterly and southeasterly trade winds converge, generally between 5 and 20 degrees north of the equator. They form during the summer and early autumn months, and are carried westward by the trade winds and where the dynamics of the upper atmosphere is more conducive to the development of these storms. The wind speed of hurricanes ranges from 74 miles per hour, which is the minimum speed separating hurricanes from tropical storms, to in excess of 157 miles per hour, the base for today's definition of a Category 5 storm on the Saffir-Simpson Hurricane Wind Scale. In addition to pounding winds and driving rains, the most dangerous element of the hurricane is often the storm surge, floodwaters that can exceed twenty feet in height. Although loss of lives from tropical cyclones has significantly decreased over the recent years, especially in developed countries, the loss of property has increased substantially. Reductions in fatalities are usually attributed to improvement in the tropical cyclone forecasting and warning systems, while increases in property losses are attributed to accelerated property development in coastal zones.

Hurricanes originate in warm sunny seas in approximately seven general areas north and south of the equator. These storms start out innocently enough as mere disturbances of gently whirling winds and slightly lowering pressures. Given a spin from the rotating earth, young hurricanes travel leisurely at first, somewhat parallel to the equator and then they eventually take a more northwesterly turn as they travel through the Caribbean. Then, fed by immense amounts of energy from warm moist air and nurtured by certain conditions of wind, temperature and pressure within the earth's atmosphere, these storms deepen in intensity and develop into full-fledged hurricanes which sweep towards the North and South Poles in great curves before losing their energy in colder regions of the earth and dying out. Hurricanes in the North Atlantic occur mainly between June through November and the peak of the season is in early September. Although, meteorologists have the basic knowledge and understanding of where and when hurricanes can occur, they are unable to predict the exact location of a hurricane before it develops. Hence, a hurricane's path can be forecast only after it is formed. These storms have killed thousands of people, flattened buildings, destroyed towns, flooded vast regions of land, sunk armadas, and even changed the course of history.

Hurricanes have brought much misery, but they can also be beneficial. Hurricanes often provide much-needed rain to drought-stricken coastlines. Their ocean interactions can flush out bays of pollutants and restore the ecosystem's vitality. For example, after the record rainfall from Hurricane Claudette in 1979 over Texas, many fish were being caught in the northern industrialized reaches of Galveston Bay that had vanished for several years. Finally, in cruel Darwinian fashion, the weak sea life and plants perished during the hurricane, leaving only the genetically strong to survive and reproduce. In addition, sometimes hurricanes often 'correct' mankind's mistakes. For example, in the early 1900's non-native foliage, such as Australian pine trees, had been introduced and planted on the tip of Key Biscayne, Florida (now the Bill Baggs State Park). These non-native species of plants had just a few natural enemies in their new environment, and they immediately dominated the plant life there, resulting in a loss of many native species in that habitat. However, these Australian non-native plants lacked the ability to withstand hurricane force winds, and Hurricane Andrew virtually destroyed them all in 1992. The park officials immediately seized the opportunity to replant the park with native species of plants, shrubs and trees.

Weather forecasting has dramatically improved in recent years because of faster and more advanced supercomputers, better satellites and radars, and a clearer understanding of how the atmosphere works. With these weather instruments and equipment rapidly becoming more precise and advanced, meteorologists are exploring every dimension of these mighty storms. They do this by testing their vast reserves of energy and probing the complex mysteries of how they are created, develop, and dissipate. Compared to the hurricane forecasting of yesteryear hurricane forecasting of today has been greatly improved. Forecasters now enjoy access to satellites, radars and survey dozens of advanced and super-fast computer models. With satellites, they can monitor storms as they develop from small disturbances to monster hurricanes. Forecasters also rely on a constant stream of information about atmospheric conditions around the world. Day and night, a huge network of weather observatories is at work taking millions of measurements every three hours. They fly into a hurricane in a $50 million jet, dropping instrument packages from over 8 miles up that send data faster than the human eye can follow. They employ everything from special radios to televisions and the Internet to warn people of the potential dangers associated with hurricanes. It is fair to say that weather forecasting will never be 100 percent accurate. The atmosphere, with all of its clouds, wind systems, storms, fronts, and spinning air patterns, is impossible to predict perfectly. Forecasts will continue to improve, however, as we build faster computers and find better ways to accurately measure the atmosphere.

Fortunately, increasing awareness and preparation, better building codes and the advent of mass communications have dropped average hurricane deaths from thousands per year at the beginning of the twentieth century to generally less than 500 a year now. But property damage has risen sharply. The geographic range of possible landfalls established when a storm is five days away from striking is now about as wide as forecasters thirty years ago could set for a storm that was three days from hitting land. As yet, man cannot control their powerful forces or changes in their direction and he may not wish to, for far more harm than good may come from tampering with such vast, complex and dynamic storms. Hurricanes have the ability to profoundly affect the planet's entire dynamic and complex climatic and weather patterns. Episodes of violent weather events such as, hurricanes remind us that much of the natural world is still outside human control. Meteorologists call the global climate a non-linear system, which is just another fancy way of saying that gradual changes are not all gradual. Some of them can, and have in the past, come suddenly, in huge and sudden movements with severe weather events such as hurricanes.

Meteorologists say that the world's weather is best understood as a kind of heat engine for redistributing heat from the equator to the poles. Much more solar energy is absorbed by the earth between the Tropic of Cancer and the Tropic of Capricorn because the sun is directly overhead everyday all year long. By contrast, the sun's rays strike only glancing blows at the North and South Poles. Each receives the sunlight for only half of the year, during which time the other is completely in darkness. In the simplistic term, this is perhaps the main reason why the tropics are constantly hot and the poles are constantly cold. Hurricanes play one of the most important roles in this process of redistributing this heat from the equator to the poles. In addition, this redistribution of heat from the equator to the poles drives the wind and ocean currents-like the Jet Stream and the Gulf Stream. These driving forces of nature have allowed much of the same weather patterns to exist here on earth since the beginning of time and disrupting them will perhaps wreak havoc to life here on earth.

Every once in a long while, the Caribbean is hit by what we meteorologists call a *'Great'* hurricane that leaves an embedded set of footprints in the sands of this region's history for generations to follow. In October 1780, the Caribbean was ravaged by three violent hurricanes, the second of which ranks as the deadliest storm ever to affect the Western Hemisphere. These events greatly altered the political and economic history of the region and further weakened the British Navy at the time when it was engaged in the American War of Revolution. The North Atlantic hurricane season of 1780 was quite distinct and unique in the sense that at least three of these *'Great'* hurricanes made their presence felt here in the Caribbean in a significant way during the month of October. This book will showcase the most powerful and destructive of these three powerful storms which caused widespread devastation on many of the islands here in the Caribbean.

CHAPTER TWO
FUNDAMENTALS OF A HURRICANE

Tropical cyclones are the broad class of all low-pressure systems that form in the tropics and have a closed wind circulation with sustained winds of at least 39 mph. When sustained winds reach 74 mph, the storm is classified according to its geographical location:

1. Hurricane (the North Atlantic Ocean, the Northeast Pacific Ocean east of the International Dateline or the South Pacific Ocean east of 160E);
2. Typhoon (the Northwest Pacific Ocean west of the International Dateline);
3. Severe Tropical Cyclone (the Southwest Pacific Ocean west of 160E or Southeast Indian Ocean east of 90E);
4. Severe Cyclonic Storm (the Southwest Indian Ocean).

For the ease of describing these intense tropical cyclones I will simply refer to them as hurricanes, unless there's a specific geographical focus. Once winds in a closed tropical low-pressure system reach 39 mph, the system is named either a tropical storm or tropical cyclone depending upon its location. Then, a name is assigned according to WMO's international naming conventions. These names are drawn from the Region IV naming list for the North Atlantic. Names are used to help focus attention to particular storms, especially when several storms are occurring at the same time. The names also provide easy recognition for the past historical and destructive hurricanes. Storms that are especially deadly or destructive have their names retired. Evolving from a tropical wave, through a tropical depression, to a tropical storm and finally a hurricane, tropical cyclones often capture our attention not only because of their power but also because of their wide-ranging societal, economic and physical impacts.

What distinguishes hurricanes from other types of low-pressure or another storm system is that hurricanes are 'warm-core' systems. This means that the entire storm system is compose of warm air. Middle-latitude low-pressure systems often have cold and warm sectors separated by weather fronts. Most hurricanes form over warm tropical oceans during the summer and early fall months. The peak of the hurricane season is usually about two months after the summer solstice. Hurricane season extends far beyond the warmest months of the year because ocean waters warm more slowly and retain their heat longer than either air or land. Scientists now realize that hurricanes are most likely to form and intensify when ocean water temperatures are at least 80°F.

Tropical cyclones are systems of large, rotating thunderstorms that forms over warm tropical waters where the winds and the seas are conducive to the development and growth of these storms. There is nothing like hurricanes in the atmosphere. Even seen by remote sensors on satellites thousands of miles above earth, the uniqueness of these powerful, tightly coiled storms is clear. Hurricanes are not the largest storm systems on earth, nor the most violent-but they do combine those qualities as no other phenomenon does, as if they were designed to be powerful engines of death and destruction. Due to the effects of the earth's rotation, these storms rotate in a counter clockwise direction in the northern hemisphere, and rotate clockwise in the southern hemisphere. They are found in all areas of the tropical regions of the world with the exception of the southern Atlantic Ocean (although there was a case where a tropical cyclone called Cyclone Catarina formed there in 2005 but this was a rare exception to the rule). These tropical cyclones are called hurricanes in the North Atlantic once they exceed the seventy-four-mile-per-hour threshold.

In the northern hemisphere, these storms are called hurricanes, a term that echoes colonial Spanish and Caribbean Indian words for evil spirits and big winds created by their gods. The word 'hurricane' has its origins in the names given to the storm gods by various tribes of local Indians within this region. In the Bahamas, it is certain that the Lucayan Indians who were the first people to inhabit the land we now call the Bahamas experienced the high winds, rough seas and heavy rains of these storms. Unfortunately, they left no written accounts of their experiences with these storms. According to the edited abstracts taken from Spanish Priest Bartholomew de Las Casas he said that these Indians believed that the islands of the Bahamas were comprised of one giant complete landmass but had been separated by the howling winds and rough seas of the hurricane.

When the Europeans first attempted to establish permanent settlements in the Caribbean, they quickly learned about these storms when it destroyed their first built settlements in the New World on the island of Hispaniola. In the Bahamas, Christopher Columbus was lucky enough to not have encountered any storms on his first voyage but in 1499 Vicente Yañez Pinzón captain of the Columbus's ship *'the Niña'* lost two ships in the fleet in the Exuma Cays due to a hurricane. Furthermore, she was the only ship to survive the famous 1495 hurricane, battered but safely returning to Spain in 1496. In 1495, Christopher Columbus encountered a hurricane near Hispaniola and it was the earliest hurricane reported by Christopher Columbus, who also encountered a tropical storm on one of his voyages to the New World.

Fortunately, here in the Caribbean, as time passed and these European settlers learned more about their new homeland, they experienced these storms on such a regular basis that they became accustomed to them. Eventually, they began calling them 'equinoctial storms,' as the storms normally hit in the weeks around the period of the fall equinox, which in the northern hemisphere occurs in late September. Now thanks in part to over four hundred years of observations and advances in technology, we now know that hurricanes can strike at any time between June and November. The peak of the season in the North Atlantic is on September 11, of each year, and August and September are the most active months for hurricanes to strike any part of this region. These storms are products of the tropical oceans and atmosphere: powered by heat from the sea, steered by the easterly trades and temperate westerlies, and driven by their own fierce energy. Around their tranquil core called the eyewall, winds blow with lethal velocity and the ocean develops an inundating surge. In addition, as they move ashore, tornadoes may descend from the advancing bands of the surrounding thunderstorms. Hurricanes, as poorly understood as they are today, seem to have two main benefits—first, they are a major source of rain for many tropical and subtropical land areas and second, they are responsible for redistribution heat from the equator to the poles which allow us as humans to live and survive on an otherwise very volatile planet.

A hurricane represents the most advanced stage of a tropical cyclone. A cyclone refers to those types of storms having low atmospheric pressure at the center and cyclonic or rotating wind circulation. Thus a tropical cyclone is a low pressure storm system that originates in tropical (or less often subtropical) areas. The tropics are defined as that area of the earth which lies between the Tropic of Cancer, 23.5 degrees north of the equator, and the Tropic of Capricorn, 23.5 degrees south of the equator. Hurricanes vary greatly in size, intensity, behavior and path, but they have enough characteristics in common that some generalizations can be made. A hurricane can be visualized as an organized system of thunderstorm-type clouds generally assembled into spiral bands, called rainbands. Much of the rain generated by a hurricane occurs within these spiraling bands of clouds, with rainfall between the bands generally being much less intense or even absent. Thunder and lightning are not always present, but when occurring will generally be found within those rainbands and the eyewall. There are generally from one to seven bands in a hurricane, with each band commonly 50 miles long. This accounts for the average diameter of the major area covered by a hurricane being roughly 100 miles, although diameters have ranged from less than 100 miles to over 500 miles. Tropical storm force winds (39 to 73 miles per hour) may occur at a distance from the center of the storm that is several times the diameter of the major cloudy portion of the hurricane.

One of the most distinctive features shared by nearly all hurricanes is the eye. This central portion of the storm varies greatly in size among hurricanes, with some only 3 miles in diameter and others extending to well over 38 miles across. The average eye is about 15 to 20 miles in diameter. The winds in the eye are greatly reduced, often blowing only 15 miles per hour, and the sky may be nearly rain and cloud free. Many people who have been in the eye of a hurricane tell of finding clear blue skies above them as the eye passed over. The eye is also where the lowest atmospheric pressure and highest temperatures of the storm occur and in many cases birds are frequently trapped in the eye, often found in large numbers clinging in desperation to the rigging of ships. They are blown into the eye and trapped there as the storm intensifies, then cannot escape through the violent winds which surround the eye. As a matter of fact, several bird species have entered the United States especially Florida in this manner from the Bahamas and other Caribbean countries, including the Black Anis from Haiti, the Bahamas Honeycreeper, the Bahamas Shallow, the Cuban Cliff Swallow, several West Indian Doves and Pigeons, and most recently the Cattle Egret from the Antilles.

The eye is completely surrounded by the most intense portion of the hurricane, the eyewall. The clouds that compose this imposing feature of the storm reach heights of over 50,000 feet. The eyewall consist of very intense cumulonimbus clouds and within these clouds contains massive amounts of water vapour brought into this area by the rainbands which are forced upwards, converting the water vapour into water and in the process releasing a tremendous amount of heat. This process helps to produce the high winds and the torrential rainfall found within the hurricane. The strongest winds and the heaviest rainfall are often found within or near the eyewall. Many persons have been fooled as the eye passes them into thinking that the storm is over, individuals venture out, only to be surprised as the other side of the eyewall approaches, bringing winds of equal destruction but now blowing from the opposite direction. Together, the eye and eyewall represents the heart of a hurricane.

For a tropical disturbance to develop into a hurricane, there must be several environmental factors that must be present, and they must interact in rather specific ways. This interaction is most likely to occur in late summer/early fall, which is the main reason for the higher incidence hurricanes forming during this time. The official hurricane season for the North Atlantic runs from June 1 to November 30. September is especially significant, since more hurricanes have hit this region during this month than any other month and as stated before, the peak of the hurricane season in the North Atlantic is September 11th of each year. As previously mentioned, a hurricane represents the ultimate stage of a tropical cyclone. The different stages of a tropical cyclone development can be described in a number of ways. The classification scheme most commonly used in this region recognizes four stages, based on formation and intensity. The stages of the tropical cyclone are:

1. Tropical disturbance: no strong winds (this stage is actually a precursor to a tropical cyclone).
2. Tropical depression: some rotary circulation at the surface and sustained winds speed of less than 39 miles per hour.
3. Tropical storm: distinct rotary circulation with highest sustained wind speed of 39 to 73 miles per hour.
4. Hurricane: very pronounced rotary circulation with sustained winds of 74 miles per hour or greater.

Several factors account for this particular seasonality. Hurricanes nearly always develop from low-pressure disturbances within the trade-wind belt, the area from approximately 30 degrees north latitude to within five degrees of the equator which experiences consistent winds blowing from east to west. Several mechanisms are known to produce areas of low pressure in the trades, and these mechanisms are most prevalent during the summer and early fall. If the Bermuda or subtropical high pressure system is particularly weak and displaced south of this normal position, a condition quite common in early summer and fall, a region of low pressure may be introduced into the trade-winds belt. For example, higher-latitude low pressure systems can more easily penetrate into the tropics when the Bermuda high is displaced southward. The southern end of such systems may become trapped in the trades and provide the seeds of a hurricane.

Another mechanism generating low-pressure disturbances in the trades involves a low-pressure belt called the Intertropical Convergence Zone (ITCZ), which is located near the equator. In the summer, most frequently during the month of August, the ITCZ is at its northernmost location, about 12 degrees north latitude. A rotating low-pressure system forming where the ITCZ meets the trades can become a westward-migrating system in the trades. When this happens the conditions are favorable for the necessary rotation of the newly formed low-pressure system to be achieved.

One more extremely common type of low-pressure disturbance is an easterly wave. This is not an oceanic wave, but an atmospheric low-pressure feature, embedded in the trade winds belt, that moves east to west. The eastern portions of these waves are often very cloudy with heavy rain showers. These systems are nearly always present in abundant numbers during the hurricane season in the North Atlantic. The African continent, especially the very southern edge of the Sahara Desert, is the dominant source for easterly waves in the North Atlantic during the peak of the hurricane season. In fact, it is a bit ironic that one of the driest places on earth is the birthplace for storms that have produced some of the greatest rainfall records on earth. These easterly waves in any given year often number somewhere between 50 to 70 (but can be as high as 80) per year, and are very common during May through November. Hurricanes that develop in this manner are called Cape Verde-type hurricanes.

After a hurricane develops, a tremendous amount of energy is released. A moderate hurricane is capable of taking up from the ocean approximately 15 million tons of water vapour per minute through the process of evaporation. The amount of energy release into the atmosphere by the transformation of this vapour back into liquid by the hurricane is the major driving force of the hurricane, and a true driving force it is. An average hurricane will release in 24 hours the energy equivalent to one-half million Nagasaki-type atomic bombs or 400 20-megaton hydrogen (fusion) bombs. This energy, if converted to electricity, would satisfy the electrical needs of the United States for more than six months. This transformation of tremendous amounts of energy is why tropical cyclones are called 'heat engines.' One of the most important requirements for the growth and development of a hurricane is the need for warm oceanic waters of 80°F or higher to supply the system with a continuing supply of warm and moisture rich air to allow the system to develop and strengthen.

In the North Atlantic, there are four different types of hurricanes that influence us in some way or the other. Each is uniquely different and has unique and different characteristics that are found in that type of hurricane alone in terms of formation and strength. The first is the Cape Verde Type hurricane which as its name suggests originates off the African Coast in the vicinity of the Cape Verde Islands. Initially it moves in a westerly direction and then in a west-northwest to a northwesterly direction as it makes its way through the Caribbean, Central America, the Bahamas and the United States. The Cape Verde Islands is an archipelago about 400 miles off the West African Coast and are volcanic in nature. It was colonized by Portugal in the fifteenth century and became an independent country in 1975. At one point in their history, these islands served as an outpost station for the movement of African slaves on the 'Middle Passage' to the Americas. This type of hurricane forms over the Atlantic mainly during the early to mid-part of the season, June through mid-September months when the easterly waves are the most dominant weather features in the Caribbean region. This type of hurricane tend to produce the strongest hurricanes in this category because of the great distance they have in traversing the warm waters of the Atlantic before they get to any landmass giving them the time and the opportunity to strengthen before hitting some landmass in the Caribbean, North or Central America.

At the beginning and the middle of the hurricane season, storms also tend to form near the Bahamas mainly from upper-level systems or TUTT low pressure systems and this type of hurricane has come to be known as '*Bahama Busters*' according to world renowned Professor William Gray from Colorado State University who gave it that name. An example of this type of storm was Hurricane Katrina in 2005, which formed just east of the Bahamas from the remnants of Tropical Depression #10 and became Tropical Depression #12. This system initially moved westward and then northwestward into the Gulf of Mexico and then over Louisiana. This type of storm tend to produce hurricanes of moderate to intense hurricanes and it all depends on the environmental factors at the time but also how long it remains in the Gulf of Mexico before hitting any landmass on the Gulf Coast States.

Another type of hurricane is the Gulf of Mexico type, which as its name suggest originates in the Gulf of Mexico and travels northward or westward from its inception and mainly influences Latin America, and the Gulf Coast of the United States. This type of hurricane tends to be the weakest of all four types of hurricanes because of the short distance from its formation to the time it hits any land area and began the weakening or dissipating stage. Finally, there is the Western Caribbean type which forms during the early and late parts of the hurricane season and forms in the most favoured location near the Gulf of Honduras or the southern Caribbean Sea mainly in May through June, and mid-September through late November. The formations of these cyclones are due in part to the seasonal movement of the Inter-Tropical Convergence Zone, also known as the Equatorial Trough. From its inception, this type of hurricane seems to take a westward or northward movement, which normally takes a track over Central America if it moves westward or over the island of Cuba and into the Bahamas if it moves northward. The severity of which is influenced by how long the storm remains over the mountainous terrain of Cuba. One notable example of this type of storm affecting the region was Hurricane Michelle in 2001.

Hurricanes are born in low latitudes and are nurtured by warm tropical waters. They die by moving into higher latitudes with colder waters, or by leaving the water and crossing over land, or occasionally by coming under the influence of unfavorable upper-air wind flow. Hurricanes exists an average of about nine days, although life spans have varied from less than 12 hours to more than 28 days. During this time they cover about 300 to 400 miles a day, for a total of approximately 2,700 to 3,600 total miles during their lifetime. Nearly all hurricanes in the North Atlantic are eventually steered by large-scale, global wind patterns onto land or into higher latitudes, where the process of decay begins. Most of these storms recurve, that is, change direction from a predominantly west or northwest track to a more northerly and even a northeasterly direction. This recurvature, which occurs on average at about 25 degrees latitude, is produce largely by clockwise moving winds around the Bermuda high pressure system in the Atlantic, and by interaction of the hurricane with the prevailing westerlies of the mid-latitudes. A hurricane will often reach its maximum intensity just before or at the point of recurvature, at which time many hurricanes slow their forward progress. Once the path of the hurricane has change it will often increase its forward speed, attaining its greatest speed soon after recurvature.

As a hurricane moves into higher latitudes while still over water, the ocean temperatures become too cold to sustain the heat engine of the storm and some would eventually become 'extra-tropical' in nature. The decaying process is especially evident once the storm moves up to oceanic regions of approximately 40 degrees latitude. Hurricane decay due to landfall is a much more complicated process. Once over land, several processes combine which together lead to the demise of the storm. Friction is involved, but to a much lesser degree than originally thought. In fact, the friction that a hurricane encounters from the extremely agitated ocean surface and tremendous amounts of spray thrown into the air is greater than the friction a hurricane would encounter over relatively flat terrain such as, the Florida Everglades.

Much more significant than friction, and the prime reason for a hurricane's demise over land, is the rapid cooling experienced by the inner core of the hurricane soon after it makes landfall. This cooling results from the loss of a hurricane's major energy source, which are heat and moisture derived from the ocean, and the conversion of water vapour into liquid water. The cooling of the inner core is immediately followed by a process called filling. During this process more air is coming in toward the central portion of the storm than is being exhausted upward through the system. The pressure in the central part of the hurricane increases, the area of maximum winds becomes more spread out and diffuse, and eventually the hurricane simply 'unravels' and dies. Some hurricanes are transformed into extratropical cyclones or combine with existing middle-latitude storms once they move into higher latitudes. Extratropical cyclones, sometimes called mid-latitude cyclones, baroclinic storms or wave cyclones, are a group of cyclones defined as synoptic scale low pressure weather systems that occur in the middle latitudes of the earth (outside of the tropics) having neither tropical nor polar characteristics, and are connected with fronts and horizontal gradients in temperature and dew point otherwise known as "baroclinic zones." When a hurricane combines with such a storm there may actually be a brief period of intensification of the hurricane, but this is often short-lived, as the cool air quickens the demise of the hurricane and it quickly dies or turns into a much weaker mid-latitude storm.

The movement of hurricanes from the lower to higher latitudes serves a very useful, in fact essential purpose in the world's climate on a global scale. Between about 35 degrees north and south of the equator, heat (shortwave radiation) from the sun absorbed by the earth and atmosphere is greater than the heat (longwave radiation) that is radiated from the earth and atmosphere back into space. If the heating that results from this imbalance is not carried away, the tropical and subtropical regions of the earth would be constantly growing warmer. Fortunately, nature has provided two mechanisms to transfer this excess energy to the higher latitudes, where there is an energy deficit, and therefore, maintain a global balance. A portion of this excess heat is carried away by ocean currents. For example, the Gulf Stream carries warmth away from the equatorial areas into coolers waters of the North Atlantic. However, most of the heat transfer is accomplished in the atmosphere. Tropical cyclones are a part of this atmospheric heat movement process. Hurricanes are therefore necessary for the earth to maintain an energy balance to support life on this planet. In this respect, these generally hated and despised storms might be viewed as 'necessary evils' of nature.

Furthermore, these storms also have other advantages in addition to helping to maintain an energy balance for the earth and that is, they provide much needed rainfall to many parched areas of the earth. A typical hurricane usually brings about 10 to 15 inches or greater of rainfall to much of the areas affected, and in the process produces over 200 billion tons of rainwater each day, an amount equal to the average annual flow of the Colorado River. Although rainfall is often a major cause of damage associated with hurricanes, the effects are not always undesirable. Over a six month hurricane season of June-November, tropical systems generally account for 45% to 60% of the seasonal rainfall in the Caribbean. Hurricanes often provide this much-needed rain to drought-stricken coastlines.

Their ocean interactions can flush bays of pollutants, restoring the ecosystem's vitality. After the record rainfall from Hurricane Claudette in 1979 in Texas, fish were being caught in the northern industrialized reaches of Galveston Bay that had vanished for several years. Finally, in cruel Darwinian fashion, weak sea life and plants perish during a hurricane, leaving only the strong to survive and reproduce. In this same manner, sometimes hurricanes 'correct' humanity's mistakes. For example, in the early 1900's non-native foliage, such as Australian pine trees, had been planted on the tip of Key Biscayne, Florida (now the Bill Baggs State Park). These non-native plants had very few natural enemies in their new environment, and quickly dominated the plant life, resulting in a loss of the natural habitat of that area. However, these Australian non-native trees lacked the ability to withstand hurricane-force winds because of their shallow roots, and Hurricane Andrew came along and destroyed them all in 1992. It was only then that park officials seized the rare opportunity to replant the park with native foliage.

Virtually all literal use of the word hurricane in literary works evokes violent wind. Yet some of the worst tropical cyclone catastrophes are caused not by winds but by torrential rain (e.g. Hurricane Katrina in 2005). The rainfall associated with hurricanes is both beneficial and harmful. Although the rains contribute to the water needs of the areas traversed by the hurricane, the rains are harmful when the amount is so large as to cause extensive flooding. There are about four factors that determine how much rain will fall in a given place: the amount of water vapour in the air, topography, the vertical extent and duration of the updraft. In fact, some of the most devastating floods are produced by tropical cyclones of sub-hurricane strength. The torrential rainfall which normally accompanies a hurricane can cause serious flooding. A recent and especially tragic example of this is Hurricane Mitch of 1998, the deadliest North Atlantic hurricane since the Great Hurricane of 1780. Floods produced by Mitch killed more than 11,000 people in Central America, and the President of Honduras declared that Mitch destroyed 50 years of progress in that country. Whereas, the storm surge and high winds are concentrated near the eye, the rain may extend outward for hundreds of miles away from the center and may last for several days, affecting areas well after the hurricane has diminished or passed over a particular area.

An average of 10 to 15 inches of rain falls over coastal areas during the passage of a well-developed hurricane, but over 20 inches have been recorded and rain may fall at the rate of one inch an hour. In twenty-four hours a record of 32.67 inches of rain fell at Belize City in Belize from Hurricane Keith in 2000, for comparison, the average annual rainfall of Belize is about 74.4 inches. Furthermore, Hurricane Camille dumped over 760 millimeters (30 inches) of rainfall over Central Virginia, drowning 109 persons in the process with flash flooding. For comparison, the average annual rainfall of Central Virginia is about 45.22 inches. The Cedar Key Hurricane of September, 1950, poured nearly 39 inches of rain in 24 hours on Yankeetown, Florida, off the Gulf Coast. This 9-day hurricane traced an unusual double loop in the Cedar Keys area, and the coast from Sarasota northward suffered extensive wind and flood damage. The coastal areas inland from Yankeetown to Tampa were flooded for several weeks. In 1963 Pacific hurricane season, Typhoon Gloria dumped 49.13 inches of rainfall in Baxin, Taiwan. While in the 1967 Pacific typhoon season 65.83 inches felled at Xinliao in Taiwan during a 24 hour period from Typhoon Carla. For comparison, the average annual rainfall of Xinliao, Taiwan is about 85 inches. However, Tropical Cyclone Denise in Foc-Foc in the La Reunion Island on January 7th and 8th of 1966 holds a world record of 45 inches in just 12 hours and 71.80 inches of rainfall in 24 hours in the same location for the total amount of rainfall over a particular location from a tropical cyclone.

Of all the tropical cyclone damaging agents, strong winds are perhaps the best understood of all of them. Damaging winds will accompany any hurricane, no matter what category it is. A hurricane by definition has winds of at least 74 miles per hour. This wind speed alone is enough to cause great damage to poorly constructed signage and knock over some of the sturdiest trees and other vegetation. Obviously, the stronger the hurricane (higher winds), the more potential there is for wind damage to exists. The fierce winds which blow in an anti-clockwise direction around the center of the central calm in the northern hemisphere may reach 100 to 200 mph. Wind speeds are the greatest near the surface around the central calm or eye. However, whenever a hurricane touches a landmass its wind speed is significantly reduced. The strongest winds (one minute sustained winds) reported in the Caribbean during the passage of a hurricane were, Hurricane Camille in 1969(190mph), Hurricane Allen in 1980 (190mph), Hurricane Wilma of 2005(185mph), and Hurricane Gilbert of 1988(185mph).

Once a hurricane makes landfall, there is a significant drop in the surface and upper level winds. Two factors accounts for this abrupt drop in wind speeds once a hurricane makes landfall. Over land a hurricane is no longer in contact with its energy source of warm ocean water. Furthermore, the increased surface roughness over land weakens the system. The land surface is rougher than the sea surface so that when a hurricane moves over land, its surface winds are slowed and blow at a greater angle across the isobars and toward the storm center. This wind shift causes the storm to begin to fill, that is, the central pressure rises, the horizontal pressure gradient weakens, and the winds slacken. The energy released in a normal hurricane is great. An average hurricane winds are so great that it is equipped with some 1.5 trillion watts of power in its winds which if converted to electricity would be equivalent to about half of the world's entire electrical generating capacity. In fact, in a single day, a hurricane can release the amount of energy necessary to supply all of the United States electrical needs for about six months. One second of a hurricane's energy is equivalent to about ten Hiroshima atomic bombs and in total, a single hurricane during its lifetime can dissipate more energy than that contained in thirty thousand atomic bombs. The hurricane which hit Galveston, Texas, in September, 1900, during its lifespan had sufficient energy to drive all the power stations in the world for four years. A large hurricane stirs up more than a million miles of atmosphere every second.

The force of the wind can quickly decimate the tree population, tear down power lines and utility poles, knock over signs, and may be strong enough to destroy some homes and buildings. Flying debris can also cause damage, and in some cases where people are caught outdoors, injuries and death can prevail. When a hurricane first makes landfall, it is common for tornadoes to form which can cause severe localized wind damage. In most cases, however, wind is a secondary cause of damage. Storm surge is normally the primary cause. The right front quadrant is strongest side of the hurricane; this is the area where there is positive convergence. In this quadrant the winds are typically the strongest, the storm surge is highest, and the possibility of tornadoes is the greatest. The right side of a hurricane is the strongest side because the wind speed and the hurricane speed-of-motion are complimentary there; meaning on this side, the wind blows in the same direction as the storm's forward motion.

On the left side, the hurricane's speed of motion subtracts from the wind speed because the main bulk of the storm is moving away from it. The storm's angle of attack is a key factor in its impact. Just as in an automobile accident, the highest level of destruction is caused by a hurricane hitting the coastline head-on. If a storm travels up the coast, with its left side brushing the seashore, the most dangerous part of the storm stays offshore and the net effect will be much less damage. The worst-case scenario would be a hurricane arriving onshore at high or spring tide. With the ocean level already at its highest point of the day, the storm surge from a Category 4 or 5 hurricane can add another 15 to 20 feet of water, with abnormally large waves breaking on top of that. Water weighs around 1,700 pounds per cubic yard, and there are very few structures that can stand up to the force a high storm surge can produce.

Violent hurricane winds may produce storm surges of up to 45 feet high at sea, and storm surges of over twenty feet may crash against the shores at speeds of up to 40 mph. Long swells may move outwards from the eye of a hurricane for more than 1,000 miles. These long swells are often the first visible signs of an approaching hurricane and are known as the *storm surge*. A storm surge, also called a *hurricane surge*, is the abnormal rise in the sea level caused by wind and pressure forces of a hurricane. It can be extremely devastating, and is in fact a major cause of damage and danger to life during the passage of a hurricane. It is estimated that 75% of all hurricane related deaths and injuries are caused by the storm surge and the remaining 20% of the 25% is simply caused by negligence. For example, persons out of curiosity venturing out into the peak of the storm and being killed by flying debris, or stepping on a live wire and getting electrocuted before the 'all-clear' is given.

The storm surge isn't just another wave pushed ahead of a storm; it acts like a gigantic bulldozer that can destroy anything in its path. Think of the storm surge as a moving wall of water weighing millions of tons. The storm surge itself is caused by the wind and pressure 'pushing' the water into the continental shelf and onto the coastline caused by a hurricane. The height of the storm surge is the difference between the observed level of sea surface and its level in the absence of the storm. In other words, the storm surge is estimated by subtracting the normal or astronomical tide from the observed or estimated storm tide. The astronomical tide is the results from the gravitational interactions between the earth, moon, and sun, generally producing two high and two low oceanic tides per day. Should the storm surge coincide with the high astronomical tide, several additional feet could be added to the water level, especially when the sun and moon are aligned, which produces the highest oceanic tides (known as syzygy).

Hurricanes have a vacuum effect on the ocean. The water is pulled toward the hurricane, causing it to 'pile up' like a small mountain. A mound of water forms under the center of a hurricane as the intensely low pressure draws water up. The shape of the shoreline and the ocean bottom has a great deal to do with a storm surge's magnitude. Over the ocean, this mound of water is barely noticeable, but it builds up as the storm approaches land. The surge's height as it reaches land depends upon the slope of the ocean floor at the coast. The more gradual the slope, the less volume of sea there is in which the surge can dissipate and further inland the water is displaced. This is why Hurricane Katrina did so much damage in 2005 and why areas like New Orleans in the United States will continue to remain vulnerable to future hurricanes. This dome of water can be up to 40 to 60 miles long as it moves onto the shoreline near the landfall point of the eye. A cubic yard of sea water weighs approximately 1,700 pounds and this water is constantly slamming into shoreline structures, even well-built structures get quickly demolished because this water acts like a battering ram on these vulnerable shoreline structures.

The highest storm surge ever recorded was produced by the 1899 Cyclone Mahina, which caused a storm surge of over 13 meters (43 feet) at Bathurst Bay, Australia. This value was derived from reanalysis of debris sightings and eyewitness reports, as a result it is controversial within the meteorological community, but clearly a phenomenal storm surge occurred. In the United States, the greatest recorded storm surge was generated by 2005's Hurricane Katrina, which produced a massive storm surge of approximately 9 meters (30 feet) high in the town of Bay St. Louis, Mississippi, and in the surrounding coastal counties. Hurricane Camille came in second with 24 feet of water in 1969. The worst storm surge, in terms of loss of life, was the 1970 Bhola Cyclone, which occurred in the area of the Bay of Bengal. This area is particularly prone to tidal surges and is often referred to as the 'storm surge capital of the world' which produced 142 moderate to severe storm surge events from 1582 to 1991. These surges, some in excess of eight meters (26 feet), have killed hundreds of thousands of people, primarily in Bangladesh. The Caribbean Islands have endured many devastating surges as well. Unfortunately, the records for storm surge effects in the Caribbean are sadly lacking or virtually non-existent. These powerful hurricanes listed above caused very high storm surge. However, worldwide storm surge data is sparse. Hurricanes and the accompanying storm surge they produce can even affect the very depths of the ocean. In 1975, some meteorological and oceanographic instruments were dropped from a research reconnaissance airplane in the Gulf of Mexico, which showed that Hurricane Eloise disturbed the ocean hundreds of feet down and created underwater waves that persisted for weeks.

CHAPTER THREE

THE HISTORY BEHIND THE WORD 'HURRICANE' AND OTHER TROPICAL CYCLONE NAMES

What is a hurricane? Simply put, it is a large, violent storm that originates in a tropical region and features extremely high winds-by definition, in excess of 74 miles per hour and blow anti-clockwise about the center in the northern hemisphere. It also brings drenching rains and has the ability to spin off tornadoes. Hurricanes are storms that form between the tropics of Cancer and Capricorn in the Atlantic, Pacific and Indian Oceans. They have different names depending on where they are formed and located throughout the world. In the Atlantic they are called hurricanes, in the north-west Pacific, typhoons, in the Indian Ocean they are known as tropical cyclones, while north of Australia they are sometimes called Willy Willies. However, by any name, they are impressive to behold. To form, hurricanes need sea surface temperatures of 26.5°C or greater, abundant moisture and light winds in the upper atmosphere. The hurricane season in the North Atlantic lasts from June 1st to November 30th. Around 80 tropical storms form each year with most of them occurring in the south or south-east of Asia. The North Atlantic region accounts for only a mere 12 percent of the worldwide total of tropical cyclones. These storms are enormous creatures of nature, often between 120 and 430 miles in diameter. They may last from a few days to a week or more and their tracks are notoriously unpredictable.

A tropical cyclone is a powerful storm system characterized by a low pressure center and numerous severe thunderstorms that produce strong winds and flooding rainfall. A tropical cyclone feeds on the heat released (latent heat) when moist air rises and the water vapour it contains condenses. They are fueled by a different heat mechanism than other cyclonic windstorms such as nor'easters, European windstorms, and polar lows, leading to their classification as "warm core" storm systems. The term 'tropical' simply refers to both the geographic origin of these systems, which forms almost exclusively in tropical regions of the earth, and their formation in maritime tropical air masses. The term "cyclone" refers to a family of such storms' cyclonic nature, with anti-clockwise rotation in the northern hemisphere and clockwise rotation in the southern hemisphere. Depending on their location and strength, tropical cyclones are referred to by other names, such as, hurricanes, typhoons, tropical storms, cyclonic storms, tropical depressions and simply cyclones which all have low atmospheric pressure at their center. A hurricane consists of a mass of organized thunderstorms that spiral in towards the extreme low pressure of the storm's eye or center. The most intense thunderstorms will have the heaviest rainfall, and the highest winds occurring outside the eye, in the region known as the eyewall. In the eye itself, the air is warm, winds are light, and skies are generally clear and rain free but can also be cloudy to overcast.

Captain George Nares, a nineteenth century Scottish naval officer and polar explorer, was always on the lookout for hurricanes. "June-too soon," he wrote. "July-stand by; August-look out you must; September-remember; October-all over." Whatever you think about the dynamics of hurricanes-two things can be said about them and that is they are very unpredictable and extremely destructive. The forces of nature such as, deadly hurricanes have shaped the lives of people from the earliest times. Indeed, the first 'meteorologists' were priests and shamans of ancient communities. Whatever lifestyles these ancient people followed, they all developed beliefs about the world around them. These beliefs helped them to explain how the world began, what happen in the future, or what happened after a person died. The world of spirits was very important. Those people, who became noted for their skills at interpreting signs in the world around them, became spiritual leaders in their communities. All religions and different races of people recognized the power of the weather elements and most scriptures contain tales about or prophecies foretelling, great natural disasters sometimes visited upon a community because of the sins of its citizens. Ancient peoples often reacted to the weather in a fearful, superstitious manner. They believed that mythological gods controlled the weather elements such as, wind, rain and sun which governed their existence. When weather conditions were favorable, there would be plenty of game to hunt, fish to catch, and bountiful harvests. But their livelihood was at the mercy of the wild weather because fierce hurricanes could damage villages of flimsy huts, destroy crops and generate vast floodwaters that could sweep away livestock.

In times of hurricanes, food shortages and starvation were constant threats as crops failed and game animals became scarce when their food supplies dried up due to a hurricane. These ancient tribes as you will see later believed that their weather fortunes were inextricably linked with the moods and actions of their gods. For this reason, they spent a great deal of time and effort appeasing these mythological weather gods. Many of these ancient tribes tried to remain on favorable terms with their deities through a mixture of prayers, rituals, dances and sometimes even human sacrifices. In some cultures such as the Aztecs of Central America, they would offer up human sacrifices to appease their rain-god Tláloc. In addition, Quetzalcoatl, the all-powerful and mighty deity in the ancient Aztec society, whose name means 'Precious Feathered Serpent,' played a critical role; he was the creator of life and controlled devastating hurricanes. The Egyptians celebrated Ra, the Sun god. Thor was the Norse god of thunder and lightning, a god to please so that calm waters would grace their seafaring expeditions. The Greeks had many weather gods; however, it was Zeus who was the most powerful of them all.

The actual origin of the word 'hurricane' and other tropical cyclone names were based on the many religions, cultures, myths, and races of people. In modern cultures, 'myth' has come to mean a story or an idea that is not true. The word 'myth' comes directly from the Greek word 'mythos'(μύθος), whose many meanings include, 'word', 'saying', 'story', and 'fiction.' Today, the word 'myth' is used any and everywhere and people now speak of myths about how to catch or cure the common cold. But the age-old myths about hurricanes in this book were an important part of these people's religions, cultures, and everyday lives. Often they were both deeply spiritual and culturally entertaining and significant. For many of these ancient races, their mythology was their history and there was often little, if any distinction between the two. Some myths were actually based on historical events, such as, devastating hurricanes or even wars but myths often offer us a treasure trove of dramatic tales. The active beings in myths are generally gods and goddesses, heroes and heroines, or animals. Most myths are set in a timeless past before recorded and critical history began. A myth is a sacred narrative in the sense that it holds religious or spiritual significance for those who tell it, and it contributes to and expresses systems of thought and values. It is a traditional story, typically involving supernatural beings or forces or creatures, which embodies and provides an explanation, aetiology (*origin myths)*, or justification for something such as the early history of a society, a religious belief or ritual, or a natural phenomenon.

The United Nation's sub-body, the World Meteorological Organization estimates that in an average year, about 80 of these tropical cyclones kills up to 15,000 people worldwide and cause an estimate of several billion dollars' worth of property damage alone. Meteorologists have estimated that between 1600 to today, hurricanes have caused well over 200,000 deaths in this region alone and over 8 million deaths worldwide. Hurricanes, typhoons and cyclones are all the same kind of violent storms originating over warm tropical ocean waters and are called by different names all over the world. From the Timor Sea to as far as northwestern Australia they are called cyclones or by the Australian colloquial term of 'Willy-Willies' from an old Aboriginal word (derived from whirlwind). In the Bay of Bengal and the Indian Ocean, they are simply called Cyclones (an English name based on a Greek word meaning "coil" as in "coil of a snake" because the winds that spiral within them resembles the coil of a snake) and are not named even to this day.

They are called Hurricanes (derived from a Carib, Mayan or Taínos/Arawak Indian word) in the Gulf of Mexico, Central and North America, the Caribbean and Eastern North Pacific Oceans (east of the International Dateline). A Hurricane is the name given to these intense storms of tropical origin, with sustained winds exceeding 64 knots (74 miles per hour). In the Indian Ocean all the way to Mauritius and along the Arabian Coasts they are known as 'Asifa-t.' In Mexico and Central America hurricanes are also known as El Cordonazo and in Haiti, they are known as Tainos. While they are called Typhoons [originating from the Chinese word 'Ty-Fung' (going back to as far as the Song (960-1278) and Yuan (1260-1341) dynasties) translated to mean 'Big or Great Wind'...] in the Western North Pacific and in the Philippines and the South China Sea (west of the International Dateline) they are known as 'Baguios' or 'Chubasco'(or simply a Typhoon). The word Baguio was derived from the Philippine city of Baguio, which was inundated in July, 1911, with over 46 inches of rain in a 24-hour period. Also, in the scientific literature of the 1600s, including the book *Geographia Naturalis* by geographer Bernhardus Varenius, the term whirlwind was used, but this term never achieved region or worldwide acceptance as a name for a hurricane.

In Japan they are known as 'Repus,' or by the more revered name of a Typhoon. The word "taifū" (台風) in Japanese means *Typhoon*; the first character meaning "pedestal" or "stand"; the second character meaning wind. The Japanese term for "divine wind" is Kamikaze (神風). The Kamikaze, were a pair or series of typhoons that were said to have saved Japan from two Mongol invasion fleets under Kublai Khan which attacked Japan in 1274 and again in 1281. The latter is said to have been the largest attempted naval invasion in history whose scale was only recently eclipsed in modern times by the D-Day invasion by the allied forces into Normandy in 1944. This was the term that was given to the typhoon winds that came up and blew the Mongol invasion fleet off course and destroyed it as it was poised to attack Japan.

On October 29, 1274, the first invasion began. Some 40,000 men, including about 25,000 Mongolians, 8,000 Korean troops, and 7,000 Chinese seamen, set sail from Korea in about 900 ships to attack Japan. With fewer troops and inferior weapons, the Japanese were far outmatched and overwhelmed and were sure to be defeated. But at nightfall just as they were attacking the Japanese coastal forces, the Korean sailors sensed an approaching typhoon and begged their reluctant Mongol commanders to put the invasion force back at sea or else it would be trapped on the coast and its ships destroyed at anchor by this typhoon. The next morning, the Japanese were surprised and delighted to see the Mongol fleet struggling to regain the open ocean in the midst of a great typhoon. The ships sadly, were no match for this great storm, and many foundered or were simply dashed to bits and pieces on the rocky coast. Nearly 13,000 men perished in this storm mostly by drowning. This Mongol fleet had been decimated by a powerful typhoon as it was poised to attack Japan.

With the second storm, even as Kublai Khan was mounting his second Japanese offensive, he was waging a bitter war of conquest against southern China, whose people had resisted him for 40 years. But finally, in 1279, the last of the southern providences, Canton, fell to the Mongol forces, and China was united under one ruler for the first time in three hundred years. Buoyed by success, Kublai again tried to bully Japan into submission by sending his emissaries to the Japanese asking them to surrender to his forces. But this time the Japanese executed his emissaries, enraging him even further and thereby paving the way for a second invasion. Knowing this was inevitable; the Japanese went to work building coastal fortifications, including a massive dike around Hakozaki Bay, which encompasses the site of the first invasion.

The second Mongol invasion of Japan assumed staggering proportions. One armada consisted of 40,000 Mongols, Koreans, and north Chinese who were to set sail from Korea, while a second, larger force of some 100,000 men was to set out from various ports in south China. The invasion plan called for the two armadas to join forces in the spring before the summer typhoon season, but unfortunately the southern force was late, delaying the invasion until late June 1281. The Japanese defenders held back the invading forces for six weeks until on the fifteenth and sixteenth of August, history then repeated itself when a gigantic typhoon decimated the Mongol fleet poised to attack Japan again.

As a direct result of these famous storms, the Japanese came to think of the typhoon as a 'divine wind,' or 'kamikaze,' sent by their gods to deliver their land from the evil invaders. Because they needed another intervention to drive away the Allied fleet in WWII, they gave this name to their Japanese suicide pilots as nationalist propaganda. In the Japanese Shinto religion, many forces of nature are worshipped as gods, known as 'kami' are represented as human figures. The Japanese god of thunder is often depicted as a strong man beating his drum. The Japanese called it Kamikaze, and the Mongols never ever returned to attack Japan again because of their personal experiences with these two great storms. In popular Japanese myths at the time, the god Raijin was the god who turned the storms against the Mongols. Other variations say that the god Fūjin or Ryūjin caused the destructive kamikaze. This use of *kamikaze* has come to be the common meaning of the word in English.[1]

Whatever name they are known by in different regions of the world, they refer to the same weather phenomena a 'tropical cyclone.' They are all the same severe tropical storms that share the same fundamental characteristics aside from the fact that they rotate clockwise in the southern hemisphere and counterclockwise in the northern hemisphere. However, by World Meteorological Organization International Agreement, the term tropical cyclone is the general term given to all hurricane-type storms that originate over tropical waters. The term cyclone, used by meteorologists, refers to an area of low pressure in which winds move counterclockwise in the northern hemisphere around the low pressure center and are usually associated with bad weather, heavy rainfall and strong wind speeds. Whereas, a tropical cyclone was the name first given to these intense circular storms by Englishman Captain Henry Piddington (1797-1848) who was keenly interested in storms affecting India and spent many years collecting information on ships caught in severe storms in the Indian Ocean. He would later become the President of the Marine Courts of Inquiry in Calcutta, India and used the term tropical cyclone to refer to a tropical storm which blew the freighter '*Charles Heddles*' in circles for nearly a week in Mauritius in February of 1845. In his book '*Sailor's Hornbook for the Laws of Storms in All Parts of the World*,' published in 1855, he called these storms cyclones, from the Greek word for coil of a snake. He called these storm tropical cyclones because it expressed sufficiently what he described as the 'tendency to move in a circular motion.'

The word cyclone is from the Greek word 'κύκλος', meaning 'circle' or Kyklos meaning 'coils of the snake', describing the rotating movement of the storm. An Egyptian word 'Cykline' meaning to 'to spin' has also been cited as a possible origin. In Greek mythology, Typhoeus or Typhōn was the son of Tartarus and Gaia. He was a monster with many heads, a man's body, and a coiled snake's tail. The king of the gods and god of the sky and weather, Zeus, fought a great battle with Typhoeus and finally buried him under Mount Etna. According to legend, he was the source of the powerful storm winds which caused widespread devastation, loss of many lives and numerous shipwrecks. The Greek word 'typhōn' meaning 'whirlwind' comes from this legend, another possible source for the origin of the English word 'typhoon.' The term is most often used for cyclones occurring in the Western Pacific Ocean and Indian Ocean. In addition, the word is an alteration of the Arabic word, tūfān, meaning hurricane, and the Greek word, typhōn, meaning violent storm and an Egyptian word 'Cykline' meaning to 'to spin.'

The history of the word typhoon presents a perfect example of the long journey that many words made in coming to the English Language vocabulary. It travelled from Greece to Arabia to India, and also arose independently in China, before assuming its current form in our language. The Greek word typhōn, used both as the name of the father of the winds and a common noun meaning "whirlwind, typhoon," was borrowed into Arabic during the Middle Ages, when Arabic learning both preserved and expanded the classical heritage and passed it on to Europe and other parts of the world. In the Arabic version of the Greek word, it was passed into languages spoken in India, where Arabic-speaking Muslim invaders had settled in the eleventh century. Thus the descendant of the Arabic word, passing into English through an Indian language and appearing in English in forms such as touffon and tūfān, originally referred specifically to a severe storm in India.

The modern form of typhoon was also influenced by a borrowing from the Cantonese variety of Chinese, namely the word 'Ty-Fung' and respelled to make it look more like Greek. 'Ty-Fung' meaning literally 'great wind' was coincidentally similar to the Arabic borrowing and is first recorded in English guise as tuffoon in 1699. The Cantonese tai-fung and the Mandarin ta-feng are derived from the word jufeng. It is also believed to have originated from the Chinese word 'jufeng.' 'Ju' can mean either 'a wind coming from four directions' or 'scary'; 'feng' is the generic word for wind. Arguably the first scientific description of a tropical cyclone and the first appearance of the word jufeng in the literature is contained in a Chinese book called Nan Yue Zhi (Book of the Southern Yue Region), written around A.D. 470. In that book, it is stated that *"Many Jufeng occur around Xi'n County. Ju is a wind (or storm) that comes in all four directions. Another meaning for Jufeng is that it is a scary wind. It frequently occurs in the sixth and seventh month (of the Chinese lunar calendar; roughly July and August of the Gregorian calendar). Before it comes it is said that chickens and dogs are silent for three days. Major ones may last up to seven days and minor ones last one or two days. These are called heifeng (meaning black storms/winds) in foreign countries."*[2]

European travellers to China in the sixteenth century took note of a word sounding like typhoon being used to denote severe coastal windstorms. On the other hand, typhoon was used in European texts and literature around 1500, long before systematic contact with China was established. It is possible that the European use of this word was derived from Typhon, the draconian earth demon of Greek Legend. The various forms of the word from these different countries coalesced and finally became typhoon, a spelling that officially first appeared in 1819 in Percy Bysshe Shelley's play 'Prometheus Unbound.' This play was concerned with the torments of the Greek mythological figure Prometheus and his suffering at the hands of Zeus. By the early eighteenth century, typhon and typhoon were in common use in European literature, as in the famous poem *Summer* by Scottish poet James Thomson (1700-1748):

> *"Beneath the radiant line that grits the globe,*
> *The circling Typhon, whirled from point to point.*
> *Exhausting all the rage of all the sky,*
> *And dire Ecnephia, reign."*[3]

In Yoruba mythology, *Oya*, the female warrior, was the goddess of fire, wind and thunder. When she became angry, she created tornadoes and hurricanes. Additionally, to ward off violent and tropical downpours, Yoruba priests in southwestern Nigeria held ceremonies around images of the thunder and lightning god Sango to protect them from the powerful winds of hurricanes. In ancient Egyptian legend, Set was regarded as the god of storms. He was associated with natural calamities like hurricanes, thunderstorms, lightning, earthquakes and eclipses. In Iroquois mythology, Ga-oh was the wind giant, whose house was guarded by several animals, each representing a specific type of wind. The Bear was the north wind who brought winter hurricanes, and he was also capable of crushing the world with his storms or destroying it with his cold air. In Babylonian mythology, Marduk, the god of gods, defeated the bad tempered dragon goddess Tiamat with the help of a hurricane. When the other gods learned about Tiamat's plans to destroy them, they turned to Marduk for help. Armed with a bow and an arrow, strong winds and a powerful hurricane, Marduk captured Tiamat and let the hurricane winds fill her jaws and stomach. Then he shot an arrow into her belly and killed her and then became the lord of all the gods.

The Meso-American and Caribbean Indians worshipped many gods. They had similar religions based on the worship mainly agricultural and natural elements gods, even though the gods' names and the symbols for them were a bit different. People asked their gods for good weather, lack of hurricanes, abundant crops and good health or for welfare. The main Inca god was the creator god *Viracocha*. His assistants were the gods of the earth and the sea. As farming occupied such an important place in the region, the 'Earth mother' or 'Earth goddess' was particularly important. The Aztecs, Mayas, Taínos and other Indians adopted many gods from other civilizations. As with the Mayans, Aztecs and Taínos, each god was connected with some aspects of nature or natural forces and in each of these religions, hurricanes or the fear of them and the respect for them played a vital part of their worship. The destructive power of storms like hurricanes inspires both fear and fascination and it is no surprise that humans throughout time have tried to control these storms. Ancient tribes were known to make offerings to the weather gods to appease them. People in ancient times believed that these violent storms were brought on by angry weather gods. In some cultures, the word for hurricane means 'storm god', 'evil spirit', 'devil' or 'god of thunder and lightning.'

The word *hurricane* comes to us via the early Spanish explorers of the New World, who were told by the Indians of this region of an evil god capable of inflicting strong winds and great destruction on their lives and possessions. The natives of the Caribbean and Central America had a healthy respect for hurricanes and an uncanny understanding of nature. In the legends of the Mayan civilizations of Central America and the Taínos of the Caribbean, these gods played an important role in their Creation. According to their beliefs and myths, the wicked gods Huracán, Hurrikán, Hunraken, and Jurakan annually victimized and savagely ravaged their homes, inflicting them with destructive winds, torrential rainfall and deadly floods. These natives were terrified whenever these gods made an appearance. They would beat drums, blew conch shells, shouted curses, engage in bizarre rituals and did everything possible to thwart these gods and drive them away. Sometimes they felt they were successful in frightening them off and at other times their fury could not be withstood and they suffered the consequences from an angry weather god. Some of these natives depicted these fearsome deities on primitive carvings as a hideous creature with swirling arms, ready to release his winds and claim its prey.

There are several theories about the origin of the word *hurricane*; some people believe it originated from the Caribbean Arawak-speaking Indians. It is believed that these Indians named their storm god 'Huracán' and over time it eventually evolved into the English word 'hurricane.' Others believed that it originated from the fierce group of cannibalistic Indians called the Caribs, but according to some historians this seems like the least likely source of this word. Native people throughout the Caribbean Basin linked hurricanes to supernatural forces and had a word for these storms which often had similar spellings but they all signified death and destruction by some evil spirit and the early European colonial explorers to the New World picked up the native names. Actually, one early historian noted that the local Caribbean Indians in preparation for these storms often tied themselves to trees to keep from being blown away from the winds of these storms. According to one early seventeenth-century English account, Indians on St. Christopher viewed 'Hurry-Cano' as a "tempestuous spirit." These ancient Indians of this region personalized the hurricane, believing that it was bearing down on them as punishment by the gods for something they had done-or not done. These days, there is more science and less superstition to these powerful storms of nature called hurricanes. Yet we humanize hurricanes with familiar names, and the big ones become folkloric and iconic characters, their rampages woven into the histories of the Caribbean, North and Central American coastal towns and cities.

A next popular theory about the hurricane's origin is that it came from the Mayan Indians of Mexico who had an ancient word for these storms, called 'Hurrikán' (or 'Huracán'). Hurrikán was the Mayan god of the storm. He was present at all three attempts to create humanity, in which he did most of the actual work of creating human beings under the direction of Kukulkán (known by the Aztec name Quetzalcoatl) and Tepeu. Unlike the other Creators, Hurrikán was not heavily personified by the Mayans and was generally considered to be more like the winds and the storms themselves. In the Mayan language, his name means "one legged". The word *hurricane* is derived from Hurrikán's name. Hurrikán is similar to the Aztec god Tlaloc. In Mayan mythology, 'Hurrikán' ("one legged") was a wind, storm and fire god and one of the creator deities who participated in all three attempts of creating humanity. 'Hurrikán' was the Mayan god of big wind, and his image was chiseled into the walls of the Mayan temples. He was one of the three most powerful forces in the pantheon of deities, along with Cabrakán (earthquakes) and Chirakán (volcanoes). He also caused the Great Flood after the first humans angered the gods. He supposedly lived in the windy mists above the floodwaters and repeated "earth" until land came up from the seas. In appearance he has one leg, the other being transformed into a serpent, a zoomorphic snout or long-nose, and a smoking object such as a cigar, torch holder or axe head which pierces a mirror on his forehead.

Actually, the first human historical record of hurricanes can be found in the ancient Mayan hieroglyphics. A powerful and deadly hurricane struck the Northern Yucatán in 1464 wiping out most of the Mayan Indian population of that area. According to Mayan mythology, the Mayan rain and wind god, Chac, sent rain for the crops. But he also sent hurricanes, which destroyed crops and flooded villages. The Mayans hoped that if they made offerings to Chac (including human sacrifices), the rains would continue to fall, but the hurricanes would cease. Every year the Mayans threw a young woman into the sea as a sacrifice to appease the god Hurrikán and a warrior was also sacrificed to lead the girl to Hurrikán's underwater kingdom. Also, one of the sacrifices in honour of this god was to drown children in wells. In some Maya regions, Chac the god of rain and wind was so important that the facades of their buildings were covered with the masks of Chac. In actual fact, at its peak, it was one of the most densely populated and culturally dynamic societies in the world but still they always built their homes far away from the hurricane prone coast.

By customarily building their major settlements away from the hurricane-prone coastline, the Mayan Indians practiced a method of disaster mitigation that, if rigorously applied today, would reduce the potential for devastation along coastal areas. The only Mayan port city discovered to date is the small to medium sized city of Tulum, on the east coast of the Yucatán Peninsula south of Cancun. Tulum remained occupied when the Spaniards first arrived in the sixteenth century and its citizens were more prepared for the storms than for the Spaniards. As the many visitors to these ruins can see, the ceremonial buildings and grounds of the city were so skillfully constructed that many remain today and withstanding many hurricanes. The Indians of Guatemala called the god of stormy weather 'Hunrakán.' Of course, the Indians did not observe in what period of the year these hurricanes could strike their country; they believed that the devil or the evil spirits sent them whenever they pleased. Their gods were the uncontrollable forces of nature on which their lives were wholly dependent, the sun, the stars, the rains and the storms.

The Taínos were generally considered to be part of the Taíno-Arawak Indians who travelled from the Orinoco-Amazon region of South America to Venezuela and then into the Caribbean Islands of the Dominican Republic, Haiti, the Bahamas, Jamaica, Puerto

Rico, and as far west as Cuba. Christopher Columbus called these inhabitants of the western hemisphere 'Indians' because he mistakenly thought he had reached the islands on the eastern side of the Indian Ocean. The word 'Taíno' comes directly from Christopher Columbus because they were the indigenous set of people he encountered on his first voyage to the Caribbean and they called themselves 'Taíno' meaning 'good' or 'noble' to differentiate themselves from their fierce enemies-the Carib Indians. This name applied to all the Island Taínos including those in the Lesser Antilles. These so-called Indians were divided into innumerable small ethnic groups, each with its own combination of linguistic, cultural, and biological traits.

Locally, the Taínos referred to themselves by the name of their location. For example, those in Puerto Rico referred to themselves as Boricua which means 'people from the island of the valiant noble lords' their island was called Borike'n meaning 'Great land of the valiant noble lord' and those occupying the Bahamas called themselves 'Lucayo' or 'Lucayans' meaning 'small islands.' Another important consequence of their navigation skills and their canoes was the fact that the Taínos had contact with other indigenous groups of the Americas, including the Mayas of Mexico and Guatemala. What is the evidence to suggest that the Taínos had contact with the Mayan culture? There are many similarities between the Mayan god, 'Hurrikán' and Taíno god 'Huracán' also, similarities in their ballgames, and similarities in their social structure and social stratification. Furthermore, the Meso-Indians of Mexico also flattened the heads of their infants in a similar fashion to the Island based Taínos and their relatives.

The Taíno Indians believed in two supreme gods, one male, and the other female. They also believed that man had a soul and after death he would go to a paradise called *Coyaba* where the natural weather elements such as droughts and hurricanes would be forgotten in an eternity of feasting and dancing. In the Taíno Indians culture, they believed in a female zemí (spirit) named Guabancex who controlled hurricanes among other things but when angered she sent out her herald Guataba to order all the other zemis to lend her their winds and with this great power she made the winds and the waters move and cast houses to the ground and uprooted trees. Representations of Guabancex portrayed her head as the eye of the storm, with twisting arms symbolizing the swirling winds. The international symbol that we use today for hurricanes was derived from this zemi. The various likenesses of this god invariably consist of a head of an indeterminate gender with no torso, two distinctive arms spiraling out from its sides. Most of these images exhibit cyclonic (counterclockwise) spirals. The Cuban ethnologist Fernando Ortiz believes that they were inspired by the tropical hurricanes that have always plagued the Caribbean. If so, the Taínos discovered the cyclonic or vortical nature of hurricanes many hundreds of years before the descendents of European settlers did. How they may have made this deduction remains a mystery to this day.

The spiral rain bands so well known to us from satellites and radars were not officially 'discovered' until the meteorological radar was developed during World War II, and they are far too big to be discerned by eye from the ground. It is speculated that these ancient people surveyed the damage done by the hurricane and, based on the direction by which the trees fell, concluded that the damage could only have been done by rotating winds. Or perhaps they witnessed tornadoes or waterspouts, which are much smaller phenomena whose rotation is readily apparent, and came to believe that all destructive winds are rotary. They also believed that sickness, or misfortunes such as devastating hurricanes were the works of malignant or highly displeased zemis and good fortune was a sign that the zemis were pleased. To keep the zemis pleased, great public festivals were held to propitiate the tribal zemis, or simply in their honour. On these occasions everyone would be well-dressed in elaborate outfits and the cacique would lead a parade beating a wooden drum. Gifts of the finest cassava were offered to the zemis in hopes that the zemis would protect them against the four chief scourges of the Taínos existence: fire, sickness, the Caribs and most importantly devastating hurricanes.

The language of the Taínos was not a written one, and written works from them are very scarce. Some documentation of their lifestyles may be found in the writings of Spanish priests such as, Bartholomew de Las Casas in Puerto Rico and the Dominican Republic during the early 16th century. Some of the Taíno origin words were borrowed by the Spanish and subsequently found its way into the English Language, and are modern day reminders of this once proud and vigorous race of people. These words include; avocado, potato, buccaneer, cay, manatee, maize, guava, *barbacoa* (barbecue), *cacique* (chief), jamaca (hammock), Tabacú (tobacco), caniba (cannibal), *canoa* (canoe), Iguana (lizard), and *huracán* or *huruká* (hurricane). Interestingly, two of the islands in the Bahamas, Inagua and Mayaguana both derived their names from the Lucayan word 'Iguana.' Bimini (meaning "two small islands" in English), another island here in the Bahamas also got its name from these Indians; however most of the other islands here in the Bahamas and the rest of the Caribbean were also given Indian names but they have been changed over the many years and centuries by various groups of people who settled or passed through the Bahamas or other Caribbean islands. For example in the Bahamas, the Lucayans called Exuma-*Yuma*, San Salvador was called *Guanahani*, Long Island was called *Samana*, Cat Island was called *Guanima*, Abaco was called *Lucayoneque*, Eleuthera was called *Cigateo*, Rum Cay was called *Manigua* and Crooked Island was called *Saomere*. Christopher Columbus when he came to the Bahamas and landed on Guanahani he renamed it San Salvador, Manigua he renamed it Santa Maria de la Concepcion, Yuma he renamed it Fernandina, Saomete he renamed it Isabella and the Ragged Island chain he renamed Islas de Arenas.[4] However, for the early Spanish explorers, the islands of the Bahamas were of no particular economic value, so therefore they established only temporary settlements mainly to transport the peaceful Indians to be used as their slaves in East Hispaniola and Cuba to mine the valuable deposits of gold and silver and to dive for pearls.

Jurakán is the phonetic name given by the Spanish settlers to the god of chaos and disorder that the Taíno Indians in Puerto Rico (and also the Carib and Arawak Indians elsewhere in the Caribbean) believed controlled the weather, particularly hurricanes. From this we derive the Spanish word *huracán* and eventually the English word *hurricane*. As the spelling and pronunciation varied across various indigenous groups, there were many alternative names along the way. For example, many West Indian historians and indigenous Indians called them by the various names including, Juracán, furacan, furican, haurachan, herycano, hurachano, hurricano, and so on. The term makes an early appearance in William Shakespeare's King Lear (Act 3, Scene 2). Being the easternmost of the Greater Antilles, Puerto Rico is often in the path of many of the North Atlantic tropical storms and hurricanes which tend to come ashore on the east coast of the island. The Taínos believed that Juracán lived at the top of a rainforest peak called El Yunque (literally, the anvil but truly derived from the name of the Taíno god of order and creation, Yuquiyú) from where he stirred the winds and caused the waves to smash against the shore.

In the Taíno culture, it was said that when the hurricane was upon them, these people would shut themselves up in their leaky huts and shouted and banged drums and blew shell trumpets to keep the evil spirits of the hurricane from killing them or destroying their homes and crops. According to Taíno legend, the goddess Atabei first created the earth, the sky, and all the celestial bodies. The metaphor of the sacred waters was included because the Taínos attributed religious and mythical qualities to water. For example, the goddess, Atabei, was associated with water. She was also the goddess of water. Yocahú, the supreme deity, was also associated with water. Both of these deities are called *Bagua*, which is water, the source of life. This image of water as a sacred entity was central to their beliefs. They were at the mercy of water for their farming. Without rain, they would not be able to farm their *conucos*.

These Indians prayed to the twin gods of rain and fair weather so that they would be pleased and prayed to these gods to keep the evil hurricane away from their farms and homes. To continue her (Atabei) work, she bore two sons, Yucaju and Guacar. Yucaju created the sun and moon to give light, and then made plants and animals to populate the earth. Seeing the beautiful fruits of Yucaju's work, Guacar became jealous and began to tear up the earth with powerful winds, renaming himself Jurakan, the god of destruction. Yucaju then created Locuo, a being intermediate between a god and a man, to live in peaceful harmony with the world. Locuo, in turn, created the first man and woman, Guaguyona and Yaya. All three continued to suffer from the powerful winds and floods inflicted by the evil god Jurakán. It was said that the god Jurakán, was perpetually angry and ruled the power of the hurricane. He became known as the god of strong winds, hence the name today of hurricane. He was feared and revered and when the hurricanes blew, the Taínos thought they had displeased Jurakán. Jurakán would later become *Huracán* in Spanish and *Hurricane* in English.

The origin of the name "Bahamas" is unclear in the history of these islands. Some historians believe it may have been derived from the Spanish word *baja mar*, meaning lands of the *'shallow seas'*; or the Lucayan Indian word for the island of Grand Bahama, *ba-ha-ma* meaning *'large upper middle land.'*[5] The seafaring Taíno people moved into the uninhabited Southeastern Bahamas from the islands of Hispaniola and Cuba sometime around 1000-800 A.D. These people came to be known as the Lucayans. According to various historians, there were estimated reports of well over 20,000 to 30,000+ Lucayans living in the Bahamas at the time of World famous Spanish Explorer Christopher Columbus's arrival in 1492. Christopher Columbus's first landfall in the New World was on an island called San Salvador which is generally accepted to be present-day San Salvador (also known as Watlings Island) in the Southeastern Bahamas. The Lucayans called this island Guanahaní but Columbus renamed it as San Salvador (Spanish for "Holy Saviour").[6] However, Columbus's discovery of this island of San Salvador is a very controversial and debatable topic among historians, scientists and lay-people alike. Even to this day, some of them still suggest that Columbus made his landfall in some other islands in the Bahamas such as, Rum Cay, Samana Cay, Cat Island and some even suggested he landed as far south as the Turks and Caicos Islands. However, it still remains a matter of great debate and mystery within the archeological and scientific community. Regrettably, that question may never be solved, as Columbus's original log book has been lost for centuries, and the only evidence is in the edited abstracts made by Father Bartholomew Las Casas.

In the Bahamas, Columbus made first contact with the Lucayans and exchanged goods with them. The Lucayans-a word that meant 'meal-eaters' in their own language, from their dependence upon cassava flour made from bitter manioc root as their staple starch food. They were sub-Taínos of the Bahamas and believed that all of their islands were once part of the mainland of America but had been cut off by the howling winds and waves of the hurricanes and they referred to these storms as huruká. The Lucayans (the Bahamas being known then as the Lucayan Islands) were Arawakan People who lived in the Bahamas at the time of Christopher Columbus landfall on October 12, 1492. Sometime between 1000-800 A.D. the Taínos of Hispaniola pressured by over-population and trading concerns migrated into the southeastern islands of the Bahamas. The Taínos of Cuba moved into the northwestern Bahamas shortly afterwards. They are widely thought to be the first Amerindians encountered by the Spanish.

Early historical accounts describe them as a peaceful set of people and they referred to themselves as 'Lucayos,' 'Lukku Kairi' or 'Lukku-Cairi' meaning 'small islands' or 'island people' because they referred to themselves by the name of their location. The Lucayans spoke the Ciboney dialect of the Taíno language. This assumption was made from the only piece of speech that was recorded phonetically and has been passed down to us. Las Casas informs us that the Arawaks of the Greater Antilles and Lucayans were unable to understand one another, *'here'*(in Hispaniola), he wrote *"they do not call gold 'caona' as in the main part of the island, nor 'nozay' as on the islet of Guanahani(San Salvador) but tuob."*[7] This brief hint of language difference tends to reinforce the theory that these Bahamian Islands were first settled by people coming from eastern Cuba of the sub-Taíno culture.

Before Columbus arrived to the Bahamas, there were about 20,000 to 30,000+ Lucayans living there, but because of slavery, diseases such as smallpox and yellow fever (to which they had no immunity), and other hardships brought about by the arrival of the Europeans, by 1517, they were virtually non-existent. As a matter of fact, when Spanish Conquistador Ponce de Leon visited those islands in 1513 in search of the magical 'Fountain of Youth,' he found no trace of these Lucayan Indians, with the exception of one elderly Indian woman. These Indians of the Caribbean and Central America lived in one of the most hurricane prone areas of the earth; as a result most of them built their temples, huts, pyramids and houses well away from the hurricane prone coastline because of the great fear and respect which they had for hurricanes.

Many early colonists in the Caribbean took solace by displaying a Cord of Saint Francis of Assisi, a short length of rope with three knots with three turns apiece, in their boats, churches and homes as a protective talisman during the hurricane season. Various legends and lore soon developed regarding Saint Francis and his connection with nature, including tropical weather and hurricanes. According to tradition, if these residents untied the first knot of the cord, winds would pick up but only moderately. Winds of 'half a gale' resulted from untying the second knot. If all three knots were untied, winds of hurricane strength were produced. Today, some descendants of African slaves in the West Indies still tie knots in the leaves of certain trees and hang them in their homes to ward off hurricanes.

Similar accounts also emerged from encounters with the Carib Indians. In old historical accounts these Indians were referred to by various names such as, *'Caribs' 'Charaibes' 'Charibees'* and *'Caribbees'* and they were a mysterious set of people who migrated from the Amazon jungles of South America.[8] They were a tribe of warlike and cannibalistic Indians who migrated northwards into the Caribbean in their canoes overcoming and dominating an earlier race of peaceful set of people called the Arawaks. While Columbus explored all parts of the West Indies, his successors colonized only those parts inhabited by the Arawak or Taíno Indians, avoiding the Carib inhabited islands because they lacked gold but most importantly because the Carib Indians were too difficult to subjugate. Ironically, the region became known as the Caribbean, named after these fierce Indians. Their practice of eating their enemies so captured the imagination of the Europeans that the Caribbean Sea was also named after these Indians. The English word 'cannibal' is derived from the term, 'Caniba' used by the Arawaks to refer to the Caribs eating the flesh of their enemies. Their raids were made over long distances in large canoes and had as one of their main objectives was to take the Arawak women as their captives, wives and slaves. While on the other hand, the captured Arawak men were tortured and killed and then barbecued and eaten during an elaborate ceremony because it was believed that if they did this, they would obtain their enemies personal power and control their spirits. The French traveller Charles de Rochefort wrote that when these Caribs Indians heard the thunder clap, they would *"make all the haste they can to their little houses, and sit down on low stools about the fire, covering their faces and resting their heads on their hands and knees, and in that posture they fall a weeping and say...Maboya is very angry with them: and they say the same when there happens a Hurricane."*[9]

The Caribs were terrified of spilling fresh water into the sea because they believed that it aroused the anger of hurricanes. They had no small stone gods but believed in good and powerful bad spirits called 'Maboya' which caused all the misfortunes of their lives. They even wore carved amulets and employed medicine men to drive the evil Maboya away. When a great and powerful storm began to rise out of the sea, the Caribs blew frantically into the air to chase it away and chewed manioc bread and spat it into the wind for the same purpose. When that was no use, they gave way to panic and crouched in their communal houses moaning, with their arms held over their heads. They felt that they were reasonably safe there because they fortified their houses with corner posts dug deep into the ground. They also believed that beyond the Maboya were great spirits, the male sun, and the female moon. They believed that the spirits of the stars controlled the weather. They also believed in a bird named Savacou which was sent out by the angry Maboya to call up the hurricane, and after this task was finished this bird would then be transformed into a star.

According to a noted English Historian John Oldmixon of the late 1600's and early 1700's, he reported that the Carib Indians excelled in forecasting hurricanes. Writing about a hurricane which occurred in 1740 on the island of St. Christopher he said:- *"Hurricanes are still frequent here, and it was some time since the custom of both the English and French inhabitants in this and the other Charibbees-Islands, to send about the month of June, to the native Charibbees of Dominica and St. Vincent, to know whether there would be any hurricanes that year; and about 10 or 12 Days before the hurricane came they constantly sent them word, and it was rarely failed."* According to Carib Indians 'Signs or Prognosticks,' a hurricane comes *"on the day of the full change, or quarters of the moon. If it will come on the full moon, you being in the change, then observe these signs. That day you will see the skies very turbulent, the sun more red than at other times, a great calm, and the hills clear of clouds or fogs over them, which in the high-lands are seldom so. In the hollows of the earth or wells, there will be great noise, as if you were in a great storm; the stars at night will look very big with Burs about them, the north-west sky smelling stronger than at other times, as it usually does in violent storms; and sometimes that day for an hour or two, the winds blows very hard westerly, out of its usual course. On the full moon you have the same signs, but a great Bur about the moon, and many about the moon, and many about the sun. The like signs must be taken notice of on the quarter-days of the moon."[10]*

According to several elderly Carib Indians, who stated that hurricanes had become more frequent in the recent years following the arrival of the Europeans to the Caribbean, which they viewed as punishment for their interactions with them. In fact, as early as 1630s, English colonists reported that Carib Indians knew when storms would strike by the number of rings that appeared around the moon: three rings meant the storm would arrive in three days, two rings meant two days and one ring meant the storm would arrive in one day. Of course, the connection between such signs and the onset of hurricanes was indeed a very unreliable way to predict the onset of hurricanes. The Carib Indians while raiding islands in the Caribbean would kill off the Arawak men and take the Arawak women as wives and mothers to their children. Actually, when the Europeans came to the Caribbean, they surprisingly found that many Carib women spoke the Taíno language because of the large number of female Taíno captives among them. So it is speculated that a word like 'hurricane' was passed into the Carib speech and this was how these fierce people learned about the terror of these savage storms. Native Indians of the West Indies often engaged in ritual purifications and sacrifices and offered songs and dances to help ward off hurricanes.

An Aztec myth tells that when the gods created the world, it was dark and cold. The youngest of the gods sacrificed himself to create a sun. But it was like him, weak, dim and feeble. Only when more powerful gods offered themselves did the sun blaze into life and shine brightly on them. However, there was one disadvantage, and that was that these gods needed constant fuel, human lives and the

Aztecs obliged. They offered tens of thousands of human sacrifices a year, just to make sure that the sun rose each morning and to prevent natural disasters such as, devastating hurricanes from destroying their communities and villages. Tlaloc was an important deity in Aztec religion, a god of rain, fertility, and water. He was a beneficent god who gave life and sustenance, but he was also feared for his ability to send hurricanes, hail, thunder and lightning, and for being the lord of the powerful element of water. In Aztec iconography he is usually depicted with goggle eyes and fangs. He was associated with caves, springs and mountains. He is known for having demanded child sacrifices. The Aztec god Tezcatlipoca (meaning Lord of the Hurricane) was believed to have special powers over the hurricane winds, as did the Palenque god Tahil (Obsidian Mirror) and the Quiché Maya sky god Huracán. The Aztec god Tezcatlipoca was feared for his capricious nature and the Aztecs called him Yaotl (meaning 'Adversary'). Tonatiuh was the Aztec Sun god and the Aztecs saw the sun as a divinity that controlled the weather, including hurricanes and consequently, all human life form. The Aztecs of Mexico, in particular built vast temples to the sun god Tonatiuh, and made bloody sacrifices of both human and animal, to persuade him to shine brightly on them and in particular not send any destructive hurricanes their way and to allow prosperity for their crops. When they built these temples, they were constructed according to the earth's alignment with the sun but most importantly they were always constructed with hurricanes in mind and away from the hurricane prone coastline.

The Aztec people considered Tonatiuh the leader of Tollán, their heaven. He was also known as the fifth sun, because the Aztecs believed that he was the sun that took over when the fourth sun was expelled from the sky. Mesoamerican creation narratives proposed that before the current world age began there were a number of previous creations, the Aztecs account of the five suns or world ages revealed that in each of the five creations the earth's inhabitants found a more satisfactory staple food than eaten by their predecessors. In the era of the first sun, which was governed by Black Tezcatlipoca, the world was inhabited by a race of giants who lived on acorns. The second sun, whose presiding god was a serpent god called

Quetzatzalcóatl was believed to be the creator of life and in control of the vital rain-bearing winds, and he saw the emergence of a race of primitive humans who lived on the seeds of the mesquite tree.

After the third age, which was ruled by Tláloc, in which people lived on plants that grew on water, such as the water lily, people returned to a diet of wild seeds in the fourth age of Chalchiúhtlicue. It was only in the fifth and current age, an age subject to the sun god Tonatiuh that the people of Mesoamerica learned how to plant and harvest maize. According to their cosmology, each sun was a god with its own cosmic era. The Aztecs believed they were still in Tonatiuh's era and according to their creation mythology, this god demanded human sacrifices as a tribute and without it he would refuse to move through the sky, hold back on the rainfall for their crops and would send destructive hurricanes their way. It is said that some 20,000 people were sacrificed each year to Tonatiuh and other gods, though this number however, is thought to be highly inflated either by the Aztecs, who wanted to inspire fear in their enemies, or the Spaniards, who wanted to speak-ill of the Aztecs. The Aztecs were fascinated by the sun so they worshiped and carefully observed it, and had a solar calendar second only in accuracy to the Mayans.

It was Captain Fernando de Oviedo who gave these storms their modern name when he wrote *"So when the devil wishes to terrify them, he promises them the 'Huracan,' which means tempest."*[11] The Portuguese word for them is Huracao which is believed to have originated from the original Taíno word Huracán. The Native American Indians had a word for these powerful storms, which they called 'Hurucane' meaning 'evil spirit of the wind.' When a hurricane approached the Florida coast, the medicine men of the North American Indians worked frantic incantations to drive the evil hurricane away. The Seminole Indians of Florida were actually, the first to flee from a storm, citing the blooming of the Florida Everglades sawgrass. They believed that only 'an atmospheric condition' such as a major hurricane would cause the pollen to bloom on the sawgrass several days before a hurricane's arrival, giving the native Indians an advanced warning of the impending storm.

Many other sub-culture Indians had similar words for these powerful storms which they all feared and respected greatly. For example, The Galibi Indians called these hurricanes Yuracan and Hyroacan. The Quiche people of Guatemala believed in the god Huraken for their god of thunder and lightning. Giuana Indians called them Yarukka and other similar Indian names were Hyrorokan, aracan, urican, huiranvucan, Yurakon, Yuruk or Yoroko. As hurricanes were becoming more frequent in the Caribbean, many of the colonists and natives of this region had various words and spellings all sounding phonetically similar for these powerful storms. The English called them, 'Hurricanes', 'Haurachana', 'Uracan', 'Herocano', 'Harrycane', 'Tempest', and 'Hyrracano.' The Spanish called them 'Huracán'and 'Furicane'and the Portuguese called them, 'Huracao' and 'Furicane.' The French had for a long time adapted the Indian word called 'Ouragan' and the Dutch referred to them as 'Orkan.' These various spellings were used until the word 'hurricane' was finally settled on in the English Language. Among the Caribbean, Central and South American peoples the word 'hurricane' seems to have always been associated with evil spirits and violence.

Christopher Columbus on his first voyage managed to avoid encountering any hurricanes but it wasn't until some of his later voyages that he encountered several hurricanes that disrupted these voyages to the New World. Based on his first voyage before encountering any hurricanes, Columbus concluded that the weather in the New World was benign: *"In all the Indies, I have always found May-like weather,"* he commented. Although sailing through hurricane-prone waters during the most dangerous months, he did not have any serious hurricane encounters on his early voyage. However, on his final voyages, Christopher Columbus himself weathered at least three of these dangerous storms. Columbus provided the earliest account of a hurricane in a letter written to Queen Isabella in 1494. In this letter he wrote, *"The tempest arose and worried me so that I knew not where to turn; Eyes never behold the seas so high, angry and covered by foam. We were forced to keep out in this bloody ocean, seething like a pot of hot fire. Never did the sky look more terrible; for one whole day and night it blazed like a furnace. The flashes came with such fury and frightfulness that we all thought the ships would be blasted. All this time the water never ceased to fall from the sky... The people were so worn out, that they longed for death to end their terrible suffering."[12]*

By June of 1494, the small town of Isabella, founded by Columbus on Hispaniola, became the first European settlement destroyed by a hurricane. The Spaniards who accompanied Columbus on his four voyages to the New World took back to Europe with them a new concept of what a severe storm could be and, naturally, a new word of Indian origin. It seems that the Indian word was pronounced 'Furacán' or 'Furacánes' during the early years of discovery and colonization of America. Peter Martyr, one of the earliest historians of the New World, said that they were called by the natives 'Furacanes,' although the plural is obviously Spanish. The Rev. P. du Tertre, (1667) in his great work of the middle of the seventeenth century, wrote first 'ouragan', and later 'houragan.'

After 1474 some changes in the Spanish language were made. For instance, words beginning with 'h' were pronounced using the 'f consonant.' The kingdoms of Aragon and Castile were united in 1474, before the discovery of America, and after that time some changes in the Spanish language were made. One of them involved words beginning with the letter 'h.' In Aragon they pronounced such words as 'f'. As Menéndez Pidal said, "Aragon was the land of the 'f', but the old Castilian lost the sound or pronunciation," so that Spanish Scholar Nebrija (Nebrija wrote a grammar of the Castilian language, and is credited as the first published grammar of any Romance language) wrote, instead of the lost 'f', an aspirated 'h.' Menéndez wrote concerning the pronunciation of the word 'hurricane' and its language used by Fernando Colón, son of Christopher Columbus "Vacillation between 'f' and 'h' is very marked predominance of the 'h.' And so, the 'h' became in Spanish a silent letter, as it still is today." Father Bartholomew de Las Casas, referring to one of these storms wrote: *"At this time the four vessels brought by Juan Aguado were destroyed in the port (of Isabella) by a great tempest, called by the Indians in their language 'Furacán.' Now we call them hurricanes, something that almost all of us have experienced at sea or on land..."[13]* Las Casas, outraged by the brutal treatment of the Indians on Hispaniola, declared that the wrath of the hurricane which struck Hispaniola was the judgment of God on the city and the men who had committed such sins against humanity. All other European languages coined a word for the tropical cyclone, based on the Spanish 'Huracán.' Gonzalo Fernandez de Oviedo (Oviedo y Valdes, 1851, Book VI, Ch. III) is more explicit in his writings concerning the origin of the word 'hurricane.' He says: *"Hurricane, in the language of this island, properly means an excessively severe storm or tempest; because, in fact, it is only a very great wind and a very great and excessive rainfall, both together or either these two things by themselves."* Oviedo further noted that the winds of the *'Huracán'* were so *"fierce that they topple houses and uproot many large trees."*[14]

Even in the English Language the word 'hurricane' evolved through several variations, for example, William Shakespeare mentioned it in his play 'King Lear' where he wrote *"Blow, winds, and crack your cheeks! Rage! Blow! You catracts and hurricanes, spout till you have drench'd out steeples, drown'd the cocks!"* Girolamo Benzoni, in 1565 in his Book *History of the New World* he mentioned his encounter with a hurricane in Hispaniola which at the time he referred to it as *'Furacanum.' "In those days a wondrous and terrible disaster occurred in this country. At sunrise such a horrible, strong wind began that the inhabitants of the island thought they had never seen or heard anything like it before. The raging storm wind (which the Spaniards called Furacanum) came with great violence, as if it wanted to spit heaven and earth apart from one another, and hurl everything to the ground...The people were as a whole so despairing because of their great fear that they run here and there, as if they were senseless and mad, and did not know what they did...The strong and frightful wind threw some entire houses and capitals including the people from the capital, tore them apart in the air and threw them down to the ground in pieces. This awful weather did such noticeable damage in such a short time that not three ships stood secure in the sea harbour or came through the storm undamaged. For the anchors, even if they were yet strong, were broken apart through the strong force of the wind and all the masts, despite their being new, were crumpled. The ships were blown around by the wind, so that all the people in them were drowned. For the most part the Indians had crawled away and hidden themselves in holes in order to escape such disaster."*[15]

As stated earlier, Christopher Columbus did not learn on his first voyage, the voyage of discovery, of the existence of such terrible 'tempests' or 'storms.' He had the exceptional good fortune of not being struck by any of them during this voyage. The Indians, while enjoying pleasant weather had no reason to speak about these storms to a group of strangers who spoke a language which they could not understand. Naturally, Columbus did not say one word about these awful storms in his much celebrated letter *"The letter of Columbus on the Discovery of America."* However, on his second voyage things were quite different. After arriving on November 3, 1493, at an island in the Lesser Antilles which he named Dominica, Columbus sailed northward and later westward, to Isabella Hispaniola, the first city in the New World, at the end of January, 1494. Then in June of that year, 1494, Isabella was struck by a hurricane, the first time that European men had seen such a terrible storm. Surely, for the first time, they heard the Taíno Indians, very much excited; extending their arms raised upward into the air and shouting: *"Furacán! Furacán!"* when the storm commenced. We can indeed say that it was that moment in history, when the word *'hurricane'* suddenly appeared to the Europeans. Columbus was not at that time in Isabella because he was sailing near the Isle of Pines, Cuba. So his companions of the ships *Marigalante* and *Gallega* were the first white men to hear these words, which were of Indian origin and about a phenomenon of the New World. Knowledge of 'Furacanes,' both the word and the terrifying storms it described, remained limited to Spanish speakers until 1555, when Richard Eden translated Columbus's ship report and other Spanish accounts of the New World, making it the first time it appeared in the English vocabulary.

In October of 1495, probably in the second half of the month, another hurricane struck Isabella, which was much stronger than the first. It finally gave Columbus, who was there at the time, the opportunity of knowing what a hurricane was and of its destructive abilities. It also gave him the opportunity of hearing the Indians shouting the same word with fear and anxiety on their faces, on the account of these terrible storms of the tropics, which they believed were caused by evil spirits. Christopher Columbus would later declare that *"nothing but the service of God and the extension of the monarchy would induce him to expose himself to such danger from these storms ever again."*[16] *'The Niña'* was the only vessel which was the smallest, oldest and the most fragile at the time but amazingly withstood that hurricane. The other two ships of Columbus, *'The San Juan'* and *'The Cordera,'* were in the harbour and were lost or badly damaged by this hurricane. Columbus gave orders to have one repaired and another ship known as, *India* constructed out of the wreck of the ones which had been destroyed, making it the first ship to be built in the Caribbean by Europeans.

In 1502 during his fourth voyage, Columbus warned the Governor Don Nicolas de Orvando of Santo Domingo of an approaching hurricane, but he was ignored; as a result a Spanish treasure fleet set sailed and lost 21 of 30 ships with 500 men. Columbus had a serious disagreement with the bureaucrats appointed by Spain to govern the fledgling colonies in the Caribbean to extract gold, pearl and other precious commodities from the native Indians. Among the more unfriendly of these exploiters was Don Nicolas de Orvando, the Governor of Hispaniola, with whom Columbus had been forbidden to have any contact with by the request of his Spanish sovereigns. But as Columbus approached Santa Domingo, he recognized the early signs of an approaching hurricane, such as large ocean swells and a veil of cirrostratus clouds overhead. Concerned for the safety of his men and ships, he sent a message to Governor Orvando begging him to be allowed to seek refuge in Santa Domingo Harbour. Columbus had observed that the Governor was preparing a large fleet of ships to set sail for Spain, carrying large quantities of gold and slaves, and warned him to delay the trip until the hurricane had passed. Refusing both the request and the advice, Orvando read Columbus's note out loud to the crew and residents, who roared with laughter at Columbus's advice. Unfortunately, the laughter was very short-lived and Orvando's ships left port only to their own demise when 21 of the 30 ships were lost in a hurricane between Hispaniola and Puerto Rico. An additional four of them were badly damaged but fortunately they were able to return to port where they too eventually sunk. Only one ship, the *Aguja*, made it to Spain, and that one, no doubt to Orvando's intense distress, was carrying what little remained of Columbus's own gold.

Meanwhile, Columbus, anticipating strong winds from the north from this hurricane, positioned his fleet in a harbour on the south side of Hispaniola. On June 13, the storm hit with ferocious northeast winds. Even with the protection of the mountainous terrain to the windward side, the fleet struggled. In Columbus's own words, *"The storm was terrible and on that night the ships were parted from me. Each one of them was reduced to an extremity, expecting nothing save death; each one of them was certain the others were lost."*[17] The anchors held only on Columbus's ship; the others were dragged out to sea, where their crews fought for their lives. Nevertheless, the fleet survived with only minimal damage. Almost 18 months later, Columbus returned to Santo Domingo, only to discover that it had been largely destroyed by the hurricane.

When the Europeans first attempted to create settlements in the Caribbean and the Americas, they quickly learned about these storms. As time passed and these settlers learned more about their new homeland, they experienced these storms on such a regular basis that they became accustomed to them. Eventually, they began calling them equinoctial storms, as the storms would normally hit in the weeks around the period of the fall equinox, which in the northern hemisphere occurs in late September. English explorers and privateers soon contributed their own accounts of encounters with these storms. In 1513, Juan Ponce de León completed the first recorded cruise along the Florida coast and came ashore near present-day St. Augustine to claim Florida for Spain. Famous for his unsuccessful search for the magical 'Fountain of Youth,' he might have discovered Florida earlier had it not been for the ravages of hurricanes. In August of 1508, he was struck by two hurricanes within two weeks. The first drove his ship onto the rocks near the Port of Yuna, Hispaniola, and the second left his ship aground on the southwest coast of Puerto Rico. Soon after Hernando Cortés found treasures of gold and silver in the newly discovered lands of West, expeditions to retrieve the riches of the New World for Spain began in earnest. In 1525 Cortés lost the first ship he sent to Mexico in a severe hurricane, along with its crew of over seventy persons. Famous English explorer Sir John Hawkins wrote his own encounters with these storms. Sir John Hawkins wrote that he left Cartagena in late July 1568 *"Hoping to have escaped the time of their stormes...which they call Furicanos."*[18] Hawkins did not leave soon enough, and he and his ships were bashed by an *"extreme storme"* as he referred to it, lasting several days.

English Explorer Sir Francis Drake encountered several major hurricanes while sailing the dangerous seas of the Americas and the Atlantic Ocean and in most cases these encounters changed the course of West Indian and American history. Sir Francis Drake, who travelled the seas of the globe in quest of glory and valuable loot, nearly lost his ships in the fleet on the Outer Banks of Carolina. One of his most famous encounters was with a major hurricane which occurred while he was anchored near the ill-fated Roanoke colony in present day North Carolina in June of 1586. His ships were anchored just off the banks while he checked on the progress of Sir Walter Raleigh's colonists on Roanoke Island. The hurricane lasted for three days, scattering Drake's fleet and nearly destroying many of his ships. There was no greater thorn in the side of the Spaniards than Francis Drake. His exploits were legendary, making him a hero to the English but a simple pirate to the Spaniards and for good reasons because he often robbed them of their valuable treasures. To the Spanish, he was known as *El Draque*, "the Dragon"; "Draque" is the Spanish pronunciation of "Drake." As a talented sea captain and navigator, he attacked their fleets and took their ships and treasures. He raided their settlements in America and played a major role in the defeat of the greatest fleet ever assembled, the "Spanish Armada."

No other English seaman brought home more wealth or had a bigger impact on English history than Drake. At the age of 28 he was trapped in a Mexican port by Spanish war ships. He had gone there for repairs after an encounter with one of his first major hurricanes at sea. Drake escaped but some of the sailors left behind were so badly treated by the Spanish that he swore revenge. He returned to the area in 1572 with two ships and 73 men. Over the next fifteen months he raided Spanish towns and their all important Silver train across the isthmus from Panama. Other English accounts reported ships damaged or lost in storms characterized by extreme wind and rain, some of which were definitely hurricanes. The English (including Drake and Hawkins) had a great respect for hurricanes, to such an extent that, as the hurricane season was understood to be approaching, more and more pirates went home or laid up their ships in some sheltered harbour until the last hurricane had passed and was replaced by the cool air of old man winter.

Probably those that first discovered the period of the year in which hurricanes developed were Spanish priest, officers of the navy or army, or civilians that had lived for a long time in the Caribbean. By the end of the sixteenth century they should have already known the approximate period that these hurricanes occurred. The Roman Catholic Church knew early on that the hurricane season extended at least from August to October because the hierarchy ordered that in all of the churches in the Caribbean to say a special prayer to protect them from these deadly hurricanes. The prayer which had to be said was: *'Ad repellendas tempestates,'* translated to mean *'for the repelling of the hurricanes or tempests.'* It was also ordered that the prayer should be said in Puerto Rico during August and September and in Cuba in September and October. This indicates that it was known that hurricanes were more frequent in those islands during the months mentioned. Eventually, West Indian colonists through first hand experiences with these storms gradually learned that hurricanes struck the Caribbean within a well-defined season. Initially, those early colonists believed that hurricanes could strike at any time of the year, but by the middle of the seventeenth century most of them recognized that there was a distinct hurricane season. This was because the hurricanes simply occurred too frequent within a particular time period for them to remain strange and unusual in their eyes. Numerous letters and reports written by colonists specifically discussed the period between July and October as the *'time of hurricanes.'*

The geography of hurricanes challenged the concept of these storms as 'national judgments or divine favor' by which God spoke to a specific group of people or country. Individual storms routinely struck various islands colonized by different European powers. For example, in 1707 a hurricane devastated the English Leeward Islands, the Dutch Islands of Saba and St. Eustatius, and the French Island of Guadeloupe. In 1674, a Dutch attack on the French Islands was thwarted by a hurricane, which also caused significant damage in the English Leeward Islands and in Barbados. The presence of hurricanes made colonists question their ability to transform the hostile environment of the Caribbean and by extension their ability to establish successful and stable societies here. But hurricanes raised other questions as well: What caused them? What forces gave rise to such powerful and dangerous storms? For some-probably a significant majority during the first several decades of the seventeenth century- they believed that these storms came directly from the hands of God. They interpreted hurricanes as 'wondrous events' or 'divine judgments' for human sins. Others linked hurricanes to various natural processes, including shifting wind patterns. The explosion of various natural processes, including shifting wind patterns, the explosion of various chemicals in the atmosphere, and the celestial movement of the planets and stars.

CHAPTER FOUR
THE NAMING OF HURRICANES

ATLANTIC TROPICAL CYCLONE NAMES

2012	2013	2014	2015	2016	2017
Alberto	Andrea	Arthur	Ana	Alex	Arlene
Beryl	Barry	Bertha	Bill	Bonnie	Bret
Chris	Chantal	Cristobal	Claudette	Colin	Cindy
Debby	Dorian	Dolly	Danny	Danielle	Don
Ernesto	Erin	Edouard	Erika	Earl	Emily
Florence	Fernand	Fay	Fred	Fiona	Franklin
Gordon	Gabrielle	Gustav	Grace	Gaston	Gert
Helene	Humberto	Hanna	Henri	Hermine	Harvey
Isaac	Ingrid	Ike	Ida	Igor	Irene
Joyce	Jerry	Josephine	Joaquin	Julia	Jose
Kirk	Karen	Kyle	Kate	Karl	Katia
Leslie	Lorenzo	Laura	Larry	Lisa	Lee
Michael	Melissa	Marco	Mindy	Matthew	Maria
Nadine	Nestor	Nana	Nicholas	Nicole	Nate
Oscar	Olga	Omar	Odette	Otto	Ophelia
Patty	Pablo	Paloma	Peter	Paula	Philippe
Rafael	Rebekah	Rene	Rose	Richard	Rina
Sandy	Sebastien	Sally	Sam	Shary	Sean
Tony	Tanya	Teddy	Teresa	Tomas	Tammy
Valerie	Van	Vicky	Victor	Virginie	Vince
William	Wendy	Wilfred	Wanda	Walter	Whitney

Information Courtesy of NOAA.

Hurricanes are the only weather disasters that have been given their own iconic names, such as, Hurricane Andrew, Gilbert, Katrina, Camille or Mitch. No two hurricanes are the same but like people; they share similar characteristics but yet still they have their own unique stories to tell. The naming of storms or hurricanes has undergone various stages of development and transformation. Initially, the word 'Hurricane' accompanied by the year of occurrence was used, for example, *'the Great Hurricane of 1780'* which killed over 22,000 persons in Martinique, Barbados and St. Eustatius. Another example was *'the Great Storm of 1703'* whose incredible damage of the British Isles was expertly detailed by Robinson Crusoe's author, Daniel Defoe. The naming scheme was substituted by a numbering system (e.g. Hurricane #1, #2, #3 of 1833 etc…) however; this became too cumbersome and confusing, especially when disseminating information about two or more storms within the same geographical area or location.

For the major hurricanes of this region, they were often named after the particular country or city they devastated. This was especially true for severe hurricanes which made their landing somewhere in the Caribbean. Three notable examples were, *'the Dominican Republic Hurricane of 1930'* which killed over 8,000 persons in the Dominican Republic, *'the Pointe-a-Pitre Hurricane of 1776'* which devastated the country of Guadeloupe and killed over 6,000 persons and devastated it's largest city and economic capital of Pointe-a-Pitre. Third was *'the Great Nassau Hurricane of 1926'* which devastated the city of Nassau in the Bahamas during the 1926 North Atlantic hurricane season. In some cases they were even named after the holiday on which they occurred, for example, *'the Great Labour Day Hurricane of 1935.'* The Great Labour Day Hurricane of 1935 was the strongest tropical cyclone during the 1935 North Atlantic hurricane season. This compact and intense hurricane caused extensive damage in the Bahamas and the upper Florida Keys. To this day, *the Great Labour Day Hurricane of 1935* is the strongest and most intense hurricane on record to ever have struck the United States in terms of barometric pressure. *The Great Labour Day Hurricane of 1935* was one of the strongest recorded hurricane landfalls worldwide. It was the only hurricane known to have made landfall in the United States with a minimum central pressure below 900 Mbar; only two others have struck the United States with winds of Category 5 strength on the Saffir-Simpson Scale. It remains the third-strongest North Atlantic hurricane on record, and it was only surpassed by Hurricane Gilbert (888Mbar) in 1988 and Hurricane Wilma (882Mbar) in 2005. In total, at least 408 people were killed by this hurricane.

In some cases they were named after the ship which experienced that particular storm. Two notable examples were: - *'the Racer's Storm of 1837'* and *'the Sea Venture Hurricane of 1609.'* The *1837 Racer's Storm* was a very powerful and destructive hurricane in the 19th century, causing 105 deaths and heavy damage to many cities on its 2,000+ mile path. *The Racer's Storm* was the 10th known tropical storm in the 1837 North Atlantic hurricane season. *The Racer's Storm* was named after the British war ship *HMS Racer* which encountered the storm in the extreme northwest Caribbean on September 28th. Another example was *the Sea Venture Hurricane of 1609*. In July 28th of 1609, a fleet of seven tall ships, with two pinnaces in tow carrying 150 settlers and supplies from Plymouth, England to Virginia to relieve the starving Jamestown colonists was struck by a hurricane while en route there. They had been sent by the Virginia Company of London to fortify the Jamestown settlement. Sir George Somers mission was to resupply the six hundred or so pioneers who a year before had settled in the infant British colonial settlement of King James's Town, sited in one of the estuaries south of the Potomac River. *The Sea Venture* was grounded at Bermuda which for some time was called *Somers Island* after the ship's captain, Admiral Sir George Somers. After being struck by this hurricane, *the Sea Venture* sprung a leak and everyone on board worked frantically to save this ship and their lives by trying to pump the water out of the hull of the ship. They tried to stem the flow of water coming into the ship by stuffing salt beef and anything else they could find to fit into the leaks of the ship. After this proved futile most of the crew simply gave up hope, falling asleep where they could, exhausted and aching from their relentless but futile efforts. But just as they were about to give up and face the grim reality that they would be loss to the unforgiving Atlantic Ocean, they spotted the island of Bermuda. Somers skillfully navigated the floundering *Sea Venture* onto a reef about half a mile to the leeward side of Bermuda. They used the ship's long boat to ferry the crew and passengers ashore.

The passengers of the shipwrecked *Sea Venture* became Bermuda's first inhabitants and their stories helped inspire William Shakespeare's writing of his final play *'The Tempest'* making it perhaps the most famous hurricane in early American history. *"And another storm brewing,"* William Shakespeare wrote in *The Tempest.* *"I hear it sing in the wind."[1]* Most of those venturing to the New World had no knowledge of the word or the actual storm. The lead ship, the three-hundred-ton *Sea Venture*, was the largest in the fleet and carried Sir Thomas Gates, the newly appointed governor of the colony, and Sir Georges Somers, admiral of the Virginia Company. It is interesting to note that Shakespeare did not name his play *'The Hurricane.'* He actually did know the word *"hurricano"* because it appears in two earlier plays, *King Lear* and *Troilus and Cressida.* Maybe he recognized that such a title would be confusing and unfamiliar to most of his audience, so he chose a more familiar word *'The Tempest'* instead. Though the island was uninhabited, Spaniards had visited Bermuda earlier and set ashore wild pigs. The shipwrecked passengers fed on those wild pigs, fish, berries and other plentiful game on the island. Although they yearned to stay on that island paradise, they managed to make two vessels *Patience* and the *Deliverance* out of what was left of the *Sea Venture* and ten months later they set sailed for Jamestown. However, some persons remained on the island and became the first colonists of that island, including Admiral Sir George Somers who initially left with the other Jamestown passengers but eventually returned and died on that island.

In some instances, hurricanes were named after important persons within this region; one such storm was, the *'Willoughby Gale of 1666.'* The word *'gale'* during these colonial times was often interchanged with the word 'hurricane' but they often meant the same thing-a hurricane and not the official term we now use today for the definition of a 'meteorological gale.' This storm was named after the British Governor of Barbados, Lord Francis Willoughby who lost his life aboard the flagship *Hope* along with over 2,000 of his troops in his fleet in this hurricane. He was appointed Governor of Barbados by Charles II in May of 1650 and attempted to negotiate the strained politics of that island, which also experienced a division between the Royalists and Parliamentarians. His last act on behalf of the English Crown came in July 1666 when, having learned of the recent French seizure of St. Kitts, he formed a relief force of two Royal Navy Frigates, twelve other large vessels (including commandeered merchant ships), a fire ship, and a ketch, bearing over 2,000 men.

Lord Willoughby had planned to proceed north to Nevis, Montserrat, and Antigua to gather further reinforcements before descending on the French. Leaving Barbados on July 28, his fleet waited for the French just off the coast of Martinique and Guadeloupe, where he sent a frigate to assault the harbour and ended up capturing two French merchant vessels on August 4. This success could not be exploited however, as that night most of his force was destroyed by a strong hurricane, including the flagship *Hope*, from which Willoughby drowned in this ship during the storm. This hurricane occurred in 1666 and was a very intense storm which struck the islands of St. Kitts, Guadeloupe, and Martinique. The fleet was actually caught by surprise by this hurricane after leaving Barbados en-route to St. Kitts and Nevis to aid the colonists there to help battle against the French attacks. After the storm, only two vessels from this fleet were ever heard from again and the French captured some of these survivors. All of the vessels and boats on the coast of Guadeloupe were dashed to pieces. For a period in the late seventeenth century, some colonists referred to especially powerful and deadly hurricanes as "Willoughby Gales." Personal names were also used elsewhere in this region, for example, *'Saxby's Gale'* which occurred in Canada in 1869, and was named after a naval officer who was thought to have predicted it.

Another example was, the *Daniel Defoe Hurricane of 1703* which occurred in November of 1703 and moved from the Atlantic across to southern England. It was made famous by an obscure political pamphleteer, Daniel Defoe. It was six years before he wrote the world famous book *Robinson Crusoe*. At the time the hurricane struck, he needed money so the storm gave him the idea of collecting eye-witness accounts of the storm and publishing it in a pamphlet. He printed and sold this pamphlet under the very strange and exceptionally long title of *'The storm or collection of the Most*

Remarkable Casualties and Disasters which happened in the late Dreadful Tempest both by Sea and Land.' In total, around 8,000 sailors lost their lives, untold numbers perished in the floods on shore, and 14,000 homes, 400 windmills and 16,000 sheep were destroyed. Some of the windmills burned down, because they turned so fast in the fierce winds that friction generated enough heat to set them on fire. The damage in London alone was estimated to have cost £2 million (at 18th century prices).

An additional example was, the *Benjamin Franklin Hurricane of October 1743,* which affected the Northeastern United States and New England, brought gusty winds and rainy conditions as far as Philadelphia, and produced extensive flooding in Boston. This was the first hurricane to be measured accurately by scientific instruments. John Winthrop, a professor of natural philosophy at Harvard College, measured the pressure and tides during the storm passage. This storm, which wasn't particularly powerful but was memorable because it garnered the interest of future patriot and one of the founders of the United States, Benjamin Franklin, who believed the storm was coming in from Boston. He was wrong, because it was actually going to Boston. From this information, he surmised that the storm was travelling in a clockwise manner from the southwest to northeast. Putting two and two together, Franklin concluded that the low pressure system was causing the storm to move in this manner.

One aspect of the earth's general circulation is that storms are not stationary; they move, and in somewhat predictable ways. Until the mid-eighteenth century, it had been generally assumed that storms were born, played out, and died in a single location and that they did not move across the earth's surface. Benjamin Franklin had planned to study a lunar eclipse one evening in September 1743, but the remnants of this hurricane ruined his evening. This was a big disappointment to him, because he had been looking forward to this lunar eclipse that this storm had obscured. His curiosity aroused, Franklin gathered additional details about the storm by reading the Boston newspapers and learned that the storm had moved up the Atlantic seaboard and against the surface winds. He learned that this hurricane struck Boston a day later, sending flood tides sweeping over the docks, destroying boats, and submerging waterfront streets. In the succeeding months he collected additional reports from travellers and newspapers from Georgia to Nova Scotia, and satisfied himself that at least in this part of the world, storms have a tendency to take a northeasterly path up the Atlantic Coast. Thus science took the first step toward a basic understanding of hurricanes and their movements.

Benjamin Franklin is also popularly known for his off the wall weather experiment years later where during a thunderstorm, in 1752, he carried out a dangerous experiment to demonstrate that a thunderstorm generates electricity. He flew a kite, with metal objects attached to its string, high in the sky into a thunderstorm cloud (Cumulonimbus). The metal items produced sparks, proving that electricity had passed along the wet string. After discovering that bolts of lightning were in fact electricity, with this knowledge Franklin developed the lightning rod to allow the lightning bolt to travel along the rod and safely into the ground. This discovery by Franklin is still used even to this day all over the world. A year later after Benjamin Franklin's famous kite flight, Swedish physicist G.W. Richmann conducted a similar experiment following Franklin's instructions to the letter, and as fate would have it, he was struck by a lightning which killed him instantly. Sailing home from France on the fifth of September, 1789, after his great years as a US Ambassador, Benjamin Franklin experienced a storm which may have been the same storm which devastated Dominica. He was eighty years old and suffering from "the Stone" but was busy observing the temperatures of the sea water, which would eventually lead to his discovery of the Gulf Stream.

Finally, there was the *Alexander Hamilton Hurricane of 1772*, which he experienced growing up as a boy living in the Caribbean on the island of St. Kitts in the Leeward Islands. This was an extremely powerful and deadly hurricane. He later on in life became the confidential aide to George Washington and his greatness rests on his Federalist influence on the American Constitution and much as on his financial genius as the first United States Secretary of the Treasury. Today he is featured on the U.S. ten dollar bill and he is one of two non-presidents featured on currently issued U.S. bills. The other is

Benjamin Franklin who is found on the U.S. $100 bill. A westward moving hurricane hit Puerto Rico on August 28. It continued through the Caribbean, hitting Hispaniola on August 30 and later on Jamaica. It moved northwestward through the Gulf of Mexico, and hit just west of Mobile, Alabama on the September 4. Many ships were destroyed in the Mobile area, and its death toll was very severe. In Pensacola, it destroyed most of the wharves. The most devastation occurred in the vicinity of Mobile and the Pasca Oocola River. All shipping at the Mouth of the Mississippi was driven into the marshes; this included the ship *El Principe de Orange* from which only 6 survived.

This storm was famously described by Alexander Hamilton, who was living on the island of St. Croix at the time, and wrote a letter about it to his father in St. Kitts. The letter was so dramatic and moving that it was published in newspapers locally on the island and first in New York and then in other states (please see my book- *'Rediscovering Hurricanes'* for a complete copy of this letter), and the locals on St. Kitts raised enough money to have him brought to America to receive a formal education to make good use of his intellectual abilities. This was because, this letter created such a sensation that some planters of St. Kitts, in the midst of the hurricane devastation, took up a collection to send him to America for better schooling because they saw in him great potential. By 1774 he was a student at King's College, now Columbia University, in New York. On St. Kitts, the damage was considerable and once again, many houses were flattened, and there were several fatalities and many more injuries. Total damage from this storm alone was estimated at £500,000 on St. Kitts. The second storm struck just three days later causing even more significant damage to the few remaining houses on this island already battered by the previous storm in 1772.

Several claimants have been put forth as the originators of the modern tropical cyclone 'naming' system. However, it was forecaster Clement Lindley Wragge, an Australian meteorologist who in 1887 began giving women's names, names from history and mythology and male names, especially names of politicians who offended him to these storms before the end of the 19th century. He was a colourful and controversial meteorologist in charge of the Brisbane, Australia Government weather office. He initially named the storms after mythological figures, but later named them after politicians he didn't like. For example, Wragge named some of these storms using biblical names such as, Ram, Raken, Talmon, and Uphaz or the ancient names of Xerxes and Hannibal. Wragge even nicknamed one storm Eline, a name that he thought was reminiscent of *"dusty maidens with liquid eyes and bewitching manners."* Most ingeniously, he gained a measure of personal revenge by naming some of the nastiest storms with politicians' names such as, Drake, Barton, and Deakin. By properly naming a hurricane, he was able to publicly describe a politician (perhaps a politician who was not too generous with the weather-bureau appropriations) as *"causing great distress"* or *"wandering aimlessly about the Pacific."* By naming these storms after these hated politicians he could get a degree of revenge on them without suffering any repercussions from them. During his last days in office, he fought with the Australian Government over the right to issue national forecasts and he lost, and was fired in 1902.

For a while, hurricanes in the West Indies were often named after the particular Saint's Day on which the hurricane occurred. As Christianity took hold in the West Indies, the naming system of storms here in the Caribbean was based on the Catholic tradition of naming these storms with the 'Saint' of the day (e.g. San Ciprian on September 26). This system for naming them was haphazard and not really a system at all. Powerful hurricanes hitting especially the Spanish speaking islands of the Caribbean got Catholic Saints' names. According to Historian Alejandro Tapia, the first hurricane to be named with the Saint of the day was the *Hurricane of San Bartolomé* which devastated Puerto Rico and the Dominican Republic on August 24 and 25 of 1568. The earlier tropical cyclones were simply designated by historians years later after their passages.

One example of a great storm named after a Saint of the day was, *'Hurricane San Felipe'* which struck Puerto Rico on September 13, 1876. Another example was *'Hurricane San Felipe the Second'* which occurred strangely enough on the very same date 52 years later on September 13, 1928 and was responsible for well over 3,433 deaths. Another hurricane which was named the *'Hurricane of Santa Elena'* struck Puerto Rico on August 18, 1851 and caused massive casualties. Then there was the *'Hurricane of Santa Ana'* (in English, Saint Anne) which struck Puerto Rico and Guadeloupe on July 26, 1825, the date of the feast in honour of the Mother of the Blessed Virgin, which killed over 1,300 persons. In addition, there was the *'Hurricane of San Ciriaco'* which killed 3,369 persons in Puerto Rico on August 8, 1899 (feast day of Saint Cyriacus) and remains one of the longest duration tropical storms(28 days) to hit the Caribbean or anywhere in the world.

The tradition of naming storms after the Saint of the day officially ended with Hurricane Betsy in 1956 which is still remembered as the *'Hurricane of Santa Clara.'* However, years later with the passage of Hurricane Donna in 1960, the storm was recognized as the *'Hurricane of San Lorenzo.'* At this time, only the major hurricanes were given names so most storms especially the minor storms before 1950 in the North Atlantic never received any kind of special designation. This is why this hurricane in 1780 was never named but was simply referred to as *'the Great Hurricane of 1780.'* The word 'Great' simply meant that the hurricane was a powerful storm and that it had sustained winds of 136 mph or greater and a minimum central pressure of 28.00 inches or less (see later chapter on the classification of hurricanes).

Later, latitude-longitude positions were used. At first they listed these storms by the latitude and longitude positions where they were first reported. This was cumbersome, slow, open to error and confusing. For example, a name like *'Hurricane 12.8°N latitude and 54.7°W longitude'* was very difficult to remember, and it would be easy to confuse this storm with another that was seen two months later, but almost at the same location. In addition, this posed another significant problem, in the 1940's when meteorologists began airborne studies of tropical cyclones, ships and aircrafts communicated mainly in Morse code. This was fine for the letters of the alphabet, but it was awkward at dealing with numbers because it was slow and caused confusion among its users.

In this region, these early storms were often referred to as, *Gales, Severe Gales, Equinoctial Storms*, or *Line Storms*. The latter two names referred to the time of the year and the location from which these storms were born (referring to the Equatorial line). Gauging the strength and fury of a seventeenth or eighteenth-century storm was quite a difficult task because at the time these colonists had no means of measuring the wind speeds of a hurricane. Contemporaries recognized a hierarchy of winds ranging from *'a stark calm'* to *'a small Gale'* to *'a Top-Sail Gale'* to *'a fret of wind'* and *'a Tempest.'* These terms were later replaced by the word 'hurricane' but such terms offered little help in interpreting the power of hurricanes or differentiating lesser tropical storms from hurricanes. Furthermore, increased development of the built environment over time meant that the potential for damage, even from minor storms, increased as well, making damage estimates a questionable foundation for judging the power of storms.

Experience has shown that using distinctive names in communications is quicker and less subject to error than the cumbersome latitude-longitude identification methods. The idea was that the names should be short, familiar to users, easy to remember and that their use would facilitate communications with millions of people of different ethnic races threatened by the storm. This was because a hurricane can last for a week or more, and there can be more than one storm at a time, so weather forecasters starting naming these storms so that there would be absolutely no confusion when talking about a particular storm. Names are easier to use and facilitate better communications among individuals and meteorologists with language barriers within the same geographical region, such as within the Caribbean, Central America and North America.

The first U.S. named hurricane (unofficially named) was Hurricane George which was the fifth storm in 1947 season. George had top winds of 155 mph as it came ashore around midday on September 17, between Pompano Beach and Delray Beach. The second hurricane unofficially named was Hurricane Bess (named for the outspoken First Lady of the USA, Bess Truman, in 1949). The third storm was nicknamed by the news media 'Hurricane Harry' after the then President of the United States Harry Truman. United States Navy and Air Force meteorologists working in the Pacific Ocean began naming tropical cyclones during World War II, when they often had to track multiple storms. They gave each storm a distinctive name in order to distinguish the cyclones more quickly than listing their positions when issuing warnings.

Towards the end of World War II, two separate United States fleets in the Pacific lacking sufficient weather information about these storms were twice badly damaged when they sailed directly into them resulting in massive causalities. Three ships were sunk, twenty one were badly damaged, 146 planes were blown overboard, and 763 men were lost. One of the results that came out of these tragedies was the fact that all US Army and Navy planes were then ordered to start tracking and studying these deadly storms, so as to prevent similar disasters like those ones from occurring again. During World War II this naming practice became widespread in weather map discussions among forecasters, especially Air Force and Navy meteorologists who plotted the movements of these storms over the wide expanses of the Pacific Ocean. Using the convention of applying 'she' to inanimate objects such as vehicles, these military meteorologists beginning in 1945 in the Northwest Pacific started naming these storms after their wives and girlfriends. However, this practice didn't last too long for whatever reason, but my guess is that those women rejected or took offense to being named after something that was responsible for so much damage and destruction. Another theory was that this practice was started by a radio operator who sang *"Every little breeze seems to whisper Louise"* when issuing a hurricane warning. From that point on that particular hurricane and future hurricanes were referred to as Louise, and the use of female names for hurricanes became standard practice.

An early example of the use of a woman's name for a storm was in the best selling pocketbook novel "Storm" by George R. Stewart, published by Random House in 1941, and has since been made into a major motion picture by Walt Disney further promoting the idea of naming storms. It involved a young meteorologist working in the San Francisco Weather Bureau Office tracking a storm, which he called *Maria*, from its birth as a disturbance in the North Pacific to its death over North America many days later. The focus of the book is a storm named Maria, but pronounced 'Ma-Rye-Ah.' Yes, the song in the famous Broadway show *Paint Your Wagon* named "They Call the Wind Maria" was inspired by this fictional storm. He gave it a name because he said that he could easily say 'Hurricane Maria' rather than, *'the low pressure center which at 6pm yesterday was located*

Wayne Neely

at latitude one-seventy four degrees east and longitude forty-three degrees north' which he considered too long and cumbersome. As Stewart detailed in his novel, *'Not since at any price would the Junior Meteorologist have revealed to the Chief that he was bestowing names-and girls' names-upon those great moving low-pressure areas.'* He unofficially gave the storms in his book women names such as, Lucy, Katherine and Ruth after some girls he knew because he said that they each had a unique personality. It is not known whether George Stewart was indeed the inspiration for the trend toward naming hurricanes which came along later in the decade, but it seems likely.[2]

In 1950 military alphabet names (e.g. Able, Baker, Charley, Dog, Easy, Fox etc...) were adopted by the World Meteorological Organization (WMO) and the first named Atlantic hurricane was Able in 1950. The Joint Army/Navy (JAN) Phonetic Alphabet was developed in 1941 and was used by all branches of the United States military until the promulgation of the NATO phonetic alphabet in 1956, which replaced it. Before the JAN phonetic alphabet, each branch of the armed forces used its own phonetic alphabet, leading to difficulties in inter-branch communications. This naming method was not very popular, and caused a lot of confusion because officials soon realized that this naming convention would cause more problems in the history books if more than one powerful Hurricane Able made landfall and caused extensive damage and death to warrant retirement. This was because hurricanes that have a severe impact on the lives or the economy of a country or region are remembered for generations after the devastation they caused, and some go into weather history, so distinguishing one storm name from another is essential for the history books.

The modern naming convention came about in response to the need for unambiguous radio communications with ships and aircrafts. As air and sea transportation started to increase and meteorological observations improved in number and quality, several typhoons, hurricanes or cyclones might have to be tracked at any given time. To help in their identification, in 1953 the systematic use of only regular women names were used in alphabetical order and this lasted until 1978. The 1953's Alice was the first real human-named storm. At the

74

time they named them after women because these meteorologists reasoned that people might pay more attention to a storm if they envisioned it as a tangible entity, a character, rather than just a bundle of wind. But the use of only women names eventually was rejected as sexist and forecasters finally went with both male and female names. Beginning in 1960, four semi-permanent sets of names were established, to be re-cycled after four years. This list was expanded to ten sets in 1971, but before making it through the list even once; these sets were replaced by the now familiar 6 sets of men and women names.

This naming practice started in the Eastern Pacific in 1959 and in 1960 for the remainder of the North Pacific. It is interesting to note that in the Northwest Pacific Basin the names, by and large, are not personal names. While there are a few men and women names, the majority of the Northwest Pacific tropical cyclone names generally reflect Pacific culture and the names consists of flowers, animals, birds, trees, or even foods while some are just descriptive adjectives. In addition, the names are not allotted in alphabetical order but are arranged by the contributing nation with the countries being alphabetized. For example, the Cambodians have contributed Naki (a flower), Krovanh (a tree) and Damrey (an elephant). China has submitted names such as Yutu (a mythological rabbit), Longwang (the dragon king and god of rain in Chinese mythology), and Dainmu (the mother of lightning and the goddess in charge of thunder). Micronesian typhoon names include Sinlaku (a legendary Kosrae goddess) and Ewiniar (the Chuuk Storm god). Hurricanes in the central Pacific have name lists for only four years and use Hawaiian names.

In the North Atlantic Basin in 1979, gender equality finally reached the naming process of hurricanes when thousands of sexism complaints written to the WMO and feminists groups in the USA and worldwide urged the WMO to add men's names, hence both men and women names were used alternately and this practice is still in use today. That year would also herald the practice of drawing up list of names in advance of the hurricane season and today an alphabetical list of 21 names is used. Hurricane Bob was the first North Atlantic storm named after a man in the 1979 hurricane season, however it was not retired (it would eventually be retired in the 1991 hurricane season). Hurricane David was the second storm named after a man and it was the first male storm to be retired in the North Atlantic Region. This was due to the great death toll and substantial damage it inflicted to the countries of Dominica, the Dominican Republic and the Bahamas during the last week of August and the first week of September in 1979.

Since 1979, the naming list now includes names from non-English speaking countries within this region, such as, Dutch, French and Spanish names which also have a large presence here in the Caribbean. This is done to reflect the diversity of the different ethnic languages of the various countries in this region, so the names of Spanish, French, Dutch, and English persons are used in the naming process. The names of storms are now selected by a select committee from member countries of the World Meteorological Organization that falls within that particular region of the world, and we here in the Caribbean comes under Region IV for classification purposes. This committee meets once a year after the hurricane season has passed and before the beginning of the new hurricane season to decide on which names that are to be retired and to replace those names with a new set of names when and where necessary.

The practice of giving different names to storms in different hurricane basins has also led to a few rare circumstances of name-changing storms. For example, in October of 1988, after Atlantic Hurricane Joan devastated Central America, it proceeded to move into the Pacific and became Pacific tropical storm Miriam. Hurricane Joan was a powerful hurricane which caused death and destruction in over a dozen countries in the Caribbean and Central America. Another example was Hurricane Hattie, which was a powerful Category 5 hurricane that pounded Central America on Halloween during the 1961 North Atlantic hurricane season. It caused $370 million in damages and killed around 275 persons. Hattie is the only hurricane on record to have earned three names (Hattie, Simone, Inga) while crossing into different basins twice. Hattie swept across the Caribbean and came ashore in the town of Belize City, British Honduras (now called Belize), on October 31. It was a strong Category 4 hurricane at landfall, having weakened from a Category 5 hurricane just offshore. After making landfall, its remnants crossed over into the Pacific and attained tropical storm status again under the name Simone. In a remarkable turn of events, after Simone itself made landfall, its remnants crossed back over to the Gulf of Mexico, where the storm became Tropical Storm Inga before dissipating. However, it is debatable whether Inga in fact formed from the remnants of Simone at all.

It is interesting to note here that the letters Q, U, X, Y, and Z are not included in the hurricane list because of the scarcity of names beginning with those letters. However, in other regions of the world some of these letters are used, for example; only "Q" and "U" are omitted in the Northeastern Pacific Basin. When a storm causes tremendous damage and death, the name is taken out of circulation and retired for reasons of sensitivity. It is then replaced with a name of the same letter and of the same gender and if possible, the same language as the name being retired (e.g. neither Hurricane Irene in 2011 or Hurricane Katrina in 2005 will ever be used again). Since 1950, there were 76 hurricanes which had their names retired. The list includes one tropical storm, Allison of 2001, which caused billions in damage from its heavy rains.

The name used the most (at least with the same spelling is Arlene (seven times), while Frances and Florence have been used seven and six times respectively. However, considering different spellings of the same name, Debbie/Debby has been used seven times, and Anna/Ana has been used eight times. The first name to be called into use five times was Edith, but that name hasn't been used since 1971. After the 1996 season, Lilly has the distinction of being the first 'L' name to be used three times, while Marco is the first 'M' name to be used more than once. The name Kendra was assigned to a system in the 1966 hurricane season, but in post-season analysis it was decided it had not been a bona fide tropical storm. This storm marked the birth of reclassification of storms in the post-hurricane season (Hurricane Andrew was a storm that was reclassified from a Category four hurricane to a Category five hurricane in the off season).

In only three years (2005, 1995, 2010) have names beginning with the letter 'O' and beyond been used, but there have been several other years in which more than 14 storms have been tracked such as: 1887-19 storms, 1933-21 storms, 1936-16 storms, 1969-18 storms, 1995-19 storms, 2005-28 storms and 2010-19 storms. The 2010 Atlantic hurricane season has been extremely active, being the most active season since 2005. It must be noted that the 2010 season ties the record with the 1995 North Atlantic hurricane season and the 1887 North Atlantic hurricane season for the third most named storms (19). Furthermore, 2010 also ties the record with the 1969 North Atlantic hurricane season and 1887 for the second most hurricanes (12). The first three of these years were well before the naming of storms began, but 1969 requires an explanation. This was early in the era of complete satellite coverage, and forecasters were still studying the evolution of non-tropical systems (sub-tropical) into warm-core, tropical-type storms. Several systems that year were not named as tropical because they began at higher latitudes and were initially cold-cored.

Formal classification of subtropical(hybrid type) cyclones and public advisories on them began in 1972, and a few years later, a review was made of satellite imagery from the late 60's and early 70's and several of these systems were included as tropical storms. In fact, two of the storms added in 1969 were hurricanes, so 1969 now stands as having 12 hurricanes. Today, subtropical storms are named using the same list as tropical storms and hurricanes. This makes sense because subtropical cyclones often take on tropical characteristics. Imagine how confusing it would be if the system got a new name just because it underwent internal changes. There is no subtropical classification equivalent to a hurricane. The assumption is that once a storm got that strong it would have acquired tropical characteristics and therefore be called a hurricane or would have merged with an extratropical system in the North Atlantic and lost its name altogether. For example, on October 24, 1979, a subtropical storm briefly reached hurricane strength as it neared Newfoundland, Canada. It quickly combined with another low-pressure system but it was never named.

Whenever a hurricane has had a major impact, any country affected by the storm can request that the name of the hurricane be 'retired' by agreement of the World Meteorological Organization (WMO). Prior to 1969, officially, retiring a storm name actually meant that it cannot be reused for at least 10 years, to facilitate historic references, legal actions, insurance claim activities, etc... and to avoid public confusion with another storm of the same name. But today these storms are retired indefinitely and if that happens, it is replaced with a storm's name with the same gender because the retired storm often becomes household names in the regions or countries they affected. When that list of names is exhausted, the Greek Alphabet (Alpha, Beta, Gamma, Delta, Epsilon, Zeta, Eta, Theta, Iota, Kappa and Lambda) is used. It must be noted that so far this list has only been used once in either the Pacific or the Atlantic Basins, which was in the North Atlantic hurricane season of 2005. It is important to note here that there were a few subtropical storms which used the Greek Alphabet in the 1970's but they were really not truly tropical in nature.

If a storm forms in the off-season, it will take the next name on the list based on the current calendar date. For example, if a tropical cyclone formed on December 29, it would take the name from the previous season's list of names. If a storm formed in February, it would be named from the subsequent season's list of names. Theoretically, a hurricane or tropical storm of any strength can have its name retired; retirement is based entirely on the level of damage and death caused by a storm. However, up until 1972 (Hurricane Agnes), there was no Category 1 hurricane which had its name retired, and no named tropical storm had its name retired until 2001 (Tropical Storm Allison). Allison is the only tropical storm to have its name retired without ever having reached hurricane strength. This is at least partially due to the fact that weaker storms tend to cause less damage, and the few weak storms that have had their names retired caused most of their destruction through heavy rainfall rather than winds.

While no request for retirement has ever been turned down, some storms such as Hurricane Gordon in 1994 caused a great deal of death and destruction but nonetheless was not retired as the main country affected-Haiti did not request retirement. Hurricane Gordon in 1994 killed 1,122 persons in Haiti, and 23 deaths in other nations. Damage in the United States was estimated at $400 million, and damages in Haiti and Cuba were severe. Despite the tremendous damage caused, the name 'Gordon' was not retired and was reused in both the 2000 and 2006 North Atlantic hurricane seasons. Since 1950, 76 storms have had their names retired. Of these, two (Carol and Edna) were reused after the storm for which they were retired but were later retroactively retired, and two others (Hilda and Janet) were included on later lists of storm names but were not reused before being retroactively retired. Before 1979, when the first permanent six-year storm names list began, some storm names were simply not used anymore. For example, in 1966, 'Fern' was substituted for 'Frieda,' and no reason was cited.

In the North Atlantic Basin in most cases, a tropical cyclone retains its name throughout its life. However, a tropical cyclone may be renamed in several situations. First, when a tropical storm crosses from the Atlantic into the Pacific, or vice versa, before 2001 it was the policy of National Hurricane Center (NHC) to rename a tropical storm which crossed from the Atlantic into the Pacific, or vice versa. Examples included Hurricane Cesar-Douglas in 1996 and Hurricane Joan-Miriam in 1988. In 2001, when Iris moved across Central America, NHC mentioned that Iris would retain its name if it regenerated in the Pacific. However, the Pacific tropical depression developed from the remnants of Iris was called Fifteen-E instead. The depression later became Tropical Storm Manuel. NHC explained that Iris had dissipated as a tropical cyclone prior to entering the eastern North Pacific Basin; the new depression was properly named Fifteen-E, rather than Iris. In 2003, when Larry was about to move across Mexico, NHC attempted to provide greater clarity: *"Should Larry remain a tropical cyclone during its passage over Mexico into the Pacific, it would retain its name. However, a new name would be given if the surface circulation dissipates and then regenerates in the Pacific."*[3] Up to now, it is extremely rare for a tropical cyclone to retain its name during the passage from the Atlantic to the Pacific, or vice versa.

Second, storms are renamed in situations where there are uncertainties of the continuation of storms. When the remnants of a tropical cyclone redevelop, the redeveloping system will be treated as a new tropical cyclone if there are uncertainties of the continuation, even though the original system may contribute to the forming of the new system. One example is the remnants of Tropical Depression #10 reforming into Tropical Depression #12 from the 2005 season which went on to become the powerful and deadly Hurricane Katrina. Another example was a storm which had the most names as stated earlier; in 1961 there was one tropical storm which had three lives and three names. Tropical Storm Hattie developed off the Caribbean Coast of Nicaragua on October 28, 1961, and drifted north and west before crossing Central America at Guatemala. It re-emerged into the Pacific Ocean on November 1 and was re-christened Simone. Two days later it recurved back towards the coastline of Central America and crossed over into the Atlantic via Mexico, re-emerging into the Gulf of Mexico as Inga.

CHAPTER FIVE

THE NEW CLASSIFICATION OF HURRICANES IN THE NORTH ATLANTIC BASIN

THE NEW SAFFIR-SIMPSON HURRICANE WIND SCALE

The Saffir-Simpson Hurricane Wind Scale is a 1 to 5 rating based on a hurricane's sustained wind speed. This scale estimates potential property damage. Hurricanes reaching Category 3 and higher are considered major hurricanes because of their potential for significant loss of life and damage. Category 1 and 2 storms are still dangerous, however, and require preventative measures. During the open public comment period for the draft of the Saffir-Simpson Hurricane Wind Scale in 2010, many people suggested that the National Hurricane Center (NHC) in Miami develop a storm surge specific scale as well as improve its forecasting of storm surge. It is acknowledged that there are some researchers who advocate developing another scale for hurricanes specifically geared toward storm surge impact by incorporating aspects of the system's size. However, the National Hurricane Center does not believe that such scales would be helpful or effective at conveying the storm surge threat.

It must be noted that the Saffir-Simpson Hurricane Wind Scale (SSHWS) went under minor modifications for the 2012 North Atlantic

Hurricane season in order to resolve the awkwardness associated with conversions among the various units used for wind speed in advisory products. The change broadens the Category 4 wind speed range by one mile per hour (mph) at each end of the range, yielding a new range of 130-156 mph. It must be noted here that this change does not alter the category assignments of any storms in the historical record, nor will it change the category assignments for future storms. The reasoning behind this change and a tabulation of the old and new scales is given below. The new summary table is shown below.[1]

Category	Sustained Winds	Types of Damage Due to Hurricane Winds
1	74-95 mph 64-82 kt 119-153 km/h	Very dangerous winds will produce some damage: Well-constructed frame homes could have damage to roof, shingles, vinyl siding and gutters. Large branches of trees will snap and shallowly rooted trees may be toppled. Extensive damage to power lines and poles likely will result in power outages that could last a few to several days.
2	96-110 mph 83-95 kt 154-177 km/h	Extremely dangerous winds will cause extensive damage: Well-constructed frame homes could sustain major roof and siding damage. Many shallowly rooted trees will be snapped or uprooted and block numerous roads. Near-total power loss is expected with outages that could last from several days to weeks.
3 (major)	111-129 mph 96-112 kt 178-208 km/h	Devastating damage will occur: Well-built framed homes may incur major damage or removal of roof decking and gable ends. Many trees will be snapped or uprooted, blocking numerous roads. Electricity and water will be unavailable for several days to weeks after the storm passes.
4 (major)	130-156 mph 113-136 kt 209-251 km/h	Catastrophic damage will occur: Well-built framed homes can sustain severe damage with loss of most of the roof structure and/or some exterior walls. Most trees will be snapped or uprooted and power poles downed. Fallen trees and power poles will isolate residential areas. Power outages will last weeks to possibly months. Most of the area will be uninhabitable for weeks or months.
5 (major)	157 mph or higher 137 kt or higher 252 km/h or higher	Catastrophic damage will occur: A high percentage of framed homes will be destroyed, with total roof failure and wall collapse. Fallen trees and power poles will isolate residential areas. Power outages will last for weeks to possibly months. Most of the area will be uninhabitable for weeks or months.

The New Saffir-Simpson Hurricane Wind Scale.

The Saffir-Simpson Hurricane Wind Scale (SSHWS) is a 1 to 5 categorization based on a hurricane's intensity at an indicated time, according to the National Hurricane Center (NHC). Essentially, the new modification is to help clarify categorization of wind speed measurements based on miles per hour (mph), kilometers per hour (km/h) and knots. There is an inherent uncertainty when estimating wind speeds for tropical cyclones. Generally, wind speeds are rounded because it's unrealistic to identify exact wind speeds. So, these numbers are rounded to the nearest "5." For example, 132 mph would be rounded to 130 mph, while 138 knots would be rounded to 140 knots.

Category	Winds	Summary
1	74-95 mph 64-82 kt 119-153 km/h	Very dangerous winds will produce some damage
2	96-110 mph 83-95 kt 154-177 km/h	Extremely dangerous winds will cause extensive damage
3	111-129 mph 96-112 kt 178-208 km/h	Devastating damage will occur
4	130-156 mph 113-136 kt 209-251 km/h	Catastrophic damage will occur
5	157 mph or higher 137 kt or higher 252 km/h or higher	Catastrophic damage will occur

The New Saffir-Simpson Hurricane Wind Scale.

This provides a problem, specifically for Category 4 classification. Category 4 used to be defined as 131 to 155 mph (or 114 to 135 knots or 210 to 259 km/h). This has caused a problem in conversions. For example, if a reading is 115 knots, it is a Category 4 hurricane. However, when 115 knots is converted to mph (132.3 mph), and it is rounded to the nearest "5" (130 mph), the hurricane is then defined as a Category 3 hurricane.

The new scale will alleviate this issue. Category 1 (64 to 82 knots) and Category 2 (83 to 95 knots) will remain the same, but Category 3 (formerly 96 to 113 knots) will now be measured as 96 to 112 knots (or 111 to 129 mph or 178 to 208 km/h). Category 4 will now be identified as 113 to 136 knots (or 130 to 156 mph or 209 to 251 km/h), and Category 5 will be defined as 137 knots or higher (or 157 mph or higher or 252 km/h or higher).[2]

The Saffir-Simpson Hurricane Wind Scale as it is now called (previously called the Saffir-Simpson Hurricane Damage Potential Scale) is a classification used for most western hemisphere tropical cyclones which exceed the intensities of "tropical depressions" and "tropical storms," and thereby become hurricanes. The scale divides hurricanes into five categories distinguished by the intensities of their sustained winds. Hurricanes are ranked according to strength and by the amount of damage they cause. The weakest hurricane is designated a Category 1 status with maximum sustained winds from 74 mph to 95 mph. In contrast, a Category 5 hurricane has maximum sustained winds of greater than 157 mph.

Only a few Atlantic hurricanes have made landfall with winds estimated to have reached the rarefied extreme of 200 mph, at least in gusts. These includes, the Great Labour Day Hurricane of 1935 which passed over the Florida Keys (inspiring the classic Humphrey Bogart movie *Key Largo*); Hurricane Camille, which came ashore at Pass Christian, Mississippi in 1969, and Hurricane Andrew in 1992, which struck the Bahamas and the lower Florida Peninsula. Some top wind speeds from some of these powerful Atlantic storms will never ever be known because in most cases the instruments were destroyed before they measured the worst of their respective winds. This is because very few anemometers are capable of accurately measuring the winds of a Category 5 hurricane. The list of Category 5 Atlantic hurricanes encompasses 32 tropical cyclones that reached the extremely rare Category 5 intensity on the Saffir-Simpson Hurricane Wind Scale within the North Atlantic. They are the most catastrophic hurricanes that can form on planet earth. They are relatively rare in the North Atlantic Basin, and generally occur only about once every three years on average in this region. Only four times-in the 1960, 1961, 2005 and 2007 hurricane seasons-have multiple Category 5 hurricanes formed. Only in 2005 have more than two Category 5 storms formed, and only in 2007 has more than one made landfall at Category 5 strength. The two most intense Category 5 hurricanes were, Hurricane Wilma in 2005 (882mb) and Hurricane Gilbert in 1988 (888mb).

Summary of the SSHWS change (highlighted in yellow):

Category	Previous range	New range
1	74-95 mph 64-82 kt 119-153 km/h	74-95 mph 64-82 kt 119-153 km/h
2	96-110 mph 83-95 kt 154-177 km/h	96-110 mph 83-95 kt 154-177 km/h
3	111-130 mph 96-113 kt 178-209 km/h	111-129 mph 96-112 kt 178-208 km/h
4	131-155 mph 114-135 kt 210-249 km/h	130-156 mph 113-136 kt 209-251 km/h
5	156 mph or higher 136 kt or higher 250 km/h or higher	157 mph or higher 137 kt or higher 252 km/h or higher

This breakdown from the National Hurricane Center shows the differences between the old scale and the new version. Now, when knot-based measurements are used to categorize hurricanes, the conversion will not affect to which category the hurricane belongs. The NHC has stated that this new scale will not affect any previous categorizations of past hurricanes and has only been implemented to make classifications easier.

The Saffir-Simpson Hurricane Wind Scale is a classification used for most western hemisphere tropical cyclones which exceed the intensities of "tropical depressions" and "tropical storms," and thereby become hurricanes. The scale divides hurricanes into five categories distinguished by the intensities of their sustained winds. Hurricanes are ranked according to strength and by the amount of damage they cause. The weakest hurricane is designated a Category

1 status with maximum sustained winds from 74 mph to 95 mph. In contrast, a Category 5 hurricane has maximum sustained winds of greater than 157 mph.

As a result of the difficulty in relating the different and varying factors or characteristics of a hurricane to the destruction potential, the Saffir-Simpson Damage Potential Scale was developed in 1969 and completed in 1971. The scale was introduced to the general public in 1973, and saw widespread use after Neil Frank replaced Simpson at the helm of the National Hurricane Center in 1974. This scale was named for Herbert Saffir a civil engineer in Coral Gables, Florida and Robert Simpson, a meteorologist and the then Director of the National Hurricane Center in Miami, Florida. It has been used for well over 37 years to estimate the relative damage potential of a hurricane due to wind and storm surge. However, it must be noted that the new scale doesn't include storm surge but just wind speeds alone. The initial scale was developed by Mr. Herbert Saffir (who at the time was well known as the father of the Miami's building codes) while working on commission from the United Nations to study low-cost housing in hurricane-prone areas. While performing the study, Saffir realized that there was no simple scale for describing the likely effects of a hurricane. Knowing the usefulness of the Richter Magnitude Scale in describing earthquakes, he devised a similar 1-5 scale based on wind speed that showed expected damage to structures. Saffir looked at the scale from an engineering point of view because he was well-versed in Miami's building codes. Saffir then gave the scale to the National Hurricane Center, and Simpson added in the likely effects of storm surge and flooding. Simpson became the Director of the National Hurricane Center in 1968 and he was already one of the world's leading authorities on tropical cyclones and a veteran of numerous Air Force and Navy flights into these hurricanes. Simpson later recalled that the National Hurricane Center at the time was having difficulty telling disaster agencies how much damage to expect from particular storms.

Using a mixture of structural engineering and meteorology, they constructed the Saffir-Simpson Damage Potential Scale because both men had first-hand experiences with hurricanes. It does not take into account rainfall or location, which means that a Category 3 hurricane which hits a major city will likely do far more damage than a Category 5 hurricane which hits a rural area. The old Saffir-Simpson Scale classified hurricanes into Categories 1,2,3,4, and 5, depending on the barometric pressure, wind speed, and storm surge and destruction. A Category 1 hurricane, for example, would inflict minimal damage, mainly to shrubbery, trees, foliage, unanchored structures, mobile homes, small craft, and low-lying areas that could become flooded. Whereas, a Category 5 hurricane would cause catastrophic damage, such as blown down trees, power lines, and poles; overturned vehicles; torn down or blown away buildings; complete destruction of mobile or manufactured homes and massive flooding.

According to Robert Simpson, there is no reason for a Category 6 on the Saffir-Simpson Scale because it is designed to measure the potential damage of a hurricane to man-made structures. If the speed of the hurricane is above 156 mph, then the damage to a building will be "serious no matter how well it's engineered." However, the result of new technologies in construction leads some to suggest that an increase in the number of categories is necessary. This suggestion was emphasized after the devastating effects of the 2005 Atlantic hurricane season. During that record year Hurricane Emily, Hurricane Katrina, Hurricane Rita, and Hurricane Wilma all became Category 5 hurricanes. A few newspaper columnists and scientists have brought up the idea of introducing a Category 6 and amending the scale to include the risk of flooding but in most cases it is often rebuffed.

In 2012 the National Hurricane Center revised the old Saffir-Simpson Scale and renamed it the *Saffir-Simpson Hurricane Wind Scale* (SSHWS). It went through minor modifications in order to resolve awkwardness associated with conversions among the various units used for wind speed in advisory products. The change broadens the Category 4 wind speed range by one mile per hour (mph) at each end of the range, yielding a new range of 130-156 mph. This change does not alter the category assignments of any storms in the historical record, nor will it change the category assignments for future storms. The reasoning behind this change and a tabulation of the old and new scales was based on the outcry from the public, media, meteorologists and others about the flaws in the previous scale. The change broadens the Category 4 wind speed range by one mile per hour (mph) at each end of the range, yielding a new range of 130-156 mph. This change does not alter the category assignments of any storms in the historical record, nor will it change the category assignments for future storms.

The reasoning behind this change and a tabulation of the old and new scales is given below. As a result of the inherent uncertainty in estimating the strength of tropical cyclones, the National Hurricane Center and the Central Pacific Hurricane Center assign tropical cyclone intensities in 5-knot (kt) increments (e.g., 100, 105, 100, 115 kt, etc.). Some advisory products, however, require intensity to be given in units of mph and kilometers per hour (km/h). For these products, the intensity in knots is converted into mph and km/h and then rounded to 5-mph and 5-km/h increments, so as not to suggest that the intensity of the storm can be known to unrealistic precision (e.g., 127 mph).

Unfortunately, this conversion and rounding process doesn't work well at the Category 4 boundaries. Category 4 has historically been defined to be 131-155 mph (with corresponding ranges in other units given as 114-135 kt, and 210-249 km/h). A hurricane with an assigned intensity of 115 kt, therefore, is a Category 4 hurricane. However, when 115 kt is converted to mph (132.3 mph) and then rounded to the nearest 5 mph (130 mph), the result falls in the Category 3 mph range. In order for the hurricane to appear as Category 4 in both kt and mph, NHC is forced to incorrectly convert 115 kt to 135 mph in its advisory products. A similar problem occurs when the Category 4 intensity of 135 kt is converted to km/h. To solve these rounding issues, the new SSHWS broadens the Category 4 wind speed range by one mph at each end of the range, yielding a new range of 130-156 mph (113-136 kt, 209-251 km/h). With this change, a 115-kt Category 4 hurricane can have its intensity properly converted to mph and rounded to the nearest 5 mph (130 mph) – and remain within the Category 4 mph range.

It's important to reiterate that because NHC assigns intensity using 5-kt increments (and will be doing so for the foreseeable future), neither storms in the historical record nor any future storms would have their SSHWS category changed as a result of this adjustment. Changing the Category 4 range to 130-156 mph, 113-136 kt, and 209-

251 km/h simply allows all unit conversions from knots to be done correctly and keep storms in the correct Category, regardless of the units used. During the open public comment period for the draft of the Saffir-Simpson Hurricane Wind Scale in 2010, many people suggested that the National Weather Service develop a storm surge specific scale as well as improve its forecasting of storm surge. It is acknowledged that there are some researchers who advocate developing another scale for hurricanes specifically geared toward storm surge impact by incorporating aspects of the system's size. However, the National Hurricane Center does not believe that such scales would be helpful or effective at conveying the storm surge threat.

The practical usefulness of the Saffir-Simpson Scale is that it relates properties of the hurricane to previously observed damage. Until the Saffir-Simpson Damage Potential Scale was developed, hurricanes were referred to as, *Great (or Extreme) Hurricanes, Severe Hurricanes, or Minor, Minimal or Major Hurricanes.* A Minor Hurricane had maximum winds of 74 mph and a minimum central pressure of 29.40 inches. A Minimal hurricane had maximum winds of between 75 to 100 mph and a minimum central pressure of between 29.03 to 29.39 inches. A Major hurricane had winds between 101 to 135 mph and a minimal central pressure of 28.01 to 29.02 inches. An Extreme or Great hurricane had winds of 136 mph or over and a minimum central pressure of 28.00 inches or less. However, these terms are no longer used but may appear in historical materials now and then.[4] It is important to note that when dealing with narrative descriptions of historical events, these determinations must be somewhat subjective. For the purposes of this book, these categories will be any storm causing devastating damage through either wind action or storm surge. Some authors over the years have used the word or terminology 'extreme' very loosely to describe the worst of these events but I will refrain from using that terminology. The word 'extreme' in my opinion would imply the 'peak' or 'maximum' of a very powerful and destructive storm. For this book, I prefer to use the more acceptable and more appropriate word of 'Great' to label these very destructive and powerful storms but I will mention it when it is only necessary. It is important to note that tropical storms are named but are not assigned a Saffir-Simpson category number.

THE CLASSIFICATION OF TROPICAL CYCLONES AROUND THE WORLD

Term	Meaning
Cyclone (Generic term for a low-pressure system Tropical Cyclone)	Cyclone is a generic term to refer to a low-pressure system. Typhoons and other types of low pressure systems are all cyclones. The direction of rotation is opposite in the northern hemisphere and the southern hemisphere, but other essential features of a cyclone are shared in both hemispheres.
Tropical Cyclone	Tropical cyclone is in general a cyclone formed in the tropical areas. However, the word "tropical" does not refer to the place of formation, and it actually refers to the structure of a cyclone. This means that a cyclone with the structure of a tropical cyclone is called a "tropical cyclone" regardless of the place. Typhoons, hurricanes and others are all "intense" tropical cyclones, so they are regarded as same meteorological phenomena (classification of intensity). A unique convention for tropical cyclones is that each tropical cyclone is named.
Extratropical Cyclone	Extratropical cyclone literally means a cyclone outside of the tropical areas. Most of the low pressure systems that pass around Japan belong to this type. Just like a tropical cyclone, this term also does not refer to the place of formation, but refers to the structure of a cyclone. The fundamental difference between a tropical cyclone and this type is that the former consists of warm air only, while the latter consists of both cold air and warm air. This difference also leads to the different source of energy for intensification. Finally, we often see a tropical cyclone transformed into an extratropical cyclone, but the inverse is extremely rare.
Typhoon	Typhoon is a tropical cyclone located in the western north Pacific basin (between 100E and 180E in the northern hemisphere). The category of a typhoon is decided by the maximum sustained winds, but please note that the typhoon in Japanese standard and the typhoon in international standard is not the same. Finally, among tropical cyclones in the world, the typhoon is the most frequent and the strongest tropical cyclone. Typhoons are named.
Hurricane	Hurricane is a tropical cyclone located in the north Atlantic, eastern or central north Pacific (east of 180E (180W) in the northern hemisphere), eastern south Pacific (east of 160E in the southern hemisphere). The category of a hurricane follows the same international standard as the typhoon based on the maximum sustained wind. When a hurricane reaches the 180E (180W) degree line and enters into the basin of the typhoon, it starts to be called a typhoon. Hurricanes are named.
Cyclone(Abbreviation of a tropical cyclone)	Cyclone is a generic term for a cyclonic system, but the same word is also used as an abbreviation of 'tropical cyclone' as long as a special term to represent a tropical cyclone does not exist. In northern Indian ocean (west of 100E), the term "cyclonic storm" is used, and in southern Indian ocean, around Australia, and in the southern Pacific ocean, the term "tropical cyclone" is in use. If a typhoon moves westward to pass 100E, then it starts to be called as a cyclone. It seems that the first tropical cyclone in the south Atlantic in 2004 is called either a cyclone or a hurricane. Cyclones are named.
Willy-Willy	Willy-Willy is often introduced as the name of a tropical cyclone around Australia, but it seems that it actually means something like a dust devil, and has little relationship with a tropical cyclone.

*Unfortunately, there are at least two definitions of this term in widespread use. Most countries (including us here in the Bahamas) use the World Meteorological Organization's definition, which is a ten-minute sustained average wind at an elevation of ten meters. But the United States uses a one-minute average, which is almost always higher.

Tropical cyclones are ranked according to their maximum winds using several scales and methods depending on which area of the world they are located. These scales are provided by several bodies, including the World Meteorological Organization, the U.S. Joint Typhoon Warning Center, the National Hurricane Center in Miami, and the Bureau of Meteorology in Australia. The National Hurricane Center uses the Saffir-Simpson Hurricane Wind Scale for hurricanes in the eastern Pacific and Atlantic Basins. Australia uses a different set of tropical cyclone categories for their region. Many basins have different names of hurricane/typhoon/cyclone strength. The United States National Hurricane Center, the main governing body for hurricanes in the North Atlantic region classifies hurricanes of Category 3 and above as Major Hurricanes. Whereas, the U.S. Joint Typhoon Warning Center classifies typhoons with wind speeds of at least 150 mph (67 m/s or 241 km/h, equivalent to a strong Category 4 storm) as *Super Typhoons*. The term *'Major Hurricane'* supplants the previously used term of *'Great Hurricane'* which was used throughout the 1950's and the 1960's.

The use of different definitions for maximum sustained winds creates additional confusion into the definitions of cyclone categories worldwide. The Saffir-Simpson Hurricane Wind Scale is used only to describe hurricanes forming in the Atlantic Ocean and Northern Pacific Ocean east of the International Date Line. Other areas use their own classification schemes to label these storms, which are called 'cyclones' or 'typhoons' depending on the area where they occur around the world. The Australian Bureau of Meteorology uses a 1-5 scale called *Tropical Cyclone Severity Categories*. Unlike the Saffir-Simpson Scale, severity categories are based on the strongest wind gusts and not sustained winds. Severity categories are scaled somewhat lower than the Saffir-Simpson Scale. A Category 1 storm features gusts less than 126 km/h (78 mph), with a severity Category 2 tropical cyclone, being roughly equivalent to a Saffir-Simpson Category 1 hurricane, while gusts in a Category 5 cyclone are at least 280 km/h (174 mph).[5]

The U.S. Joint Typhoon Warning Center classifies West Pacific typhoons as tropical cyclones with wind speeds greater than 73 mph (118 km/h). Typhoons with wind speeds of at least 150 mph (67 m/s or 241 km/h, equivalent to a strong Category 4 hurricane) are dubbed *Super Typhoons*. In the Southwestern Indian Ocean: (1) a "tropical depression" is a tropical disturbance in which the maximum of the average wind speed is 28 to 33 knots (51 to 62 km/h); (2) a "moderate tropical storm" is a tropical disturbance in which the maximum of the average wind speed is 34 to 47 knots (63 to 88 km/h); (3) a "severe tropical storm" is a tropical disturbance in which the maximum of the average wind speed is 48 to 63 knots (89 to 117 km/h); (4) a "tropical cyclone" is a tropical disturbance in which the maximum of the average wind speed is 64 to 89 knots (118 to 165 km/h); (5) an "intense tropical cyclone" is a tropical disturbance in which the maximum of the average wind speed is 90 to 115 knots (166 to 212 km/h); and (6) a "very intense tropical cyclone" is a tropical disturbance in which the maximum of the average wind speed is greater than 115 knots (greater than 212 km/h).[6]

The Beaufort Wind Scale was a scale that was developed by Sir Francis Beaufort in 1805 of the British Navy and was based solely on human observation. The Beaufort Wind Scale is now universally used around the world by seamen and lay persons alike. In 1805-06 Commander Francis Beaufort (Later Admiral Sir Francis Beaufort) devised a descriptive wind scale in an effort to standardize wind reports in ship's logs. As a result of this scale we have hurricane winds starting at 64 knots. His scale divided wind speeds into 14 Forces (later reduced to thirteen) with each Force assigned a number, a common name, and a description of the effects such a wind would have on a sailing ship. Since the worst storm an Atlantic sailor was likely to run into was a hurricane that name was applied to the top Force on the scale. During the 19th century, with the manufacture of accurate anemometers, actual numerical values were assigned to each Force Level, but it wasn't until 1926 (with revisions in 1939 and 1946) that the International Meteorological Committee (predecessor of the World Meteorological Organization) adopted a universal scale of wind speed values. It was a progressive scale with the range of speed for Forces increasing as you go higher. Thus, Force 1 is only 3 knots in range, while the Force 11 is 8 knots in range and Force 12 starts out at 64 knots (74 mph). There is nothing magical in this number, and since hurricane force winds are a rare experience, chances are the committee which decided on this number didn't do so because of any real observations during a hurricane.

Another wind scale called the Smeaton-Rouse Wind Scale which was developed in 1759 pegged hurricane force winds at 70 knots (80 mph). Just the same, when a tropical cyclone has maximum winds of approximately these speeds we do see the mature structure (eye, eyewall, spiral rainbands) begin to form, so there is some unity with setting hurricane force winds in this neighbourhood. For example, if whole trees moved and resistance was felt while walking against the wind and the waves produced white foam with streaks on it then the observer would categorize it as a gale. In the 1800's and early 1900's Caribbean fishermen used this Beaufort Wind Scale almost exclusively to gauge the intensity of a storm. Even in historical records in the Caribbean, many of these storms were simply referred to as 'gales' or 'severe gales' rather than hurricanes or tropical storms. This often resulted in many of these storms going unreported or under-reported because a gale in meteorological terms simply meant that these storms had sustained wind speeds of between 34 to 47 knots (39 to 54 mph) as opposed to 64 knots (74 mph) or greater for a hurricane. Although the traditional definition of a hurricane is Beaufort Force 12 winds ('air filled with foam, sea completely white with driving spray, visibility greatly reduced'), nowadays the Saffir-Simpson Hurricane Wind Scale is used, especially in this region of the world. It is a scale which is used as a quick means of informing not only meteorologists, but also the public, of the relative intensity of an approaching storm.

In Meteorology as in nature, the elements always try to achieve a perfect balance but thankfully they never do. For example, a hurricane's main objective is a simple one, to take heat from the equator to the poles and likewise, the cold front's objective is similarly to take cold air from the poles to the equator but thankfully none of them ever get to achieve their objectives so they continue trying in this never ending cycle and the result is life here on earth as we know it today. The sun is our only source of heat on a global scale. Around 70% of the earth's surface is covered in water-mostly the oceans. Since water holds heat energy better than the land, our tropical oceans are extremely efficient in storing energy transmitted by the sun. So the heat generated by the sun and stored in the oceans is the first major ingredient for fueling hurricanes. Hurricanes form over tropical waters where the winds are light, the humidity is high in a deep layer, and the surface water temperature is warm, typically 26.5 degrees Celsius or greater over a vast area, often between latitudes 5 degrees to 25 degrees north or south of the equator. Over the tropical and subtropical North Atlantic and North Pacific oceans these conditions prevail in the summer and early fall; hence, the hurricane season normally runs from June through November. At this time the water is hot enough to create atmospheric convection that casts moisture 10 miles up into the atmosphere.

These extremely hazardous weather systems occur most commonly across the low-latitude Northwest Pacific and its 'downstream' land areas, where on average just over a third of the global total of such storms develop. In an average year there are approximately 80 of these tropical cyclones which form over warm tropical oceans with 48 of them becoming hurricanes and 20 of them becoming intense hurricanes. Many residents within this region perceive the North Atlantic Ocean basin a prolific producer of hurricanes because of the worldwide publicity these storms generate. In reality, the North Atlantic is generally only a marginal basin in terms of hurricane activity. Every tropical ocean except the South Atlantic and Southeast Pacific contains hurricanes; several of these tropical oceans produce more hurricanes annually than the North Atlantic. Hurricanes are generally a summer phenomenon, but the length of the hurricane season varies in each basin, as does the peak of activity. The Northeast Pacific averages 17%, the Northwest Pacific averages just over 33%, while the North Atlantic typically sees about 12% of the world's total of tropical cyclones, while the other regions accounts for the remaining 38%(the percentages may vary from year to year and basin to basin but these are just conservative averages) of the world total of hurricanes. Additionally, most basins use a 10-minute average of sustained wind speeds to determine intensity, as recommended by the WMO, but this is not the case in the North Atlantic and Northeastern Pacific regions, where 1-minute averages, almost always higher, are used.[7&8]

TROPICAL CYCLONE MAP

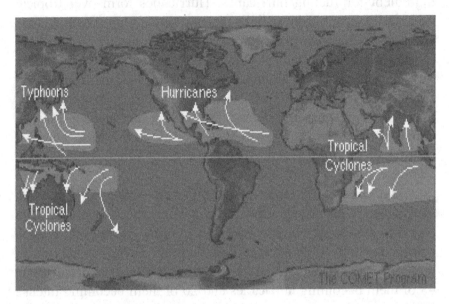

(Courtesy of www.comet.ucar.edu)

- **Northern Atlantic Ocean:** The most-studied of all tropical basins and accounts for approximately 12% of the world's total tropical cyclones. Tropical cyclone formation here varies widely from year to year, ranging from twenty eight to one per year with an average of around ten. The United States Atlantic and Gulf Coasts, Mexico, Central America, the Caribbean Islands, and Bermuda are frequently affected by storms in this basin. Venezuela, the south-east of Canada and Atlantic "Macaronesian" islands are also occasionally affected. Many of the more intense Atlantic storms are Cape Verde-Type hurricanes, which forms off the west coast of Africa near the Cape Verde Islands. On rare occasions, a hurricane can reach the European mainland such as, Hurricane Lili, which dissipated over the British Isles in October of 1996 and Tropical Storm Vince in September 2005, which made landfall on the southwestern coast of Spain in the record breaking 2005 North Atlantic hurricane season. In an average year, about 10 storms form in this basin with 6 of them becoming hurricanes and of that total 2 of them becoming intense hurricanes. In this basin, the hurricane season runs from June 1 to November 30 with the peak of the season occurring around September 10.

- **Northeastern Pacific Ocean:** This is the second most active basin in the world accounting for approximately 17% of the worlds' total tropical cyclones, and the most compact (a large number of storms for such a small area of ocean). Storms that form here can affect western Mexico, Hawaii, northern Central America, and on extremely rare occasions, California and Arizona. There is no record of a hurricane ever reaching California; however, to some meteorologists, historical records in 1858 indicate that there was a storm which struck San Diego with winds of over 75 mph. In an average year, about 17 storms form in this basin with 10 of them becoming hurricanes and of that total 5 of them becoming intense hurricanes. In this basin, the hurricane season runs from May 15 to November 30 with the peak of the season occurring around August 25.

- **Northwestern Pacific Ocean:** Tropical cyclone activity in this region frequently affects China, Japan, Hong Kong, the Philippines, and Taiwan, but also many other countries in Southeast Asia, such as Vietnam, South Korea, and parts of Indonesia, plus numerous Oceanian islands. This is by far the most active basin, accounting for over 33% of all tropical cyclone activity in the world. The coast of China sees the most land falling tropical cyclones worldwide. The Philippines receives an average 18 typhoon landings per year. Rarely does a typhoon or an extratropical storm reach northward to Siberia, Russia. In an average year, about 27 storms form in this basin with 17 of them becoming hurricanes and of that total 8 of them becoming intense hurricanes. It is interesting to note that in this basin, the hurricane season occurs year-round with the peak of the season occurring around September 1 and the minimum occurring in February.

- **Northern Indian Ocean:** This basin is sub-divided into two areas, the Bay of Bengal and the Arabian Sea, with the Bay of Bengal dominating (5 to 6 times more activity). This basin's season has an interesting and rare double peak season; one in April and May before the onset of the monsoons, and another in October and November just after the monsoons. Tropical cyclones which form in this basin has historically cost the most lives — most notably, the November, 1970 Bhola Cyclone killed approximately 300,000 to 500,000 persons mainly in Bangladesh and coastal India from drowning. Nations affected by this basin include India, Bangladesh, Sri Lanka, Thailand, Myanmar, and Pakistan. Rarely, a tropical cyclone formed in this basin will affect the Arabian Peninsula. This basin accounts for about 12% of the worlds' total of tropical cyclones. In an average year about 5 storms form in this basin with 2 of them becoming hurricanes and of that total 1 becoming an intense hurricane. In the North Indian basin, storms are most common from April to December 30, with peaks in May 15 and November 10.

- **Southwestern Pacific Ocean:** Tropical activity in this region largely affects Australia and Oceania. On rare occasions, tropical storms reach the vicinity of Brisbane, Australia and into New Zealand, usually during or after extratropical transition. This basin accounts for about 11% of the worlds' total of tropical cyclones. In an average year about 10 storms form in this basin with 5 of them becoming hurricanes and of that total 2 of them becoming intense hurricanes. In this basin, the hurricane season runs from October 15 to May 1 with the peak of the season occurring around March 1.

- **Southeastern Indian Ocean:** Tropical activity in this region affects Australia and Indonesia. According to the Australian Bureau of Meteorology, the most frequently hit portion of Australia is between Exmouth and Broome in Western Australia. This basin accounts for about 7% of the worlds' total of tropical cyclones. In an average year about 7 storms form in this basin with 3 of them becoming hurricanes and of that total 1 becoming an intense hurricane. In this basin, the hurricane season runs from October 15 to May 1 with the peak of the season occurring January 15 and February 25.

- **Southwestern Indian Ocean:** This basin is often the least understood, due to a lack of historical data. Cyclones forming here impact Madagascar, Mozambique, Mauritius, Reunion, Comoros, Tanzania, and Kenya. This basin accounts for about the remaining 8% of the worlds' total of tropical cyclones. In an average year about 10 storms form in this basin with 5 of them becoming hurricanes and of that total 2 of them becoming intense hurricanes. In this basin, the hurricane season runs from October 15 to May 15 with the peak of the season occurring January 15 and February 20.

A hurricane is a circular, cyclonic system with a diameter anywhere from 100 to 500 miles extending upwards to heights of 40,000 to 50,000 feet. They draw their energy from latent heat from the warm tropical seas and they are generally smaller than middle-latitude cyclones, which on the other hand depend on the tropics-to-pole temperature gradient for their energy. At the base of the hurricane, air is sucked in by the very low pressure at the center and then spirals inward. Once within the hurricane structure itself, air rises rapidly to the top and spirals outward. It is this rapid upward movement of great quantities of moisture rich air that produces the enormous amounts of rain during a hurricane. A hurricane consists of huge swirl of clouds rotating around a calm center-the eye-where warm air is sucked down. Clouds, mainly cumulonimbus clouds are arranged in bands around the eye, the tallest forming the wall of the eye. The eyewall as it is commonly called is the area of highest surface winds in the tropical cyclone. It is composed of many strong updrafts and downdrafts. The mechanisms by which the eyewall and the eye are formed are not very well understood but it is generally thought that the eye feature is a fundamental component of all rotating fluids.

Hurricanes have very strong pressure gradients with isobars that decrease in value toward the center of the very low pressure. The strong pressure gradients are the main reason behind the powerful winds of the hurricane. In addition, the resulting latent heat of condensation that is released provides the power to drive the storm. High pressure air in the upper atmosphere (above 30,000 feet/9,000m) over the storm's center also removes heat from the rising air, further driving the air cycle and the hurricane's growth. As high pressure air is sucked into the low-pressure center of the storm, wind speeds increase. At the center of the hurricane is the eye of the storm, which is an area of calm, usually warm and humid, but rainless air. Spiral rain bands and these bands of heavy convective showers that spiral inward toward the storm's center surround hurricanes. Cumulus and Cumulonimbus clouds ascend and lightning develop.

Although a great deal of time, money and effort has been spent on studying the development, growth, maturity and tracks of hurricanes, much is still not known about these mysterious but powerful storms. For example, it is still not possible to predict the exact track of a hurricane with pinpoint accuracy, even though it can be tracked with weather radars and studied through reconnaissance aircrafts, computer models and weather satellites. Furthermore, meteorologists can list factors that are favorable for development of a hurricane or list pre-conditions that are necessary for the formation of a hurricane but they can't say with a degree of certainty or pin-point accuracy that in a certain situation or scenario that a hurricane will definitely develop and travel along a particular path. However numerical weather predictions models are becoming more accurate and precise in trying to predict the movement and strength of these storms. Meteorologists from all around the world have come to rely on the accuracy of these weather models to help predict the movement and strength of these storms and to improve the overall hurricane forecast.

CHAPTER SIX
THE 1780 NORTH ATLANTIC HURRICANE SEASON

Thousands of British sailors drowned, and dozens of British warships were destroyed by three successive deadly hurricanes that roared through the Caribbean in 1780.

The season officially began on June 1, 1780, and lasted until November 30, although it effectively persisted into at least late October due to continued storm activity and a very active season. Among the deadliest and most intense of these storms were, the *Great Hurricane of 1780* and the *Savanna la Mar Hurricane*. The 1780 Atlantic hurricane season was extraordinarily destructive. The impact of the season was widespread and ruinous with record damages. It was also the deadliest North Atlantic hurricane season in recorded history with well over 30,000+ deaths and repeatedly shattered numerous records. The Caribbean felt the most catastrophic effects of the season. In October 1780, the Caribbean was devastated by at least three violent hurricanes, the second of which ranks as the deadliest storm ever to affect the Western Hemisphere. These events greatly changed the political and economic history of the region and further weakened the British Navy at a time when it was deeply engaged in the American Revolutionary War. These three different hurricanes, all in October, caused at least 1,000 deaths each. This event was so rare that it was only repeated in the 1893 and 2005 North Atlantic hurricane seasons. The season also held the record as the deadliest North Atlantic hurricane of all time. The major destructive hurricanes of that year were:

1) On June 13, a major hurricane struck the island of Puerto Rico and caused tremendous deaths and losses. An English war frigate, that was forced to leave Saint Lucia, got stranded and was lost on the coast of Guayama, some persons died but 100 men and officers were rescued by the assistance that was given by the residents of that town. This storm was probably a short distance northwest of St. Lucia on the 12th and it originated from the Atlantic. Historian Ramírez de Arellano, in his list of hurricanes of Puerto Rico, says that it occurred on June 13, giving as his source the work of Pedro Tomás de Córdova. Here is what another historian Salivia in his book on this storm, part of which was written by Córdova had to say about this storm:

'On the 13th of that month (June) a furious hurricane was experienced that caused considerable damage in the country...An English war frigate, that was forced to leave Saint Lucia, stranded and was lost on the coast of Guayama, 100 men and officers were

saved by the assistance that was given by the neighbors(inhabitants) of that town.'[1]

2) New Orleans experienced a powerful hurricane on August 24, causing winds gusting to over 160 mph completely destroying 39 of the 43 buildings in Grand Isle, Louisiana. The eye then passed over New Orleans that night, severely damaging structures in what is known as the French Quarter, causing harvest-ruining crop damage, severe flooding, and tornadoes. This was from an entry from Count de Lafreinire's Diary.

3) On August 25, St. Kitts in the Leeward Islands was struck by a storm.

4) A hurricane hit Jamaica on the afternoon of October 3 and completely destroyed the settlement of Savanna-la-Mar (commonly known as Sav-la-Mar, or simply *Sav* by the locals). This storm was called the *'Savanna-la-Mar Hurricane'* named after the settlement it devastated. It remains one of the worst natural disasters to hit this country. It is the main town and the capital of the Westmoreland Parish, Jamaica. It is a coastal town and contains a fort, constructed in the 18th century for defence purposes against pirates. As the storm approached the Jamaican port city of Savanna-la-Mar, curious residents lined up to watch the building seas. With no warning, a storm surge estimated to have been 20 feet high swept across the coast, engulfing the onlookers and hurling large ships inland. The storm totally destroyed the city and the surrounding sugar plantations. Few structures withstood the terrible onslaught, and many people perished in the collapsing buildings, including the city's courthouse. In the port town of Lucea, about 20 miles north of Savanna-la-Mar, 400 persons died and all but two houses were demolished; even the trees and shrubs were swept away. Further north, at Montego Bay, another 360 persons were killed. It continued steady in its direction, and hit central Cuba. As the storm approached, it wrecked the British frigate *Phoenix,* dashing it ashore at Cabo de la Cruz and killing 200 of its' crew. The ships *Victor* and *Barbadoes,* which had sailed from Montego Bay on September 29, were never heard from again; nor was the *Scarborough,* which had left on October 1. The *HMS Ulysses,* also out of Montego Bay, was saved by her crew, who tossed all the guns off her upper deck, thus lowering her center of gravity.

The *Sterling Castle* was also overtaken and crippled by the storm, but she struggled valiantly onward, only to be overtaken and sunk in the central North Atlantic by the second hurricane. The storm then moved over the Bahamas before entering the shipping lanes between Cape Hatteras and Bermuda. The storm caused an estimated 3,000 lives and among them more than 1,500 sailors and destroyed two British fleets with one being the ship the *Monarch*, killing all of its crew as well as several hundred Spanish prisoners onboard. The following account of the Savanna-la-Mar Hurricane, October 5th is taken from the *Jamaican Annual Register,* as given by Reid:

"About 1pm the gale began (at Savanna-la-Mar), from the southeast, and continued increasing with accumulated violence until four in the afternoon, when it veered to the south and became a perfect tempest, which lasted in full force until near eight; it then abated. The sea during the last period exhibited a most awful scene; the waves swelled to an amazing height, rushed with an impetuosity not to be described on the land, and in a few minutes determined the fate of all the houses in the Bay. About ten, the waters began to abate, and at that time a smart shock of earthquake was felt. All the small vessels were driven ashore and dashed to pieces. The ships 'Princess Royal (Captain Ruthven),' 'Henry,' and 'Austin Hall,' were forced from their anchors and carried so far into the morass that they will never be got off. The earthquake lifted the 'Princess Royal' from her beam-ends, righted her, and fixed her on a firm bed. This circumstance has been of great use to the surviving inhabitants, for whose accommodation she now serves as a house.

At Queen Bay only two houses remain; and H.M.S sloop 'Badger,' lying in that harbour has lost all her masts, and run on shore. At Montego Bay, the tempest increased to such an amazing degree as at dark to threaten general ruin and destruction. The prodigious flashes of lightning which regularly succeeded each other, was an alleviation. From midnight the storm began to abate."[2]

The Jamaican planter William Beckford recalled that in the immediate aftermath of this 1780 hurricane, slaves took advantage of the chaotic conditions to loot whatever they could from the ruins of stores and dwellings, especially in urban areas. He stated that, *"poured down in troops to the scene of devastation...and having made free with the rum that was floating in the inundations, began to grow insolent and unruly; and, by their exertion and caution, at once to suppress."*[3]

In terms of expenses, this storm was perhaps one of the most deadly and costliest hurricanes to ever impact Jamaica. Here's an account of what Matthew Mulcahy had to say about this storm in his book, *"Hurricanes and Society in the British Greater Caribbean, 1624-1783":*

"The two hurricanes that struck Jamaica on October 3 and Barbados on October 10, 1780, rank among the worst disasters ever to hit the West Indies. The first, the Savanna-la-Mar Hurricane, was the lesser of the two storms. It struck the western parishes of Jamaica, causing severe damage throughout Westmoreland and Hanover parishes and in parts of St. James's and St. Elizabeth's parishes. Hundreds of colonists and slaves died, and reports estimated property damage in Westmoreland parish alone at £950,000 currency (£678,571 sterling)..."[4]

The morning of October 3, 1780, dawned a crisp and clear typical Jamaican day. In the southwestern part there was a slight wind and a few intermittent showers, but all in all things were calm and looking to remain so. By mid-day, all that changed. Here is how the Governor, Colonel John Dalling described this change of events in his official report to London:

"The sky all of a sudden became very much overcast, and an uncommon elevation of the sea immediately followed. Whilst the unhappy settlers at Savanna-la-Mar were observing this extraordinary phenomenon, the sea broke suddenly in upon the town, and on its retreat swept every thing away with it, so as not to leave the smallest vestige of Man, Beast, or House behind."[5]

That was only the beginning of the destruction. The catastrophe Dalling described above was followed by what many called the most devastating hurricane to have hit the island up to that point in its history. By midday, buildings on the southwest coast of the island began to sway back and forth as if they were balancing on a tightrope. Fires broke out and spread. By 4 pm the full force of the hurricane had arrived and the town of Savanna-la-Mar was directly in its path. It was reported that, a mighty wave rose out of the boiling sea and swept over the coast for a mile. Along with the debris of the homes and businesses, two ships and a schooner were carried along and left stranded among some mango trees. By nightfall, not one building was left standing in the town or for 30-40 miles on either side. In addition, all of the buildings in the parishes of Westmoreland, Hanover, and some in parts of St. James and St. Elizabeth, were demolished. Property owners were unable to identify their estate boundaries or in some cases not even their houses. Slave provision grounds were demolished. Trees and plants were blown away and flattened, mountains and valleys, denuded, the majority of its population, drowned or crushed to death. Rivers were running through new channels; large lakes were seen in districts which a day before had been covered in cane fields; huge rocks were hurled down from the highest mountains; deep ravines formed across the roads, which were everywhere impassable. In the days that followed, husbands looked for wives, mothers for sons, sisters for brothers, to no avail. It is impossible to tell just how many lives were lost. The dead lay unburied and disease began to spread. The destruction of the food crops resulted in a famine, and because the American War of Independence was being waged, none could be imported from the nearby colonies. Thousands of slaves starved to death. In Kingston citizens raised £10,000 to help their countrymen in the west. The British Government sent an additional £40,000. The damage, however, was estimated at £700,000.

A graphic and very moving account of this storm was written by the Anglican clergyman George Wilson Bridges:

"The sea seemed mingled with the clouds, while the heaving swell of the earth, as it rolled beneath its bed, bore the raging floods over their natural boundaries, overwhelmed the coast, and retreating with irresistible force, bore all before them. To the distance of half a mile, the waves carried and fixed vessels of no ordinary size, leaving them the providential means of sheltering the houseless inhabitants. Not a tree, or bush, or cane was to be seen: Universal desolation prevailed, and the wretched victims of violated nature, who would obtain no such shelter, and who had not time to fly to the protecting rocks, were either crushed beneath the falling ruins, or swept away, and never heard from anymore. The sheltered remains of houses,

whose tenants were dead or dying-the maddening search for wives and children, who were lost-the terrific howling of the frightened negroes, as it mingled with the whistling but subsiding winds-and the deluged state of the earth, strewed with the wreck of nature, and ploughed into deep ravines, was the scene which daylight ushered in; and, as if to mock the misery it had caused, the morning sun was again bright and cheerful."6

There was a bit of very interesting and fascinating folklore attached to this storm. The tale involved a slave locally referred to as *Plato the Wizard*. Jamaican Folklore attached the devastation of this western town as the work of the runaway slave known as *Plato the Wizard*, from beyond the grave. Just before his 1780 execution in Jamaica, the renowned obeah man pronounced a curse on Jamaica - predicting that his death would be avenged by a terrible storm set to befall the island before the end of that same year. It is said that Plato and his band of other runaways kept the parish of Westmoreland in a state of perpetual alarm from his stronghold in the Moreland Mountains. Plato warned that whoever dared to lay a finger on him would suffer spiritual torments. It is not surprising that no slave would set traps for Plato even though the reward for his capture was great. Plato was an example of the type of spirit slavery could not hold. However, he did have one weakness and that was consuming rum. It was proved to be his downfall. At the time, Plato's usual supplies were curtailed as a result of a massive hunt conducted for his arrest. He arranged with a watchman he knew well, to go out and get him some rum. The watchman decided to use the rum as bait. It was easier than he expected. Soon after he handed Plato the rum, he fell into a drunken stupor and right into the watchman's trap. Plato was captured, tried and immediately sentenced to death. As a dreadful power was said to have descended upon him, Plato coolly cursed any and everything in sight. He terrified the jailor who tied him to the stake by announcing that he had cast an obeah spell on him and he did not have long to live. Soon after Plato's death, the jailor fell ill and died. Before the year was over, Plato's other curse came true - the island was hit by what was described as the most terrible hurricane to ever spread death and destruction in the seas of the West Indies. The region where Plato the Wizard had roamed free and died in betrayal was hardest hit.[7]

The best narrative of this great hurricane, was written by the young Lieutenant Archer of the *H.M.S. Phoenix*, which commanded by Sir Hyde Parker, known as *'Old Vinegar,'* who had also experienced typhoons in the Indian Ocean before this voyage in the West Indies. In a letter to his mother in England that was dated November 6, 1780, Archer wrote:

"The 4th of last month(October), at half-past five in the morning, H.M.S. Phoenix was wrecked on the island of Cuba, about three leagues to the eastward of Cape Cruz, in a most dreadful hurricane; H.M. sloops the Barbadoes, and Victor, and H.M.S. the Scarborough, were in the hurricane. The two former, it is apprehended, are foundered; but the latter, I am in hopes, is safe." (In his letter of December 30, 1780 he reported that the *Scarborough* was also lost in this storm)...*"At eleven at night it began to snuffle, with a monstrous heavy appearance from the eastward. Close-reefed the topsails. Sir Hyde sent for me. "What sort of weather have we, Archer?" "It blows a little, and has a very ugly look." "Don't hoist the topsails till it clears a little, there is no trusting any country." At eight in the morning I came up again, found it blowing hard from the east-northeast with close-reefed topsails upon the ship, and heavy squalls at times. Sir Hyde came upon deck. "Well, Archer, what do you think of it?" "O, Sir, it is only a hurricane in the East Indies, and the beginning of it had much the same appearance as this; so take in the topsails; we have plenty of sea-room."*[8]

These were the only men found alive of the four lost ships that had been located in Montego Bay. Sir Hyde Parker was tried and acquitted of negligence in the loss of the *Phoenix*.

Historian Southey also reported on this storm:

"October the 4th, His Majesty's ship Phoenix, Captain Sir Hyde Parker, was wrecked in Cuba, three leagues to the eastward of Cape Cruz, in a hurricane: twenty of the crew were washed overboard with the masts."[9]

Fernández Duro in his best-known work (1901, VII), made these comments with regards to this hurricane:

"A cartel ship that was carrying to Santiago de Cuba the garrison of the ship San Juan of Nicaragua,(was lost) with a hurricane, the 13th of October. Ninety-five persons perished."[10]

In addition, Lieutenant Archer, of H.M.S. *Phoenix* wrote in his log book with regards to the hurricane's impact at Montego Bay *"Many of the houses, where we had been so merry, were so completely destroyed, that scarcely a vestige remained to mark where they stood."* The *Phoenix* under Sir Hyde Parker, was driven ashore near Cape Cruz in Cuba just as she was about to founder. In addition, the *'Scarborough,' 'Barbadoes,'* and *'Victor'* which were anchored at Montego Bay were lost in the storm. Archer crossed back to Jamaica in a rickety open boat and procured assistance for the survivors. With regards to the destruction of Savanna-la-Mar, it is stated by other authorities that a fearful pestilence broke out shortly after which was due to the putrefaction of the unburied corpses. Another historian, Gardner in his account of the storm's history said that *"people would suddenly fall down when smitten with the pestilence and died within two hours."*[11]

5) The Great Hurricane of 1780 existed in early to mid-October, causing a record of well over 22,000 deaths in the eastern Caribbean Sea.

6) A powerful hurricane located in the Eastern Gulf of Mexico, which existed from October 17 to 21, killed 2,000 people. This hurricane became known as Solano's Hurricane. It was the third in a trio of intense hurricanes that occurred in October of 1780 and was first spotted near Jamaica on the 15th. Progressing northwestward into the Gulf of Mexico, it dissipated over the southeastern United States around the 22nd. In May of 1780, this great Spanish fleet arrived off Dominica on its way to Havana. The fleet's armed vessels and transport ships were loaded with thousands of men onboard who were dying by the hundreds because of the filth below the decks, bad food and ship fever. It was commanded by Admiral Solano who had dodged the British and came in at last grandly under the sun-coloured rocks of El Morro as the ancient city of Havana burst into festival.

This hurricane was most notable for having defeated a Spanish plan to take the Florida panhandle from the British. Under the command of Field Marshall Don Bernardo de Gálvez and Admiral

Don José Solano, an armada of some 64 warships, transport ships, and supply vessels carrying some four thousand soldiers, with some brought in from as far as Puerto Rico set out from Havana on the sixteenth with the objective of taking control of Pensacola, Florida from the British. Admiral Solano proceeded very well with extreme care and caution. The first thing he did before sailing was to consult the ships captains. These were practical sailors, who steered ships into or out of harbours. As a general rule these captains were seasoned middle-aged men, some even older. They possessed a considerable knowledge of the weather, its changes or deterioration especially when it came to hurricanes. They were aware of Admiral Solano's mission, and of its importance and magnitude. Surely, if they had noticed anything abnormal in the weather, they would have indicated it to the Admiral, advising him not to sail on the next day, and to wait. But they didn't so most persons speculated that at the time of their journey the weather was fine. Solano wanted to have, if possible, moderate southeasterly winds so as to make a rapid voyage going towards the Florida Peninsula. That was not the case. He wrote in his log:

"The next morning, the 16th of October, the wind being light, and more easterly, the signal was made to weigh, and fifty eight ships, out of seventy four, got out of the harbour before night, and they were all out by 9pm."[12]

It is evident that the weather at Havana was fair during the daytime of the 16th, or else the fifty eight ships would not have sailed. The enterprise was too important to have taken any chances on account of the weather. Here is what he reported in his log book:

"On October 16th, 1780, at daybreak, after a moderate land breeze from the E and ESE, the scud moving in the same direction, it fell calm...October 17th, by noon the wind freshened at NE, scud and heavy clouds closing in upon us. By 10 at night, the wind increased, and was then at NE ¼ E, with torrents of rain and some hard squalls, shifting as far as ENE...From the 18th to the 20th, continued lying-to in the fourth quadrant; the weather still dark and increasing; the wind at NE."[13]

The French were worried by the news of early hurricanes so they refused the Spanish's invitation to join them. However they sailed north in a demonstration against the British in North America and ordered the main French fleet back to France, leaving nine ships to patrol the Caribbean islands. As for Pensacola, the English under General Campbell was always fearful of a Spanish attack. They did not know until much later how lucky they were and how the hurricane had saved them. The slow-moving hurricane, known to history as 'Solano's Hurricane,' began to affect the fleet on the 17th and proceeded to wreak havoc over the succeeding five days, scattering and badly damaging the ships. Although nearly two thousand persons died, both Gálvez and Solano survived, returning finally to Havana, but Gálvez would later return to capture Pensacola the following May. "Have we so little constancy and tenacity that a single tropical storm suffices to halt us?" Gálvez wrote in a heated argument with the War Council in Havana, about another expedition against Pensacola. He fought off a British attack on Mobile. The cautious War Council had to admit that the British were too weak to attack Havana.

As a result of this hurricane, Cuba remained under the control of the Spanish even to this day rather than the British who were strategically planning to grasp control and claiming this large island nation for the King of England. The next May, after great gallantry, Gálvez moved in on Pensacola again. The first fleet commander, Calbo, refused to cooperate and it was not until Solano came up with a fleet which he put at Gálvez' orders that Pensacola finally fell and the British lost all of West Florida. This history changing hurricane was always called 'Solano's Storm' because an English Ambassador at Madrid copied and translated Solano's Log book from the Spanish records. If the full story be told, it would show that Solano was only a late comer and all of the credit should go to Gálvez. It should be rightfully called "The last Hurricane of Bernardo de Gálvez," or better yet 'Gálvez's Hurricane,' who endured much at the hands of this storm. It was during this storm that Dunbar noted how tornadoes form around tropical storms and seldom last more than 5 to 10 minutes. This was no comfort to the inhabitants of the area, who were distraught after these two storms and an excessively cold winter followed by a very rainy summer. These residents wrote the Spanish sovereign not to abandon the country regardless of the adverse blows of nature.

7) In late October, another tropical cyclone struck Barbados and then St. Lucia.

8) Around November 17, a tropical cyclone moved up the east coast of the United States disrupting the British blockade of the New England states.

The hurricane season of 1780 is one of the worst in recorded history. At least five powerful and destructive storms struck American and Caribbean shores that year. In October, three storms in three successive weeks caused unparalleled economic and military destruction. The first was named the Savanna-la-Mar Hurricane and struck a tiny settlement on the island of Jamaica on October 3. The settlement was completely destroyed by the massive storm tides and powerful winds. The storm would cross Cuba and the Bahamas before encountering the British fleet east of Daytona Beach. Another fleet of British ships would be seriously damaged off the Virginia Coast. Over 3,000 deaths were attributed to the storm.

The storm that destroyed the Windward Islands on October 10-12, 1780 is the deadliest ever in recorded Atlantic history. It became known simply as the Great Hurricane of 1780. The evening of October 10th was heralded by a fiery red sunset on the island of Barbados. A light rain began falling shortly afterwards, and by 10pm hurricane force winds were felt. All night long, winds reached the rarified Category 5 intensity as the eye passed just north of the island. The entire island was leveled and it is estimated that over four thousand people perished on this island. The hurricane then set its sights on St. Vincent, where some persons estimated that the winds gusted to well over 170 mph. Over two hundred French and British sailors were drowned as their warships foundered off the island's eastern shore. After devastating St. Lucia, this great hurricane turned its fury on Martinique, where over nine thousand people lost their lives. A supply convoy of forty ships bringing provisions to the island was dashed to bits, resulting in five thousand dead. The Great Hurricane of 1780 then moved northwestward, passing between Puerto Rico and Hispaniola. By the 16th, it was beginning to recurve, skirting the eastern Bahamas and then it passed just south of Bermuda on October 18. Spanish Admiral Solano was en-route from Havana to Pensacola in October 1780 to capture the important port city.

The third major hurricane of the month swept north through the Gulf of Mexico catching and scattering the fleet of 64 warships on October 21. Over two thousand people died along the eastern Gulf of Mexico in this storm. The 1780s were the deadliest decade in recorded North Atlantic Hurricane history. Well over 35,000 people died from hurricanes during this decade. The October storms scuttled much of the British and Spanish navies and aided the colonies in the American Revolution. The British Navy suffered more losses from these hurricanes than it did from the battles fought in the Revolutionary War itself.

CHAPTER SEVEN
NEMO REMEMBERS THE GREAT
HURRICANE OF 1780

On Friday, October 7, 2005 National Emergency Management Organization (NEMO) had a special day to celebrate the 225th Anniversary of this great storm and former Caribbean Institute of Meteorology and Hydrology (CIMH) Principal Dr. Colin Depradine made a special presentation about this storm which I found extremely informative so I will share it with you. The article was originally published in *The Barbados Advisory*, 35th Anniversary Edition of the CIMH in 2002.[1]

This destructive season should be seen against a backdrop of the US War of Independence, which involved hostilities in the Caribbean by the fleets of Spain, France and the Dutch Republic fighting a vicious battle against British fleets with the concomitant greater risk of loss of life due to increased exposure of warships and transports to hazardous weather conditions. This critical coincidence is at least partially responsible for the unprecedented losses of life inflicted, especially in the three fierce hurricanes that struck in quick succession during October. It was the deadliest North Atlantic hurricane of all time, and actually changed the course of history of the United States and the Caribbean. In October 1780, British warships were sailing to fight the French for control of the area around the Antilles Islands and to fight the rebellious American colonists for control of the American coast. As British warships moved through Barbados they were caught in a gigantic hurricane, a hurricane so powerful that they had never seen any like this before. The hurricane did more than just blow through the region; it crushed it.

THE 30 DEADLIEST HURRICANES OF THE NORTH ATLANTIC

The 30 Deadliest Tropical Cyclones for the North Atlantic		
RankName / Areas of Largest Loss	*Dates*	*Deaths*
1. "Great Hurricane of 1780": Martinique, Barbados, St. Eustatius	10-16 Oct 1780	22000+
2. "Great Galveston Hurricane of 1900": Galveston Island	8 Sep 1900	8000-12000
3. Mitch: Honduras, Nicaragua, Guatemala, El Salvador, Belize	10/22 - 11/5 1998	9086
4. Fifi: Honduras	14-19 Sep 1974	8000-10000
5. "The Dominican Republic Hurricane of 1930": Dominican Republic	1-6 Sep 1930	8000
6. Flora: Haiti, Cuba	9/30-10/8 1963	8000
7. "Pointe-a-Pitre Bay Hurricane": Guatemala	6 Sep 1776	6000
8. "Newfoundland Banks": Newfoundland	9-12 Sep 1775	4000
9. "Hurricane of San Ciriaco": Puerto Rico, Carolinas	8-19 Aug 1899	3433
10. "Great Okeechobee-San Felipe II Hurricane": Florida, Puerto Rico, Martinique, Guadeloupe, Turks & Caicos	12-17 Sep 1928	3411
11. "The Cuba Hurricane": Cuba, Cayman Islands, Jamaica	4-10 Nov 1932	3107
12. Jeanne: Haiti, Dominican Republic, Bahamas, Florida	13-29 Sep 2004	3000
13. "Central Atlantic Hurricane": Central Atlantic	16-17 Sep 1782	3000
14. Martinique	Aug 1813	3000
15. El Salvador, Honduras	4-8 Jun 1934	3000
16. Western Cuba	21-22 Jun 1791	3000
17. Barbados	10-11 Aug 1831	2500
18. Belize	6-10 Sep 1931	2500
19. Haiti, Honduras, Offshore Jamaica	19-25 Oct 1935	2150
20. David: Dominican Republic, Dominica, US	8/29-9/5 1979	2068
21. Offshore Florida (?)	1781	2000

22.	Sea Islands Hurricane: South Carolina, Georgia	27-28 Aug 1893	2000-2500
23.	Eastern Gulf of Mexico	17-21 Oct 1780	2000
24.	Cuba	7-8 Oct 1870	2000
25.	Chenier Caminanda Hurricane: Louisiana	1-2 Oct 1893	2000
26.	Guadeloupe, Martinique	14-15 Aug 1666	2000
27.	Martinique	Aug 1767	1600
28.	Mexico	28 Aug 1909	1500
29.	W Cuba, Straits of FL	Oct 1644	1500
30.	Katrina: Louisiana, Mississippi	Aug 23-31 2005	1836

References:
2004: Rappaport, Edward N. and Fernandez-Partagas, Jose; "The Deadliest Atlantic Tropical Cyclones, 1492-Present," NOAA Technical Memorandum NWS NHC-47, National Hurricane Center, 41 pp. 2) The Deadliest, Costliest, and Most Intense United States Hurricanes of This Century (and Other Frequently Requested Hurricane Facts) by Paul Hebert, Jerry Jarrell, and Max Mayfield - published by the U.S. Department of Commerce as NOAA Technical Memorandum NWS TPC-1.

On October 10, Barbados had a bright orange sunset followed by light rain. At 10:00pm the winds had reached hurricane strength. For the next several days the hurricane stopped over the islands. *"The strongest buildings and the whole houses, most of which were stone and remarkable for their solidity, gave way to the fury of the wind, and were torn up to their foundations; all the forts were destroyed, and many of the heavy cannons carried upwards of a hundred feet from the forts...more than 6,000 perished and all of the inhabitants are entirely ruined."* wrote Sir George Rodney to Lady Rodney on December 10, 1780. Among those that perished were British sailors and their warships. Eight of the twelve warships sank and their sailors drowned-a loss that ultimately benefited the American colonists in their fight for independence.

"The greatest of all Hurricanes occurred from October 10 - 16, 1780, as the storm hit virtually every island from Tobago in the south

east through the Leeward Islands across to Hispaniola. The death toll was 4,500 in Barbados, 9,000 in Martinique and 4,500 in St. Eustatius. [Source: Disaster Mitigation Guidelines by PAHO]. We remember the 225th Anniversary of the Great Hurricane, where so many died."

"The Great Hurricane of October 10, 1780, is arguably, the most destructive hurricane to have struck Barbados and the islands of the Eastern Caribbean. It is estimated that 22,000 persons lost their lives in Barbados, St. Vincent, St. Lucia and Martinique."

The following quotation from the book *'The Ocean'* by Reclus (1873) gives an approximate idea of the violence of this storm:

"Starting from Barbados, where neither trees nor dwellings were left standing, it caused the English fleet anchored off St. Lucia to disappear and completely ravaged this island, where 6000 persons were crushed under the ruins. After this, the whirlwind tending toward Martinique, enveloped a convoy of French transports, and sunk more than 40 ships carrying 4000 soldiers; on land, the town of St. Pierre and other places ere completely razed by the rind, and 9000 persons perished there. More to the north, Dominique, St. Eustatius, St. Vincent and Porto Rico were likewise devastated and most of the vessels which were on the path of the cyclone foundered, with all their crews. Beyond Porto Rico, the tempest bent to the north-east, toward the Bermudas and though its violence had gradually diminished, it sunk several English warships returning to Europe."

This illustrated painting shows several ships caught in the Great Hurricane of 1780 near Barbados.

Some indication of the violence of the storm can be gleaned from a letter written by Dr. Gilbert Blane, in Barbados, to Dr. Hunter in which he writes:

"........what will give as strong an idea of the force of the wind as anything; many of them (of the trees) were stripped of their bark."

"Dr. Jose Millas in his book 'Hurricane of the Caribbean and Adjacent Land Areas", wrote that in hurricanes in which the wind has reached 200 miles an hour in the most cases happens as a severe gusts, this phenomenon has not been mentioned before this storm. In the Great Havana Hurricane of October 18, 1944 the maximum wind velocity was measured at 163 miles an hour and the bark of the trees remained intact. He suggests that tiny water bullets would have to reach the trees with a very, very great velocity so as to be able to strip them of their bark. Probably that velocity must be greater than 200 miles an hour."

Major-General Cunninghame, Governor of Barbados, in his account of the Hurricane at Barbados wrote:

"The armory was leveled to the ground, and the arms scattered about. The buildings were all demolished; for so violent was the storm here, when assisted by the sea, that a 12 pounder gun was carried from the south to the north battery, a distance of 140 yards.. The loss to this country is immense: many years will be required to retrieve it."

The following quotation from a paper by Dr. Gilbert Blane in the Transactions of the Royal Society of Edinburgh is instructive:

"There had been nothing that could be called a hurricane felt at Barbados for more than a century before 1780, so that the inhabitants began to think themselves exempt from such calamities and accordingly had no edifices of sufficient strength to withstand the force of a hurricane."

The Editor of *"The West Indian"* - a Bajan newspaper, mentioned the Great Hurricane of 1780 in his piece on the 1831 Hurricane. He wrote:

"At dawn of day (October 10th), the wind rushing with a mighty force from the northwest... Towards evening the storm increased, and at nine o'clock had attained its height, but it continued to rage till four next morning, when there was a temporary lull. Before day-break,

the castle and forts, the church, every public building and almost every house in Bridgetown, were leveled with the earth."

It is evident that the "lull" did not correspond to the centre of the storm.

An artist sketch of a ship caught in the Great Hurricane of 1780.

Coke in his *History of the West Indies* (1808) said:

"To estimate, with accuracy, the damage which the colony received in all its departments would be an impossible task. The calculation which was made soon after the mournful occasion, estimated the loss at little less than one million and a half sterling.

- *At St. Christopher's many vessels were forced on shore.*
- *At St. Lucia, all the barracks and huts for His Majesty's troops and other buildings on the island were blown down, and the ships driven to sea; only two houses were left standing in the town. Men and animals were raised from the ground and hurled to a distance of several yards. The sea rose to such a height that it demolished the fort, and hurled a vessel against the naval hospital, which was crushed by its weight. The coral bed at the bottom of the sea was torn up, and pieces of it raised so high on their edges that they were afterwards visible above the water;*

and the harbour itself was deepened six feet, and in some places even more.

- *At Dominica, they suffered greatly. Almost all of the houses standing near the shore were carried away, and the royal bake house, the magazine, and a part of the barracks, were destroyed.*
- *At. St. Vincent, every building was blown down and the town destroyed and the French frigate was wrecked.*
- *At Grenada, nineteen sail of loaded Dutch ships were stranded and beaten to pieces.*
- *At Martinique, all the ships that were bringing troops and provisions were blown off the island. In the town of St. Pierre, every house was blown down and more than 1000 people perished. The number of people who perished in Martinique was said to be 9000. The Laurel and Andromeda were two of the many vessels which were wrecked in the harbour.*
- *At. St. Eustatia, the loss was very great. Between 4000 and 5000 persons are said to have lost their lives. Seven vessels were dashed to pieces on the rocks at North Point, and of the 19 vessels which broke lose of their moorings and drifted out to sea, only one was ever recovered."*

Meteorologist and historian José Millás estimates that the hurricane developed in the Atlantic possibly in the vicinity of 12°N and 38°W. It moved westward very slowly at little more than 6 nautical miles per hour. When its centre was about 120 nautical miles east of Barbados, it began to curve and move between west by north and west-northwest. After crossing a very short distance north of Barbados, it took a more northwesterly track passing east of St. Lucia, southwest of St. Kitts, south of Puerto Rico changing course for Mona Island, recurving and passing east of the Turks Islands. Recurving once again, it passed southeast of Bermuda, moving in a northeasterly direction.

An artist sketch of a three masted vessel floundering during the Great Hurricane of 1780.

CHAPTER EIGHT
IMPACT OF THE GREAT HURRICANE OF 1780

The Great Hurricane of 1780, also known as *Hurricane San Calixto II,* was one of the most powerful and deadliest North Atlantic hurricanes on record. It is often regarded as a cataclysmic hurricane. Its worst effects were experienced on October 10, 1780. This storm perhaps was generated in the mid-Atlantic, not far from the Equator and it was first felt in Barbados where just about every tree and house on this island was blown down. The official death toll was approximately 22,000 persons but some historians have put the death toll as high as 27,500 persons.

The storm passed through the Lesser Antilles and a small portion of the Greater Antilles in the Caribbean between October 10 and October 16 of 1780. The death toll is often assumed to be higher than the official 22,000 persons count because they included only the actual direct deaths. However, some historians suggested that the indirect deaths which occurred due to starvation, severe injuries, diseases and water contamination immediately after the storm should have also been included. Specifics on the hurricane's track and strength are unclear since the official North Atlantic hurricane database only goes back as far as 1851. This had a fatal impact on the economies in the Caribbean and parts of North American region. It decimated the British fleet and was responsible for the English presence in the

North Atlantic to be significantly reduced. From a meteorological perspective, the storm was unusual based on its track. The storm hit several of the most populous islands in the Lesser and Greater Antilles in the Caribbean. Not for more than two hundred years would the death toll of a North Atlantic hurricane exceed more than 10,000 persons and that was with Hurricane Mitch in 1998.

For a while, major hurricanes in the West Indies were often named after the particular Saint's day on which the hurricane occurred. As Christianity took hold in the West Indies, the naming system of storms here in the Caribbean was based on the Catholic tradition of naming these storms with the 'Saint' of the day (e.g. San Ciprian on September 26). This system for naming them was haphazard and not really a system at all. One example of a great storm named after a Saint of the day was, *'Hurricane San Felipe'* which struck Puerto Rico on September 13, 1876. The Great Hurricane of 1780 was known as the Hurricane of *San Calixto II* based on *Pope Callixtus I or Callistus I.* He was Pope from 217 to about 222 AD, during the reigns of the Roman Emperors Heligabalus and Alexander Severus. He was martyred for his Christian faith and is a Canonized Saint of the Roman Catholic Church. Callixtus was honoured as a Martyr in Todi, Italy, on August 14. This date and name of San Calixto II was significant because this was one of the dates that the Great Hurricane of 1780 struck the Caribbean. It was named San Calixto II, because another earlier historical hurricane struck on the same day in the Caribbean and was simply called the Hurricane of San Calixto. The Roman Catholic Church celebrates his optional memorial on 14 October, one of the days when the Great Hurricane of 1780 struck Puerto Rico at 7am causing great damage at Cabo Rojo and Lajes.

This powerful and deadly hurricane moved over Barbados with winds possibly exceeding 200 mph, before moving past Martinique, Saint Eustatius and Saint Lucia. Thousands of deaths were reported on each island. Coming in the midst of the American Revolution, the storm caused heavy losses to British and French fleets contesting for control of the area. The American Revolution was a major war which lasted from 1775 to 1783. It was fought between 13 British Colonies in North America and their parent country of Great Britain, and was made up of two related events: The War of Independence which lasted from 1775 to 1783 and the formation of the American Government as laid out by the United States Constitution in 1787. The colonies gained their Independence as the United States of America, under the Treaty of Paris of 1783. The hurricane later passed near Puerto Rico and over the eastern portion of the Dominican Republic. There, it caused significant damage near the coastal areas of this island. It ultimately turned to the northeast before being last observed on October 20 southeast of Cape Race, Newfoundland.

The death toll from the Great Hurricane of 1780 alone exceeds that of any other entire decade of North Atlantic hurricanes. It is substantially higher than that of the second-deadliest North Atlantic storm, Hurricane Mitch which had deaths between approximately 10,000 to 12,000 persons over Central America in 1998. The Great Hurricane of 1780 was part of the disastrous and very active 1780 North Atlantic Hurricane season, with two other deadly storms occurring in the month of October.[1] During this great storm the loss was enormous, 13 battle-ships were lost, and 16 more were dismasted. England and America suffered an annual loss from wrecks of more than 1,000 vessels, and nearly one half of this was on the American coast.

The exact origin of the hurricane is unknown, though a few modern historians considered it to be a classic Cape Verde Type Hurricane and was estimated to have developed somewhere between the Cape Verde Islands and the Eastern Caribbean in early October of 1780. The system strengthened and grew in size as it tracked slowly westward and first began affecting the island of Barbados late on October 9. Later on October 10, the worst of the hurricane passed over the island. Early on October 11, the hurricane turned north-northwest about 56 miles east of St. Lucia, and later that night it neared and devastated the island of Martinique. The cyclone gradually weakened as it passed to the southwest of Dominica early on October 12 and subsequently struck the island of Guadeloupe. After devastating Guadeloupe, the hurricane turned west-northwest, passing about 90 miles southwest of the island of St. Kitts.

The hurricane steadily neared Puerto Rico as it paralleled the southern coastline, and made its closest point of approach on October 14 to the southwest portion of the island. Here the cathedral, seven churches, and 1,400 houses were blown down and 1,600 sick and wounded persons were buried beneath the ruins of the hospital. Great damage was also done to the shipping industry in Puerto Rico. The *Deal Castle* was wrecked near the island of Mona, and the merchant fleet convoyed by the *Ulysses* and *Pomona* had also sustained considerable damage. It subsequently turned to the northwest, hitting the island of Mona in the Mona Passage before making landfall near the current-day Dominican Republic, Province of Samaná. After this, it moved on to Silver Keys, where the *Stirling Castle* foundered. At what spot the *Thunderer*, which was on her journey from St. Lucia to Jamaica, bearing the broad pennant of Commodore Walsingham, was lost, can never be ascertained. Late on October 15, it reached the Atlantic Ocean and after passing about 160 miles east of Grand Turk Island (in the Turks and Caicos Islands) it is estimated to have recurved to the northeast. The hurricane passed 150 miles southeast of Bermuda on October 18, where fifty British ships were driven ashore and two line-of-battle ships were destroyed, and was last observed two days later about 295 miles southeast of Cape Race, Newfoundland.

This representation of the distressed situation of His Majesty's Ship 'Egmont' when it was dismasted in the Great Hurricane of October, 1780 near the island of St. Lucia by Lt. William Elliott.

On October 19, strong winds and high tides were reported in northeastern shores of Florida. One modern historian suggested the hurricane passed much closer to the state than previously thought. Another possibility considered was an extension to a hurricane in the western Caribbean Sea. Due to lack of data, the exact track of the Great Hurricane of 1780 is still unknown to this day even with the guidance of modern technology. A study by Miller *et al.* (2006) suggests that the Great Hurricane of 1780 may have affected much more of Northern Florida than anticipated.

On October 10, 1780, a powerful hurricane slammed the islands of the West Indies at peak intensity and killing well over 22,000 persons. Known simply as the *Great Hurricane of 1780*, it was the deadliest hurricane on record in the North Atlantic Region. As stated earlier, at the time of this Great Hurricane, the American Revolution was winding down and British and French naval forces were battling for control of the West Indies. It was already a dangerous area of the world for ships. It was estimated that one out of every twenty ships sent to the West Indies met their demise at the bottom of the Caribbean Sea due to hurricanes.

The command of the British fleet in the West Indies was divided. There were then some twenty-seven British warships based among the British islands in the Caribbean. Sir Peter Parker commanded the fleet at Jamaica, and was at Port Royal but Sir George Rodney was off New York in the *Sandwich*, having gone to the coast of America with a portion of his fleet just before the storms occurred. Of Sir Peter Parker's squadron, *the Thunderer, Stirling Castle, Scarborough, Barbados, Phoenix, Deal Castle, Victor* and *the Endeavour*, were all lost; and nearly all of the crew members perished. *The Berwick, Hector, Trident, Ruby, Bristol, Ulysses,* and *Pomona*, were dismasted. British Admiral Rodney was in New York during the hurricane, and when he visited Barbados he incorrectly concluded that the storm must have been accompanied by a massive earthquake to achieve such total destruction.

He had a fleet of 12 warships patrolling the islands when the hurricane approached. He had left the command of this fleet of ships in the Leeward Islands to Admiral Hotham, who was on the flagship the *Vengeance*. The ships were no match for the storm and eight sank in the Harbour of St. Lucia, killing hundreds of sailors. Of Sir George Rodney's squadron, *the Blanche, Andromeda, Laurel, Camelion,* and *Beaver's Prize,* were lost; and *the Vengeance, Montagu, Ajax, Alemene, Egremont, Endymion, Albermarle, Venus,* and *Amazon* were dismasted or severely damaged. The *Albermarle* was located in Carlisle Bay, Barbados. The *Endymion,* with the *Andromeda* and *Laurel,* were cruising on the east side of Martinique and the *Venus, Convert,* and *Surprize* were sailing in the northern Antilles Islands. The *HMS Ulysses* and *Pomona* with a fleet of other ships encountered the hurricane while they were in the Mona Passage and many of those ships were also lost or badly damaged. The *Diamond* and the *Pelican* had been sent to Honduras to convoy British merchant ships. However, on their return to the Caribbean, they encountered the storm in the vicinity of Jamaica and these ships were badly damaged.[2]

Describing the impact of the storm on Barbados, Sir George Rodney later wrote to his wife Lady Rodney dated at St. Lucia, December 10, 1780: *"I sailed from New York on the 16th November, and arrived at Barbados on the 5th of this month. You may easily conceive my surprise, concern, and astonishment, when I saw the dreadful situation of this island and the destructive effects of the hurricane...The whole face of the country appears an entire ruin, and the most beautiful island in the world has the appearance of a country laid waste by fire, and sword, and appears to the imagination more dreadful than it is possible for me to find words to express...."[3]

Only two houses in all of St. Lucia remained standing. There were even some reports that bark was stripped from the trees by the force of the winds in some locations. Some expert meteorologists seem to agree that this would only happen if the winds are in excess of 200 miles per hour. The French fared no better, losing an estimated 40 ships and among them were the frigates *Cres* and *La Constante* and 4,000 soldiers. Martinique had the highest casualty rate of over 9,000 persons causing the Governor of Martinique to declare in French, *'Les bailments du convoy disparurent'* translated in English to mean-*The vessels of the convoy disappeared.*[4] Although there have been many deadly storms in the years since 1780, only Hurricane Mitch in 1998 can barely approach the Great Hurricane of 1780 in terms of lives lost.

The Great Hurricane of 1780 persisted near the country of Barbados for about two days, producing violent winds which were described as "so deafening that people could not hear their own voices." That was a stark contrast to the day before when the winds were almost calm, with a fiery red sunset. The rain began the night of October 9. On October 10, the wind was blowing from the northwest at daybreak, steadily increasing by 10am. At 4pm the ships at the bay broke their moorings. At 6pm, the island was feeling the full impact of the storm, and the winds were blowing from the northwest at 10pm and had reached its peak by midnight. It then went around to the west by 1am, diminishing back to normal at 8am on the October 11. It was reported the strength of the winds were so strong that the winds stripped the bark off trees before the hurricane blew down every tree on the island. This phenomenon has not been observed in any of the strongest modern-day tropical cyclones, so, according to the late great meteorologist Dr. Jose Millas, in his book *Hurricanes of the Caribbean 1492-1800,* he said for that to have occurred it would have meant that the winds were blowing at least 200 mph.

The strong winds of this storm also destroyed every house on Barbados. Most ships located in the bay broke free of their moorings from the hurricane's rough seas and all of the forts on the island were destroyed. The winds and seas moved heavy cannons about 100 feet from where they were located. About 4,326 persons died on this island and some of the dead would be burned while others would be buried in the churchyards. They were also interred in all sorts of places found convenient for that purpose. In fact, only about 30 of its 2,000 houses and other buildings remained standing. The St. Michael's Parish Church, which was erected in 1665 and rebuilt in 1752 laid in a heap of rubbles. Nine other of the 13 churches, chapels and all five Quaker meeting houses were also left in rubbles. Some of the other churches were re-established including, St. Michael's which rose again in 1786. This hurricane also brought other benefits as well. Many Barbadian colonists noted that the Great Hurricane of 1780 destroyed the sugar ants that had plagued planters and also ate the sugar canes during the previous decade. The planter William Senhouse wrote that the storm also eliminated the *"Black Blast Ants, which had been so prejudicial to the canes,"[5]* although he further commented that the hurricane also drove the hummingbirds from the island.

When this hurricane moved away from Barbados, there was nothing left but mud, debris, dead cattle and rotting corpses. On this island, the production of sugar and rum so vital to the local economy was drastically curtailed, not recovering for at least four years later. As you will see later, the Barbados Mercury reported that in most of the plantations, all the buildings and the sugar mills were destroyed and there was not a single estate on the island which entirely escaped the violence of the hurricane. Many settlers and owners of these plantations abandoned their plantations and returned to England, leaving the island's economy even further depressed. Fortunately, Lord Rodney raised the unprecedented sum of £80,000 for relief work and food from the Caribbean, North America and Europe.

A Twenty-two gun brig sloop as it near St. Lucia in 1780.

On the island of St. Vincent, located to the west of Barbados, a storm surge estimated to have been at least 20 feet high washed entire villages into the sea. On the other hand, Lord Rodney hurried to seize St. Vincent, hearing that it had been wrecked. But the French drove him away. On this island, the hurricane destroyed 584 of the 600 houses in Kingstown. On the island of Grenada, 19 Dutch ships were totally wrecked. On St. Lucia, rough waves and a strong storm surge destroyed the fleet of British Admiral George Rodney at Port Castries, with one ship destroying the city's hospital by being lifted on top of it. Of the British ships, the *Vengeance* was wrecked on the shore, the *Deal Castle* was blown to Puerto Rico and smashed to pieces, the *Thunderer* which had just arrived from England, set sail in the storm and was never heard from again. The hurricane destroyed all but two houses at Port Castries, and throughout the island about 6,000 persons died. The vortex estimated to have passed 50 to 60 miles east of St. Lucia at 7am on October 11, moving northwest towards Martinique.

The British Admiral George Brydges Rodney, 1st Baron Rodney (1718-1792), by winning notable victories in Caribbean waters over French, Spanish, and Dutch forces, contributed substantially to the supreme British command of these Caribbean seas in the late 18th century. Because of many of his notable victories against these various nations, many of these islands of the Caribbean remained under British command until the early to mid 1900's when most of them gained Independence from Great Britain. He was born in February 1718; George Rodney attended Harrow before volunteering for British Naval Service at the early age of fourteen. Stationed in the Mediterranean, he became first a lieutenant and then a post as Captain. In October 1747, in command of the 60-gun *Eagle,* he took part in Admiral Edward Hawke's victory over the French off Ushant, an island of northwest France in the Atlantic Ocean off western Brittany, and was cited for gallantry. Two years later he was named governor and commander in chief of Newfoundland with the rank of Commodore. In 1751 he was elected to Parliament.

During the Seven Years War, Rodney commanded the 74-gun *Dublin* and participated in the expedition against Rochefort in 1757. He also served under Adm. Edward Boscawen in 1758 at the siege and capture of Louisbourg, Nova Scotia. In 1759 and 1760 he destroyed many French transport ships which were intercepted along the Normandy coast for an invasion of Britain and was appointed commander in chief of the Leeward Islands station in 1761. In 1762, he reduced the French Martinique fleet and forced them to surrender the islands of St. Lucia and Grenada. Rodney was promoted to vice admiral of the blue and created a baronet. Governor of Greenwich Hospital from 1765 to 1770, he was appointed rear admiral in 1771. From then until 1774 he commanded the Jamaican station. Having fallen into debt, he lived in Paris for 3 years in order to escape his creditors. Recalled to England in 1778, Rodney was later promoted to the post of Admiral. Late in 1779, he was named Commander in Chief of the Leeward Islands. Rodney was ordered to sail with 22 ships of the line and a large convoy of transports to the West Indies and on the way to relieve Gibraltar, which had been under Spanish siege since July 1779. In January 1780 he captured a Spanish convoy off Cape Finisterre and defeated Adm. Don Juan de Langara's 11 ships in the so-called Moonlight Battle, fought off Cape St. Vincent at night. These feats relieved Gibraltar and brought Rodney international fame.

The Revolutionary War was not going well for General George Washington in 1780. By August of that year, the British had captured South Carolina. In September, traitor Benedict Arnold gave the British the plans for the fort at West Point, New York. But the winds of fortune shifted in October, when the most powerful Atlantic hurricane in recorded history struck British warships in the Caribbean. This hurricane left the British fleet in tatters and soon afterward, the tide of the American Revolution began to turn in favor of the colonists. In September 1780, leaving half of his fleet in West Indian waters, Rodney sailed to New York and foiled George Washington's designs for a Franco-American land and sea assault on the city. It was during this time that his fleet of ships was destroyed in the Great Hurricane of 1780 in the Lesser Antilles. Returning to the Caribbean in February 1781, Rodney captured the Dutch islands of St. Eustatius and St. Martin and confiscated huge stocks belonging to British merchants trading illegally with American Revolutionists, thereby crippling a contraband trade on which the Americans greatly depended. For the rest of his life he was involved in lawsuits with British merchants over this action. In April 1782, after a running engagement with a fleet of 29 ships under Adm. François de Grasse, Rodney and his 34 ships defeated the French off Dominica by bursting in an unorthodox manner through the middle of the French formation and fragmenting it. Called the Battle of the Saints, this action was Rodney's greatest victory. Britain thereby won supremacy of the seas, but the action was too late to affect the outcome of the American Revolution. When Rodney returned to England, he received a barony and a pension from the British Government. A bold and quick-tempered man who had been addicted to expensive tastes and to gambling, Rodney lived quietly in the country until he died in London on May 24, 1792. Dominating the waters of the West Indies during his periods of active service, Rodney personified the might of British naval power.

A fleet of 40 French ships involved in the American Revolutionary War capsized as a result of this hurricane off the coast of Martinique. Approximately 4,000 soldiers drowned and many of the ships, towns, churches, houses and a hospital on this island were destroyed. The hurricane produced a 25-foot (7.6 m) storm surge on Martinique, destroying all houses in the capital city of St. Pierre; and the causalities were great because well over 9,000 persons died on the island. The 25 crew members of a British vessel was blown off course and ashore on the island of Martinique. Had it occurred any other time in this war, they would have been killed, captured and thrown in jail perhaps for the duration of the war because these two countries were fierce enemies and were at war. Initially, they were captured by some French Slaves on the island but were later released by a sympathetic French Governor, Marquis de Bouillé. The Governor sent them back to St. Lucia, writing that he would not keep as prisoners' men who had suffered the same horror and misery that had overtaken them all. In the end, the French Governor describing the impact that this storm had on this French Colony by reporting to the French Government in Paris, France that, on the island of Martinique *"all of the French vessels disappeared in this storm."*[6]

Severe damages were reported on the islands of Dominica, Guadeloupe, Antigua, and St. Kitts, though it is unknown if any died on those islands. Additionally, many ships were washed ashore on

St. Kitts. A powerful storm surge affected the island of St. Eustatius, causing approximately 4,000 to 5,000 deaths. Heavy damage was reported in southern Puerto Rico, primarily in Cabo Rojo and Lajas. Severe damage also occurred on the eastern side of the Dominican Republic. At nine o'clock at night, under stars, the *Stirling Castle*, that had suffered so much already and now sailed, badly damaged in the old channel north of Santo Domingo. It was drawn by the boiling, vicious currents to strike, as so many galleons and great ships had done, on the Silver Shoals. There she broke and was sucked down among the dim spines and turrets of coral to slide into the muffled deeps. Of the entire crew, only one midshipman and four seamen were saved.

In 1780 the twenty-two gun brig ship Ontario was washed ashore and destroyed in the Great Hurricane of 1780.

The hurricane later grounded 50 ships near Bermuda. In North Carolina, the effects of this storm were felt on October 14, where Lord Cornwallis was retreating, after the American victory at King's Mountain, a heavy rain was falling. His soldiers, as hungry as the

Americans had been, plodded for days under cold gray sheets of rain, through swamps and mud holes. They huddled at night on the wet ground, for fifteen days of wretchedness. Although this undiminished and powerful storm curved to the northeast Atlantic, its long reaching gales were felt off the Delaware where Lord Rodney himself, pacing the quarterdeck of the *Sandwich*, his elegant high nose sniffing the bright October day, felt nothing of the hurricane at all. Off Long Island, however, *HMS Shrewsbury*, that had been damaged off Newport in the earlier hurricane, and was now refitted, and *HMS Resolution*, bowled along on a sunlit ocean. Sudden and powerful squalls forced them to strike their top gallant masts. The Shrewsbury split a topsail during the storm. Northeast of Bermuda the hurricane was observed only by *HMS Berwick* to be curving toward the Azores. It reached at least the latitude of Great Britain. Its winds were not strong but its width apparently covered the distance from Newfoundland all the way into the central Atlantic.

This storm is definitely the greatest North Atlantic hurricane on record. It was the first hurricane in history which today can be traced in painstaking day-to-day detailed logbooks of many of the boat captains sailing throughout the North Atlantic at the time. The British sea power in the Caribbean was so weakened by this storm that they could not carry out the pre-planned mission to capture Puerto Rico. English woodcutters and fishermen had for years tried to live of Crabs on Vieques Islands, near Puerto Rico, which were also a haven for deserting British slaves. The possession of Puerto Rico would have enhanced British prosperity as well as her control of the West Indies. The Great Hurricane of 1780 put a stop to that. In fact, until the naval victories of two years later, there was practically no strength left in the British navy, as the course of the American Revolution would show. As a result Puerto Rico remained in Spanish hands. To this day their presence is still felt on the island in their people, culture, religion and language.

CHAPTER NINE
PERSONAL RECOLLECTIONS OF THE
GREAT HURRICANE OF 1780

The Great Hurricane of 1780 was a great topic for many of the colonists living in the Caribbean during that time. After this storm, many letters were written to loved ones and government officials living in Europe and the Americas. Some of the letters gave a full report of the terrors that they had experienced: *"until the 16th we had that terrible weather of thunder, lightning, wind and heavy rain as if the four elements would unite"*[1] wrote one colonist. Others described just what they had heard and in some cases they only briefly mentioned the hurricane and its effects in passing. Another eye-witness spoke of a *'damage that no pen can describe,'* but off course they tried to give their impression. For instance in the following section from a letter written from Saint-Eustatius:

"A short while ago it pleased the Lord Almighty to show us his power. Here we had from 12 to 22 October of this year a very fierce wind and a heavy sea that ruined a lot of houses and warehouses, yes even many ships were wrecked and many people were killed... the wall has been completely washed away by the sea and the back of the house has been left only on single struts, yes it was so heavy that the sea flew over our house but we may thank the Lord for His mercy that we have come off so well."[2] Subsequently, the letter describes how severe the weather was on the other islands, for on Saint-Eustatius

the hurricane had not reached its peak yet. The next section paints the situation on Martinique at first hand:

"After we had been there for a while, on the 12th October we were forced to leave the roadstead for a while because of a fierce wind... Because of this weather we left for the island of Martinique. Great damage had been done there: 154 houses on the beach were smashed to pieces by strong breakers, but the weirdest thing was to see a ship in the houses... The inhabitants told me that there had not been such a weather within living memory and a 120 years old castle, 6 to 8 foot deep in its foundation, had fallen down by the fierce wind."[3]

Here is an account of the storm's impact on the Leeward Islands, as told in *'The Law of The Storms'*:

"In the Leeward Islands, the family at Government House retreated to the centre of the building as the tempest increased, imagining from the prodigious strength of the walls, they being three feet thick, and from its circular form, it would have withstood the wind's utmost rage; however, by half-past 11 they were obliged to retreat to the cellar, the wind having forced its passage into every part, and torn off most of the roof. The water rose to a height of four feet in the cellar, so that they fled to the batteries and sought shelter under the cannon, many of which were moved. So violent was the storm, when assisted by the sea, that a twelve-pounder gun was carried from the south to the north battery, a distance of 140 yards. When the day broke the landscape had a complete winter aspect: not a leaf, not a twig, was to be seen on the trees."[4]

Here is a copy of a few words of the narrative on the Hon. Clement William Finch, Captain of the *Amazon*. His ship was located on the western side of St. Lucia near Castries, when the hurricane began:

"About seven o'clock at night (of the 11th) the gale increased to a degree that can better conceived from the consequences, than from any description I can give."[5]

Of course many writers wanted to tell their loved ones at home that they were safe. A.J. Van Halm, for instance, wrote to his wife in Waalwijk:

"Not many islands have been free from damage so it wouldn't surprise me if these tidings (that a lot of people have been killed) have reached Holland, but be convinced of the contrary: we are all in good health; there is no illness among the crew and I have not been hurt a finger."[6]

A very touching letter was written by Captain Jan Roelofsz de Groot who lost everything. He was concerned about his livelihood and wrote to his employer:

"It hurts me utmost in my heart and soul to lose such a beautiful ship and your fortune, but I can testify to God, and at all times to you that these accidents have not been caused by my seamanship, but only by Gods hand. I hope that you will not cast me out because of this accident. I can testify to you that the Almighty God has not only shown this to me, but to hundreds of ships of all nations, and people have fallen into similar accidents. It has made me poor, my goods and cargo are gone and lost without a penny insurance."[7]

Here is a Thanksgiving Sermon preached at St. Lucia, the Sunday after the Great Hurricane of 1780 struck the Caribbean on board of His Majesty's Ship *Vengeance* Captained by Captain Holloway and Commodore Hotham. The sermon was preached by Rev. P. Toucham the Late Chaplain of His Majesty's Ships, *Aleide* and *Egmont:*

"In my memorial to the Lords of the Admiralty, I have represented, that in consequence of an order which I obtained from their Right Honorable Board, I failed passenger with His Majesty's Ship Families, in the summer of 1780, to join my ship the Aleide, at that time with the Leeward Island Fleet, under Lord Rodney: that the Families, in her way to Jamaica, landed me at Barbados, from whence I went, in Endymion, to St. Lucia. That on my arrival there, I was immediately sent for from His Majesty's Ship 'Vengeance,' on board of which Commodore Hotham had his pendant, and had been left by Lord Rodney, with the command of the squadron in those seas, until his Lordship's return from America. For which he had lately failed with the grand division of the fleet, among which was my ship. There being at that time no chaplain belonging to the 'Vengeance,' I acted in her,

as such, by particular desire (I could not otherwise) from the Sunday preceding the hurricane of October, 1780, till the spring of 1781 or about six months, when they sailed for St Eustatius and England.

This is what lies affected by me, on the table of the Right Honorable Board of Admiralty, from whom I cannot doubt of receiving speedy justice. It is what I now, in public effort. Notwithstanding the omission of the purser of the 'Vengeance,' and what I do not think, any person in London will afterwards, pretend, for their finer purposes, to call in question: especially, when I here appeal, with a certainty of their affects, from my knowledge of their honor, to every officer of the 'Vengeance' (even purser and all) for the truth of my affection. Let me extend to this appeal to everyone of those brave men, under their command who heard me preach this sermon, with the most serious attention.

And here let me embrace this first opportunity, which I have ever had in public, of thanking the Commodore, the Captain, and every officer, and every private man, whom God hath preserved alive unto this day, for all the personal civilities which I have received from them, and for that strict decorum, that manly gravity, and dutiful attention, with which they always behaved, during the whole of divine service.

I cannot think of them and allow myself to part with their idea, without bowing down before that throne where mercy fits exalted, and praying, in most fervent manner, to Almighty, for the temporal, spiritual, and eternal welfare, of their persons and families! Wherever they are, May the God of all grace, who had called us unto eternal glory, by Jesus Christ, make, and keep them forever, perfect in every good work, to do His will, working in them that which is well pleasing in his sight, through Jesus Christ.

Psalm cxvi. 12-17 "What shall I render unto the Lord for all his benefits towards me?-I will offer unto him the sacrifice of thanksgiving, and will call upon the name of the Lord." Take it, on the whole, in either the military or the moral part of it, and we cannot find upon a record a character, merely human, more amiable and more exemplary than that of David. For, whether we mark his conduct as a man or as a monarch-as a patriot or politician-as a father-a husband-a friend-or as a saint-or as a hero, we feel, with admiration, his striking excellence. Through every scene of life, through every difficult situation, from the day on which God "took him from the sheepfolds, from following the ewes great with young, and brought him to feed Jacob, his people, and Israel his inheritance, and from that memorable period, till he died in a good old age, full of days, riches and honour....After speaking of that, I shall remind you of a few considerations, calculated to enkindle in our hearts a familiar, profitable, a superior gratitude to God, for the superior mercies which he hath graciously vouched for us. I shall conclude all with an application suited to our text, and to the occasion of our being more assembled together in the land of the living, and in the place of hope.

And therefore, when Providence held out 'the terrors of the Lord' before him; when he saw, as we did in the past week from his ship, that the judgment of the Almighty were come upon the earth. In consequence of this religious, and indeed rational interpretation of Providences, we never find David repining, nor murmuring, raging nor blaspheming, in even the most trying and tragic scenes of life. As one that is dumb, he opened not his mouth, for he knew it was the doing of the Lord, of that God who is righteous in all his ways, and just in all his judgments.

What shall we render unto the Lord for his revealing this divine truth to us, with all his other benefits towards us...To give an additional fervor to our gratitude for all God's benefits towards us-we will, in the next place think, with adoration to Heaven, of another very distinguishing and memorable mercy, which a good God hath graciously vouched for us by his kind providence.

What, therefore, shall we render to the Lord, for delivering out country-our fathers, and us their progeny, from the yoke of spiritual tyranny, from the horrors of this dreadful superstition? We will offer to day, and while we have a being, the sacrifice of thanksgiving-we will call upon the name of the Lord, and implore his aid to enable us, to the end that we may be wholly free, and wholly his-to deliver ourselves from the bondage of corruption, into the glorious Liberty of the children of God.

I will but just remind you of the compassion and mercy of God manifested to you, in raising you up, when you have been laid low upon the bed of sickness in delivering you very often from dangers and differences both by land and sea-at home and abroad-in society and solitude-by night and by day-and, particularly, in preserving you alive, perhaps without a wound, in the hours of battle-while thousands have fallen by your side, and ten thousands at your right hand. The mere mention of these mercies, will, I hope, awake in your souls that gratitude, which they once excited, or ought to have excited, and which will always due for them. My brethren, since I had the honor of preaching to you last Lord's day, it hath pleased Almighty God to alarm us with the most awful dispensation of his providence, that any of us have ever seen, a few days ago.

By land, what shocking scenes of destruction have come of us seen since that time. And what terrible horrors have we all heard of from the inland part of the island. There we may behold, as we have beheld here, the houses of every kind leveled with the dust I therefore, as here, we may see the old, and the young, the invalid and the man of health, promiscuously smothered in their ruins. While their surviving relations and countrymen stand pensive, in unutterable woe, around the desolated habitations. Many, and even some of them who are strangers in a strange land have lost their all and are, at this moment, without clothing, without money, without friends, in bad health and, I may add, without so much as the most common food.

For their irrefutable tempest, which tore up the trees of the forest with their roots, hath radically destroyed those fruits of the earth which are the staff of life. But, tragic and terrible as this hurricane and earthquake proved at land, all must allow that it was no lefts to at sea. When frightened at the thunders of the Most High as he came down in judgment with the angels of his vengeance-we saw the sun, the moon, and the stars disappear and the very heavens seemed to fly away with a great noise-when the waters of the great deep rose up rapidly upon us, and had well overwhelmed our souls-when the waves were raging around us for entrance---When the windows of the firmament were opened above us. When the pillars of the world were trembling below us. When the thunders and whirlwinds roared tremendously on every side of us. When the lightning and meteors, day and night, blazed unceasingly about us. When the vessels were dashing to pieces before and behind us. When this noble, battle-

wounded ship was striking upon that rock and the angel of death, as he passed by, looked upon us and we saw all their dreary shores covered with wrecks. What anguished filled our souls! And with what a torture of pain did the terrible prospects in our eye, and the ideas of our brethrens situation at sea, harrow up every feeling mind among us! The thoughts of being cut off at once, and forever in a foreign land by an unavoidable and unnatural death from our country, from our parents, from our wives, from our children, from glory and the conquest of Britain's foes, and from everything that can make life desirable. Added, inexpressibly, to the other agonies of our souls and made each horror look more horrible! But, my brethren, true is that saying, 'Man's extremity is God's opportunity.' At this momentous and memorable crisis, our God heard the groans of our distress and he graciously saved and delivered us and hath brought all of us in health and in the peace unto this day!

On this, His holy day, have we therefore met together, to wait upon and worship to magnify and bless, with the united ardors of our hearts, the great God of our salvation—the divine and almighty author of our miraculous deliverance. Miraculous! It certainly was, for after every effort had been exerted-every means had been used, for our preservation, which naval skills, and naval spirit could possibly exert—nature's great King commanded the winds and the waves to "Be still" and they were still!

And here allow me to congratulate with all of you, officers supreme and subordinate, and with every single individual of the ship's company, upon the strength with which God strengthened your souls, during the whole of this trying scene.

From the supreme commander there is nothing so great in conduct or in courage which we had not reason to expect, from his many past displays of both—nor have our highest expectations been disappointed.

Very great eulogiums are due to the activity zeal and spirit of the captain and every other officer deserves the encomiums of praise.

And you, my brave men, who acted under their command, merit every compliment which we can bestow on an indefatigable attention, a cheerful performance of your duty—a cool intrepidity—and a

Christian resignation to heaven, when every moment seemed big with your final fate.

In my scared line, I could only pour out my soul for all of you, in ejaculatory prayer before that God whose mercy rejoiced against judgment and who sits exalted to give to penitence, pardon and salvation.

Blended with dying ardors of your repentance and devotions, they penetrated the Heavens, and were immediately presented and pleaded upon by our divine advocate—they were graciously heard, and have been speedily and mercifully answered.

Now, my brethren, what shall we render unto the Lord for this wonderful salvation of us, and for all his other signal mercies and deliverances of every kind, of which I have reminded you! Shall we continue any longer in sin when such grace does abound? Shall we go, when the ardor of our gratitude abates, and thoughtless of this very striking and uncommon interposal of providence in our favor, return, the swearer to his blasphemies—the drunkard to his bottle— the man of criminal gallantry to his intrigues—or shall any sinner, of any other passion among us, return again to the commission of his former vices—after being thus snatched by the arm of Omnipotence from the jaws of death—and, it may be from the bottomless abyss of destruction! God forbid! First that we should be so ungrateful to our greatest and best benefactor. This would be a safe return for all his loving kindness and tender mercies to us, and it would argue that we were lost to all sense of our own temporal and eternal interests.

In the hours of your fear and distress, without a doubt, all of you were full of devotional dispositions—and, it is natural to suppose, that most if not all of you, resolved, that if God, then spared your lives, you would give up your immoral follies, and act a more rational and pious part, through every period of the future time which you prayed. Well, God has, agreeable to your wishes and vows, spared and prolonged your lives—but pray remember that your vows are registered in Heaven—and that there are terrible threatenings in your Bibles against the man who neglects to perform all such vows as you have unto God—God will not be mocked—he has been ever since, marking all your thoughts, words and actions—he is, this day, marking the frame of your souls, while you are offering him the thanksgiving of your heart. He expects that you will immediately reduce your resolutions to practice—that is---that, as you were saved by his grace, ye will henceforth live to his glory—that you will lead new lives of sobriety, righteousness and Godliness.

If thus you have resolved—and will thus reform and amend your hearts—your conversation and moral conduct, then, you may confidently depend upon it, that God will in all future trials, as he has in this, 'be your strength and your hope, and a very present help in every time of trouble.' Then may we speak comfort to our souls, and in an humble dependence upon that all-powerful being, who, on many extraordinary occasions, as well as this, has been our savior and deliverer, take up that noble and heroic resolution of the royal author of my text, "Though a host of foes were led against us, yet will not our hearts be afraid—though wars surround us on every side, yet will we put our trust in God—We will not fear, though the Earth be moved—though the hills be carried into the midst of the sea—though the waves thereof rage and swell and the mountains shake at the tempest of the same. For the Lord of Host is with us, the God of Jacob is our refuge!"[8]

Other letter writers paid much attention to the hurricane, but they did not forget their own passions either. Jan Hendrik de Boer, for instance, wrote to his tenderly beloved wife about the catastrophe and the many deceased. His letter was written in great haste but Jan Hendrik assured his Gesiena that she was never from his mind, not even for an hour. He even proposed to her. Since he put his proposal in a postscript that might strike us as not very romantic:

"P.S. I hope you are willing to marry me when we arrive at home?"[9]

Lambertus de Koning was also concerned about matters of the heart. At first he gave a very detailed report of the October storm that made him face death more than once. Yet, by the end of his letter, he puts all his misery into perspective by swearing to his tenderly beloved darling that nothing caused him so much pain *'as the loss of your beautiful eyes would hurt me.'* That he has not received a letter from her amiable hand since he has left bothers him very much. Lambertus' letter may give us the impression that the hurricane was just a storm in a teacup compared to his personal grief. Yet, the many reports by eye-witnesses prove otherwise: they convince us of the devastating power shown by *The Great Hurricane of 1780*, a devastating power that made a deep and unforgettable impression.

The Great Hurricane of 1780 was first felt in Barbados on October 10, 1780. The account is taken from *'The Ocean'* by Élisée Reclus, published in 1874:

"The most terrible cyclone of modern times is probably that of the 10th of October, 1780, which has been specially named the "great hurricane." Starting from Barbados, where neither trees nor dwellings were left standing, it caused an English fleet anchored off St. Lucia to disappear, and completely ravaged this island, where 6,000 persons were crushed under the ruins. After this, the whirlwind, tending toward Martinique, enveloped a convoy of French transports, and sunk more than 40 ships carrying 4,000 soldiers; on land the towns of St. Pierre and other places were completely razed by the wind, and 9,000 persons perished there. More to the north, Dominique, St. Eustatius, St. Vincent and Porto Rico were likewise devastated, and most of the vessels which were on the path of the cyclone foundered with all their crews. Beyond Porto Rico the tempest bent to the northeast, toward the Bermudas, and through its violence had gradually diminished, it sunk several English warships returning to Europe. At Barbados, where the cyclone had commenced its terrible spiral, the wind was unchained with such fury, that the inhabitants hiding in their cellars did not hear their houses falling above their heads; they did not feel the shocks of earthquake which, according to Rodney, accompanied the storm."[10]

The first news of this disaster was carried to England in a letter from Major General Vaughn, Commander-In-Chief of His Majesty's Royal Forces in the Leeward Islands, dated October 30, 1780:

"I am much concerned to inform your Lordship, that this island was almost entirely destroyed by a most violent hurricane, which began on Tuesday the 10th instant. And continued almost without intermission for nearly forty-eight hours. It is impossible for me to attempt a description of the storm; suffice to say, that few families

have escaped the general ruin, and I do not believe that 10 houses are saved in the whole island: scarce a house is standing in Bridgetown; whole families were buried in the ruins of their habitations; and many, in attempting to escape, were maimed and disabled: a general convulsion of nature seemed to take place, and an universal destruction ensued. The strongest colours could not paint to your Lordship the miseries of the inhabitants: on the one hand, the ground covered with mangled bodies of their friends and relations, and on the other, reputable families, wandering through the ruins, seeking for food and shelter: in short, imagination can form but a faint idea of the horrors of this dreadful scene."[11]

After the *Great Hurricane of 1780*, the Barbados Mercury compared the damage that occurred on that island with the damage sustained after the Lisbon, Portugal earthquake reported that:

"Some gentlemen, now here, and who were at Lisbon a few days after the earthquake, declare that this town in proportion to its size, has suffered more from the late calamity than Lisbon did at that time."[12]

Captain Maury, in his book *'Physical Geography of the Sea,"* gives a rather exaggerated account of the effects produced by this storm in Barbados, apparently from memory-some of the details being like, but not quite the same as those actually recorded. He reported:

"("the bark was blown from trees, and the fruits of the earth destroyed; the very bottom and depths of the sea were uprooted and likewise many forts and castles were washed away, and their great guns were carried in the air like chaff." The barks of trees were removed, but, it is believed rather through the effects of electric action than by the power of the wind. Cannons were driven along the batteries, and flung into the fosse, but not "carried in the air like chaff." Those who lived in the Government Building took refuge in the central part where circular walls, nearly a yard thick, seemed to afford promise of safety. But at 11:30 o'clock the wind had broken down parts of these walls, and lifted off the roof. Terrified they sought refuge in the cellarage, but before long the water had risen there to the height of more than a yard, and they were driven into the battery,

145

where they placed themselves behind the heavier cannons, some of which were driven from their place by the force of the wind. When day broke the country looked as if it had been blasted by fire; not a leaf was spared and not even a branch, remained upon the trees. As in great floods a common terror preserves peace animals which usually war upon each other, so during the Great Storm of 1780, human passions were for the time quelled by the fiercer war of the elements.)"[13]

Here is a very descriptive account of the Governor of Barbados's experience with this storm as told by historian Poyer:

"The power of the wind was remarkably exemplified, during the Great Hurricane of 1780, which at Barbadoes forced its way into every part of the Government House, and tore off most of the roof, though the walls were three feet thick, and doors and windows had been well barricaded. Obliged to retreat from thence, the Governor and his family fled to the ruins of the foundation of the flag-staff, and compelled to relinquish that station, they with difficulty reached the cannon of the fortifications, under the carriages of which they took wind, and they dreaded every moment that the guns would be dismounted, and crush them by their fall..."[14]

Here's an account of historian Poyer in his book *'The History of Barbados'* as he further describes the impact of the *Great Hurricane of 1780* on the island of Barbados and other Caribbean islands:

"Nothing can be conceived more dismal than the aspect of a country desolated by one of those tropical blasts. The cane-fields appear as if a roller had passed over them, and the woods as if visited by some sudden blight; the rivers are swollen and discoloured, and the level lands inundated by their overflowings, and by torrents of rain that have fallen; numbers of the dwellings are laid in ruins; the plantain-walks (from which the inhabitants draw much of their subsistence) are destroyed, and even the ground provisions, or various edible roots, do not entirely escape the general devastation. The planter, in short, sees his crop destroyed; and, what is far worse, he frequently beholds his slaves perish around him for want of subsistence, or by diseases brought upon them by improper food, to which, in the

extremity of hunger, they resort. What adds to the horrors of such a situation, is the long drought usually succeeding those visitations, by which the products of the earth spared by the tempest are arrested in their growth, the vegetation being dried up and suspended by the parching heat and want of moisture. These accumulated evils were never so severely felt as after the Great Hurricane of 1780; at which time the slaves were every day perishing in numbers, partly by diseases (chiefly dysentery) produced by unwholesome food, and partly by absolute starvation. The lowest price of a barrel even of old decayed flour was fourteen pounds Jamaica currency-it was indeed a great favor to obtain it at any price. A universal scarcity of other provisions prevailed, and the miserable slaves were compelled to feed on the wild-yam (a bitter and unwholesome root), on half-ripe fruits, and other wretched vegetables, which to their craving appetites were yet sweet and gratifying.

At this time of general misery and privation, there were some avaricious monopolizers, who, regardless of the sufferings around them, kept back their flour from the market, with a view of obtaining a still higher price for it. A base avarice often defeats itself. One of these wretches kept a considerable quantity of this article on hand till the arrival of a fresh supply, which was generously sold by the importer at a moderate price; and the hoarded flour, being by this time greatly injured by keeping, was sold by public auction at about one-twentieth of the price its sordid owner expected for it...the fairest female forms stripped of their drapery by the ruthless blasts passed the dismal night, exposed almost in a state of perfect nudity, to the inclemency of contending elements while their weeping parents and affectionate husbands, in all the agonies of sympathizing tenderness, ineffectually strove to shield them from the pelting of the pitiless storm. There were not more than 30 houses standing in Bridgetown and most of these had been extensively damaged. The wind and the waves removed a cannon of twelve pound ball-one firing an iron ball weighing twelve pounds from the Pierhead to the Wharf on the opposite side, a distance of 140 yards."[15]

This account describes the loss of the Royal Navy vessel 'Ontario' in the Great Hurricane of 1780. It was taken from *Legend of the Lake:*

The 22-Gun Brig-Sloop Ontario, 1780. This account describes the impact of the loss of these British warships had on the American War of Revolution:

"The Great Hurricane of October 1780, the most devastating in a hundred years, had arisen 3,000 miles away in the Caribbean. On October 10th it sank a Royal Navy vessel the size of "Ontario" off the island of St. Lucia, the HMS Beaver's Prize formerly Oliver Cromwell. The same day HMS Cornwall [74 guns] and the HMS Vengeance [32] sank nearby, while at St. Vincent HMS Experiment [50] was lost. It was a very black month for the Royal Navy. As well, over one hundred merchant ships foundered or were driven ashore at great cost to Lloyd's of London, the insurers.

The hurricane continued northward, striking Bermuda on October 18th and taking a toll of a further fifty ships. Veering a little to the west, it crossed the New England coast and struck Lake Ontario a few days later. The north-east wind mentioned by Brigadier Powell would be the westerly part of the counter-clockwise hurricane, probably with winds upwards of 80 knots, which, after dark, would strike without warning.

Death came swiftly Halloween night, 1780. Only six months after her christening, His Majesty's 22-Gun Brig Ontario foundered in the wake of the 18th century's most violent hurricane. Her resting place, the tomb of the 100 people who died in Lake Ontario's worst maritime disaster, was discovered by scuba divers in 1995. Ontario was built at the Carleton ship yards near Kingston, Ontario, to protect British Canada from invasion by American forces travelling up through the Great Lakes and river systems during the Revolutionary War. Because she was built in wartime, her short career was wrapped in secrecy. The British admiralty did not want the revolutionaries to know the brig's capabilities, and, after her loss, they did not want George Washington to know how weak the western defenses of Canada were. Arthur Smith believes that this shroud of secrecy still hides many truths about the Ontario.

A narrow study of the brig would be interesting to naval historians but hardly worthwhile for students and general readers. However, Smith has taken a more fertile structural approach by placing the detailed aspects of the ship's manufacture and military attributes within the framework of life on Lake Ontario during the later 18th century. The story of the Ontario becomes a rich history of the Great Lake lowlands' growing and hectic life.

Ships and ship building were vital for transportation, trade and security throughout the 18th and early 19th centuries. At the time Ontario was built, regiments of British soldiers were moving through the Lake Ontario region to meet the threat of Washington's armies. Loyalists were fleeing the revolutionary colonies and establishing new roots in the peninsula, and farmers, merchants and fur traders needed to move their goods and products.

The British Admiralty ship plans of Ontario show how complex it was to build a warship of 23 tons. The master shipwrights task was a daunting endeavor. These huge ships were actually very fragile and, in the harsh environment of the Great Lakes, had, at best, a very short lifetime. Ontario's captain, James Andrews, needed to be alert to the characteristics of his ship and to the changing elements lest tragedy befall his crew at any moment."[16]

Here is an account by Samuel Hyde who was one of the few historians who actually described in such vivid details what impact this storm had on Barbados and what was done with the thousands of dead bodies:

"The merchants of Bridgetown were not prepared for this hurricane, and there was no relief committee formed nor plans for such an eventuality formulated, so from the number of dead bodies lying in the streets, and among the ruins, and the quantity of putrid fish thrown up by the sea, no unreasonable apprehensions were entertained that such a pestilence would ensue. To avert this evil, among other necessary purposes, the merchants of Bridgetown formed an association and appointed committees for the internment of the dead, and the distribution of provisions for the relief of their indigent fellow-suffers."[17]

Poyer, like Samuel Hyde, recorded the general conditions of William Senhouse, who like Reverend Edghill, recorded what took place at his home. William Senhouse was the Surveyor General of H.M's. Customs at Barbados, and he had spent many years at sea. His autobiographical manuscript which was published in the Journal of the Barbados Museum and Historical Society in August, 1935, reads:

"I had weathered many hard gales in H.M.'s. Navy but this in a manner appeared to; rain fell like a deluge possess the united force of them all. The very tone or sound of the wind, was wound up to a pitch almost bordering upon a whistle, which added great weight to the wind, and when driven in our faces felt like hail or small shot; the thunder and lightning was tremendous and incessant...The estimated damage to property was about 1.4 million pounds, and the Governor estimated the total loss of life at 4,326. The population was less than 100,000."[18]

Mr. William Senhouse records that the wind was fresh from early in the morning and the clouds were dense but he did not then observe anything unusual. The wind gradually increased during the afternoon and there was small flow of rain, but at 1pm a part of the roof of the 'Grove' blew off and he tried to secure the remainder with ropes. He and his family removed themselves to the downstairs rooms in a part of the building he thought was secure, but the falling of stones on the floor above made them move into the buttery, a space of 4 feet by 12 feet, in which he counted 38 people, half up to their knees in water.. Senhouse, records the fall of the house in the following personal account:

"I must leave thee here, oh gentle reader, to the fertility of thy own lively imagination to screw up thy mind if thou canst to such a pitch as an adequate idea of the force of that wind, the very sound of which was mere than sufficient to overpower and drown the noise and horrid crash of a falling house whilst we ourselves were in it! Singular as the fact may be, it is no less true, for not one of us were sensible of its fall!"...."The Grove house consisted of 4 lofty gables, all of which falling broke with irresistible force thro' the floor of the upper chambers, and carrying everything before them with their ponderous ruins, completely filled up and destroyed everything in the lower rooms! The kitchen was in some sort an exception, for altho' it was almost full of negroes when the house fell, yet it is miraculous to relate that not one of them was materially injured."[19]

This account was taken from *'Peeps into Barbados History'* and *'Dreadful Rampage of the 1780 Storm'* by Edward A. Stoute and W.A. Swartworth about the impact this great storm had on the island of Barbados. Edward A. Stoute was a Barbadian Historian and a Member of the Council of the Barbados National Trust and W.A. Swartworth was a U.S. Science Writer:

'PEEPS INTO BARBADOS HISTORY'

"The merchants of Bridgetown were not prepared for this hurricane, and there was no relief committee formed nor plans for such an eventuality formulated, so "from the number of dead bodies lying in the streets, and among the ruins, and the quantity of putrid fish thrown up by the sea, no unreasonable apprehensions were entertained that a pestilence would ensue. To avert this evil, among other necessary purposes, the merchants of Bridgetown formed an association and appointed committees for the interment of the dead, and the distribution of provisions for the relief of their indigent fellow sufferers."

Mr. Senhouse records that the wind was fresh from early in the morning and the clouds were dense but he did not then observe anything unusual. The wind gradually increased during the afternoon and there was small rain, but at 1pm a part of the roof of the 'Grove' blew off and he tried to secure the remainder with ropes. He and his family removed themselves to the downstairs rooms in part of the building he thought secure, but the falling of stones on the floor above made them move into the buttery, a space of 4 feet by 12 feet, in which he counted 38 people, half up to their knees in water. Mr. Senhouse records the fall of the house in the following words:

"I must leave thee here, oh! Gentle reader, to the fertility of thy own lively imagination to screw up thy mind if thou canst to such a pitch as to conceive an adequate idea of the force of that wind, the very sound of which was more than sufficient to overpower and drown the noise to overpower and drown the noise and horrid crash of a falling house whilst we ourselves were in it. Singular as the fact may be, it is no less true, for not one of us were sensible of its fall!" Mr. Senhouse describes the "Grove" house as follows"...consisted of 4 lofty gables, all of which falling broke with irrestible force thro' the floor of the upper chambers, and carrying everything before them with

their ponderous ruins, completely filled up and destroyed everything in the lower rooms! The Kitchen was in some sort an exception, for a tho' it was almost full of negroes when the house fell, yet it is miraculous to relate that not one of them was materially injured."

It is recorded that the total value of property destroyed by this hurricane was £1,350,564-5-01/2, and that two thousand and thirty three slaves were killed. The number of free negroes or people of European extract were not included in this total, as they were not considered valuable property like the slave.

The British Parliament came to the rescue of the island by voting £80,000 for the relief of the sufferers, and this amount was augmented by another £20,000 which was raised by the citizens of Dublin, Ireland.

The members of the House of Assembly sought to protect the landowners during the period of distress, for they introduced legislation to suspend for a time any legal proceedings for debt against landowners. The Speaker, Sir John Gay Alleyne, considered this to be a very unjust law, and moved the insertion of a clause excluding him by name from any benefits to be derived from the operation of this law. This resulted in the withdrawal of the Bill.

To economize and to assist the unfortunate tax-payer who had been hit hard by the destruction of their property, the House of Assembly reduced the salary of His Excellency the Governor; this resulted in his introducing a table of fees to augment his income. This was done without the agreement of the representatives of the people. Mr. Duke introduced a motion in the House of Assembly and a petition was forwarded to the King praying for the removal of the Governor on account of his arbitrary and illegal exaction. James Cunningham, the Governor, was ably supported by his patron, Lord George Germaine, and this resulted in his not being recalled until after the defeat of Lord North's Ministry in 1782. This Ministry had lasted for a period of twelve years and had caused the loss of the American Colonies."[20]

'DREADFUL RAMPAGE OF THE 1780 STORM'

"Poyer in his History of Barbados, relates that on the morning of Tuesday October, 10, 1780 the wind was very high and was

accompanied by heavy rain; it was from a north-westerly direction and continued to increase thus alarming the inhabitants; by noon of that day many houses were either materially damaged or totally destroyed.

By three o'clock in the afternoon Carlisle Bay was devoid of ships for all had broken from their moorings and some had been driven ashore and wrecked while others were driven out to sea.

As night approached the fury of this hurricane increased, "and a scene of terror and distress awaited the ruined and dismayed inhabitants in the dread hour of darkness, of which no powers of language can convey an adequate idea."

About 9pm the storm reached its apex, and from then to 4am the next day the work of destruction was completed. For "within that dreadful interval the whole Island was devastated and its unsheltered inhabitants were reduced to the last extremity of misery and despair."

The towns appeared to have suffered more than the country, where houses were concentrated there were greater casualties, as people endeavoring to escape from their own wrecked home, became endangered by the falling walls of their neighbour's homes while on their flight to open places.

"The howling of the tempest; the noise of descending torrents from clouds surcharged with rain; the incessant flashing of lightning; the roaring of thunder; the continual crash of falling houses, the dismal groans of the wounded and the dying, the shriek of despair, the lamentations of woe; and the screams of women and children calling for help on those whose ears were now closed his wife 'grievously contused by the fall of his house, and an infant only six months old, were among the midnight wanderers, who traversed the dreary waste in search of an uncertain place of shelter and repose.

"The fairest female forms stripped of their drapery by the ruthless blast passed the dismal night, exposed almost in a state of perfect nudity, to the inclemency of contending elements while weeping parents and affectionate husbands, in all the agonies of sympathizing tenderness, ineffectually strove to shield them from the pelting of the pitiless storm."

A demonstration of the force of the wind and waves is given the removal of a "cannon of twelve pound ball-one firing an iron ball weighing twelve pounds-from the pierhead to the wharf on the opposite side, a distance of 140 yards."

In Bridgetown not more than 30 houses and stores were left standing, and most of these had been extensively damaged. Of the 11 churches, only St. Andrew's, St. Peter's, three Chapels and All Saints' Chapel remained standing. Those that were not totally destroyed were materially damaged."[21]

The military commander of Barbados in 1780 reported that after the *Great Hurricane of 1780* he was forced for many days to wear the slaves' clothes which he had borrowed because all of his clothes were destroyed in the hurricane. One of the best accounts of this storm's damage in Barbados is one that was officially sent by Major-General Cunninghame, Governor of Barbados, to Secretary of State and Major-General Vaughan:

"The evening preceding the hurricane, the 9th October, was remarkably calm; but the sky surprisingly red and fiery. During the night much rain fell. On the morning of the 10th much rain and wind from the northwest. By 10am it increased very much. By 1pm the ships in the bay drove. By 4pm the 'Albemarle' frigate parted and went to sea, as did all the other vessels, about 25 in number. By 6pm the wind had torn up and blown down many trees, and foreboded a most violent tempest.

At Government House every precaution was taken to guard against what might happen: the doors and windows were barricaded, but it availed little. By 10pm the wind forced itself a passage through the house from the north-northwest, and the tempest increasing every minute, the family took to the centre of the building, imagining, from the prodigious strength of the walls, they being three feet thick, and from its circular form, it would have withstood the winds most utmost rage; however, by half past eleven they were obliged to retreat to the cellar, the wind having forced its passage into every part, and torn off most of the roof...The armory was leveled to the ground, and the arms scattered about...The buildings were all demolished; for so violent was the storm here, when assisted by the sea, that a

12-pounder gun was carried from the south to the north battery, a distance of 140 yards...the loss to this country is immense: many years will be required to retrieve it."[22]

Here is a copy of some parts of the letter written by a Dr. Gilbert Blane to Dr. William Hunter and it is dated December 22, 1780:

"There had been nothing that could be called a hurricane felt at Barbados for more than a century before 1780, so that the inhabitants began to think themselves exempt from such calamities, and accordingly had no edifices of sufficient strength to withstand the force of a hurricane...On the evening of the 10th the wind rose to such a degree of violence as clearly to amount to what is called a hurricane. At 8pm it began to make impression on all the houses, by tearing off the roofs, and overthrowing some of the walls...It was thought to be at its greatest height at midnight, and did not abate considerably until eight the next morning...Even the bodies of men and cattle were lifted from the ground, and carried several yards...A ship was driven on shore against one of the buildings of the Naval Hospital, which by this shock, and by impetuosity of the wind and sea, was entirely destroyed and swept away. At Barbadoes, indeed, the greater part of the hurricane was from the northeast; but an hour or two after midnight, it was, for a little time due west."[23]

Another historian of the Lesser Antilles, Halliday, gives a very descriptive account of the hurricane in Barbados in his writings called *'Account of the Hurricane'* in 1831:

"At dawn of the day,(October 10th), the wind rushing with a mighty force from the northwest...Towards evening the storm increased, and at nine o'clock had attained its height, but it continued to rage till four the next morning, when there was a temporary lull...Before daybreak, the castle and forts, the church, every public building, and almost every house in Bridgetown, were leveled with the earth."[24]

Here is an account of the Great Hurricane of 1780 as told by Sir Robert Hermann Schomburgk in 1848 in his book, *'The History of Barbados: comprising geographical and statistical description of the island: a sketch of the historical events since the settlement: and an account of its geology and natural productions:*

"On the morning of Tuesday the 10th of October 1780, slight apprehensions were felt by a few persons in consequences of the unusual violence of the wind, accompanied by heavy rains. The preceding evening had been hazy and the sun had set with a fiery appearance, but nothing serious was apprehended. The wind, which blew in the morning from the north-east by north, veered gradually to the westward. It increased, and at noon several houses in different parts of the island were blown down, and the ships in the bay began to drive. The Albemarle frigate, the only man-of-war then in the bay, slipped her best bower cable, and subsequently the hawser, and stood out to sea. As the night approached the wind became westerly and increased in fury. It appeared to have reached its height at midnight; but long were that hour approached the work of destruction had commenced: an eye-witness and sufferer during this dismal night, says "the havoc which met the eye contributed to subdue the firmest mind. The howling of the tempest; the noise of descending torrents from clouds surcharged with rain; the incessant flashing of lightning; the roaring of the thunder; the continual crash of falling houses; the dismal groans of the wounded and the dying; the shriek of despair; the lamentations of woe; and the screams of women and the children calling for help on those whose cars were now closed to the voice of complaint,-formed an accumulation of sorrow and the terror too great for human fortitude, too vast for human conception."

The inhabitants long here at midnight considered it unsafe to remain in their houses; they fled to the fields, to avoid being buried in the ruins of walls and roofs. The cattle had broken from their folds, and their dismal bellowing increased the scene of horror. The force of the storm surpassed all conception. Admiral Rodney stated that the heavy cannon were carried upwards of a hundred feet from the forts, and as will be observed from the letter which follows, and which was addressed by Major General Cunninghame, Governor of Barbados, to the Secretary of State, a twelve-pounder was carried by the wind and waves from the south to the north battery, a distance of 140 yards.

At daylight, October 11th, a scene of desolation was presented seldom equaled. The face of nature seemed completely changed; not a single house or building in the island, however strong or sheltered, *had escaped damage. Bridgetown was one heap of ruins; not more than thirty houses or stores were left standing, all of which had suffered more or less. The church of St. Michael, with its lofty steeple, was leveled to the ground; the town-hall, the prison, the castle and the fortifications shared a similar fate. The mole-head, which cost the island more than twenty thousand pounds, was destroyed, and the basin filled up with sand, ledges of coral reef and timber. Had it not been for the partial protection which the pier afforded, the total destruction of Bridgetown would have been unavoidable; it broke the force of the waves, which rushed with fearful impetuosity against it. A ship was driven ashore against one of the buildings at the Naval Hospital, which by this shock, combined with the fury of the winds and waves, was entirely destroyed and swept away. Of eleven churches and two chapels, only two churches and one chapel were left standing—these were the churches of St. Andrew and St. Peter, and All Saints' Chapel. The Governor's residence at Pilgrim and the residence of the Commander-in-chief were blown down. The secretary of General Vaughan had his thigh broken, and the General himself received several severe contusions. The barracks and hospital were destroyed. Speightstown suffered less than Bridgetown, or any other part of the island; the Holetown and Oistin's participated in the general havoc.*

The loss of human life has been estimated at 4326 souls, and the loss which the colony sustained, at £1,320,564 Sterling. Most of the five stock and horned cattle perished; the caries, corn and ground provisions were totally destroyed, and famine threatened those who survived the catastrophe. As if to increase the horror of the event, the slaves were actively employed in plunder; a body of 800 prisoners of war also had been liberated by the demolition of the gaol, and it was thought that these men might join the slaves, to complete the destruction of what the elements had spared. The active measures of General Vaughan however prevented this, if indeed it had been contemplated, and the survivors had at least the satisfaction of considering themselves safe under his protection, aided as he was by his troops. Don Pedro de Saint Iago, captain of the regiment of Arragon and the Spanish prisoners under him, spared no labour to contribute to the relief of the distressed inhabitants and the preservation of public order.

The loss which the two hurricanes that took place in October in the West Indies caused to the navy, may be conceived. The magnanimous conduct of the Marquis de Bouille deserves to be mentioned on this occasion. The Laurel and Andromeda, two British frigates, having been wrecked on the coast of Martinique, he sent thirty-one sailors, all that were saved of their crews, with a flag of truce to Commodore Hotham at St. Lucia, declaring that he could not consider in the light of enemies men who, in common with his people, had been partakers of the same danger, and were equally entitled to every assistance and relief that could be rendered in a season of such universal calamity; adding that he only lamented that their numbers were so small, and particularly that none of the officers were saved. Let us compare this with the conduct of Major-General Cunninghame, who, as we shall presently see from his dispatch, has just then escaped the imminent danger of the fury of the winds; a circumstance which one would have thought should have opened his heart to compassion and humane feeling. The crew of a small Spanish launch with a few mules on board, on the 12th of October sought shelter from the winds and waves in Maycock's Bay. The matrosses detained the vessel until the governor's pleasure was known; and His Excellency ordered her to be seized as a droit of Admiralty, made the crew prisoners of war, and converted the vessel and cargo to his own use. "Thus what the wretched mariners had saved from the angry elements, was torn from them by the rapacity of a human being, insensible to the tender emotions of pity and compassion."[25]

Here is another account of the Government of Barbados' response after the *Great Hurricane of 1780* as told by Sir Robert Hermann Schomburgk in 1848 in his book, *'The History of Barbados: comprising geographical and statistical description of the island: a sketch of the historical events since the settlement: and an account of its geology and natural productions.'* After the Great Hurricane of 1780 some persons felt that the Governor of Barbados should increase taxes or levy new ones to help with the governing of the country and to raise funds after the storm. Below is the heated debate that followed:

"The Governor summoned the Council to frame an address to the throne, in which they implored his Majesty's assistance. The petition was accompanied by a letter from his Excellency to Lord George Germaine; and General Vaughan addresses the Secretary of State for a similar purpose, assuring him that a famine must inevitably ensue unless some effectual assistance were rendered to prevent it. It was expected that there would be a special call of the Assembly on this melancholy occasion, in order to consult with the governor and Council how to mitigate the public distress; but his Excellency considered otherwise, and the Assembly did not meet until the 31st of October, pursuant to adjournment. It was resolved to implore the King's gracious assistance in a dutiful address, and to direct Mr. Estwick to renew his application to the ministry for the remission of the four-and-half percent duty, with which he was to combine the petition for the establishment of a free port as the means of rescuing Barbados from ruin.

The Governor took an early opportunity of desiring the Assembly to frame a proper levy-bill and to put the fortifications in order: he likewise drew their attention to the ruinous state of Pilgrim, his residence, and stated that the armoury had been entirely destroyed during the hurricane, and the arms were exposed to the weather. The Assembly answered, that what little the storm had spared was required for the bare necessities of life, and for this reason they declined to pass a levy-bill, or to incur any expense in the repair of the fortifications; His Excellency's residence however, they added, should be put in repair as speedily as circumstances would permit, and the arms which were exposed in consequence of the destruction of the armoury should be taken care of. It was certainly most unfeeling of the Governor at this moment of distress to propose the imposition of fresh taxes upon the community. Another message from him was of a similar nature; he required the Assembly, as the troops were to be withdrawn, to provide the necessary means for guarding the prisoners of war and preserving the peace of the island. The House replied that, as there was no place of sufficient security in which to lodge the prisoners, they requested that they might be sent away with the troops.

Judge Gittens, a member of the House, introduced a bill to suspend for a limited term of years the proceedings in the courts of justice and the marshal's office, until the inhabitants had recovered from the present calamity. This novel measure, the object of which was to obstruct the course of justice by law and to deprive the creditor of his legal remedy, met with becoming opposition, even from those whom the calamity had brought to the brink of ruin, and who might have materially benefited by such a measure. The bill was withdrawn, without being put to the vote of a second reading.

The Governor continuing to extort the illegal fees which he had established without the concurrence of the representatives of the people, Mr. Duke brought the subject again before the House, and proved that the levying of money without the consent of Parliament had been repeatedly and solemnly declared illegal in England. This being the case with the King, it could not be supposed that a Governor of the British colony, the inhabitants of which enjoyed by charter the rights of British subjects was at liberty to extort money from them. Several local statute proved that no old fees could be altered, nor new ones established, without the authority of the Governor, Council, and Assembly: yet his Excellency and the Council, in direct contravention of the most positive laws had presumed to establish a new table of fees. After various arguments tending to prove that the Governor and his agent Mr. Workman had been guilty of extortion, the House passed several resolutions condemning them."[26]

Major-General Cunninghame sent the following account of the Great Hurricane of 1780, to the Secretary of State and Major-General Vaughan. The Commander-in-chief refers the English Government to that account for a description of it:

Copy of a Journal of what passed at Barbados, from the 9th of October until the 16th, 1780.

"The evening preceding the hurricane, the 9th of October, was remarkably calm, but the sky surprisingly red and fiery; during the night much rain fell. On the morning of the 10th much rain fell. On the morning of the 10th much rain and wind from the north-west.

By ten o'clock it increased very much; by one, the ships in the bay drove; four o'clock, the Albermarle frigate(the only man-of-war here) parted her anchors and went to sea, as did all the other vessels, about twenty-five in number. Soon after, by six o'clock, the wind had torn up and blown many trees, and foreboded a most violent tempest."

"At the Government House every precaution was taken to guard against what might happen: the doors and windows were barricaded up but it availed little. By ten o'clock the wind forced itself a passage through the house from north-northwest, and the tempest increasing every minute, the family took to the centre of the building, imagining from the prodigious strength of the walls, they being three feet thick, and from its circular form, it would have withstood the wind's utmost rage: however, by half-past eleven o'clock they were obliged to retreat to the cellar, the wind having forced its way into every part, and torn off most of the roof. From this asylum they were soon driven out, the water being stopped in its passage, and having forced itself a course into the cellar, they knew not where to go; the water rose four feet, and the ruins were falling from all quarters. To continue in the cellar was impossible; to return to the house equally so: the only chance left, was making for the fields, which at that time appeared equally dangerous: it was however attempted, and the family were so fortunate as to get to the ruins of the foundation of the flag-staff, which soon after giving way, every one endeavored to find a retreat for himself. The Governor, and the few who remained were thrown down, and it was with great difficulty they gained a cannon, under the carriage of which they took shelter; their situation here was highly deplorable: many of the cannons were moved, and they had reason to fear that under which they sat might be dismounted, and crush them by its fall; or that some of the ruins that were flying about, would put an end to their existence; and to render the scene still more dreadful, they had much to fear from the powder-magazine, near which they were. The armoury was level with the ground, and the arms and cannon scattered about."

"Anxiously did they wait the break of day, flattering themselves that with the light they should see a cessation of the storm; yet when it appeared, little was the tempest abated, and it served but to exhibit the most melancholy prospect imaginable. Nothing can

compare with the terrible devastation that presented itself on all sides; not a building standing; the trees, if not torn up by the roots, deprived of their leaves and branches; and the most luxuriant spring changed, in this one night, to the dreariest whiter. In vain was it to look round for shelter; houses that, from their situation, it was to have been imagined would have been in a degree protected, were all flat with the earth; and the miserable owners, if they were so fortunate as to escape with their lives, were left without a covering for themselves and family. General Vaughan was early obliged to evacuate his house; in escaping he was much bruised; his secretary was so unfortunate as to break his thigh."

"Nothing has ever happened that has caused such universal desolation. No one house in the island is exempt from danger. Very few buildings are left standing on the estates. The depopulation of the negroes and the cattle, particularly of the horned kind, is very great, which must, more especially in these times, be a cause of great distress to the planters. It is as yet impossible to make any accurate calculation of the number of souls who have perished in this dreadful calamity. Whites and blacks together, it is imagined to exceed some thousands, but fortunately few people of consequence are among the number. Many are buried in the ruins of the houses and buildings; many fell victims to the violence of the storm and inclemency of the weather; and great numbers were driven into the sea, and there perished. The troops have suffered inconsiderably, though both the barracks and hospital were early blown down. Alarming consequences were dreaded from the number of dead bodies that lay uninterred, and from the quantity the sea threw up, which however are happily subsided. What few public buildings there were, are fallen in the general wreck. The fortifications have suffered very considerably. The buildings were all demolished, for so violent was the storm here, when assisted by the sea, that a twelve-pounder gun was carried from the south to the north battery, a distance of 140 yards. The loss to this country is immense; many years will be required to retrieve it."[27]

Here is another descriptive account of this storm as it passed over several Caribbean Islands as reported in *the Barbados Annual Register*:

"At St. Christopher many vessels were forced ashore. At St. Lucia, all the barracks and huts for his Majesty's troops, and other buildings on the island, were blown down, and the ships driven to sea; and the Amazon, Captain Finch, miraculously escaped foundering. At Dominica, they suffered greatly. At St. Vincent, every building was blown down and the town destroyed. At Grenada, nineteen loaded Dutch ships were stranded and beat to pieces. At Martinique, all the ships were blown off the island that were bringing troops and provisions. On the 12th, four ships foundered in Fort Royal Bay, and the crews perished. The other ships were blown out of the roads. In the town of St. Pierre every house is blown down, and more than 100 people have perished. At Fort Royal, the cathedral, seven churches, and other religious edifices, many other public buildings, and 1,400 houses, were blown down. The hospital of Nôtre Dame, in which were 1600 sick and wounded, was blown down; and the greatest part of these persons buried in the ruins. The number of persons who perished in Martinique are said to have been 9000. At St. Eustatia, the loss was very great. Seven ships were driven on shore near North Point, and their crews perished. Between 4,000 and 5,000 persons are supposed to have lost their lives in St. Eustatia."[28]

On the French Island of Martinique the situation was just as bad as those in the English speaking islands and here is the account of the Intendant of Martinique to the Minister of Marine:

"In Martinique, the wind that prevailed from the east-northeast having become very strong during the day of October 11, many of the ships of the convoy were driven. The wind became very violent. Then it changed to the east-northeast and soon to the south and then to the west. Many ships were lost or seriously damaged. In St. Pierre, the sea rose and in an instant destroyed more than 150 houses, among them 30 or 40 recently built. Fort St. Pierre built 120 years before was destroyed also. The sea in St. Pierre did greater damage than the wind; the sea reached a height of 25 feet.

The wind and the sea caused a great damage in Dominica. Many ships were stranded on the coast and almost all of the houses near the sea were destroyed...The disaster was even worse at St. Vincent and the losses greater. The frigate Juno that had just arrived was lost. Of 600 houses in King's Town only 14 remained; the others were destroyed, and the inhabitants suffered the greatest misery...It did little damage in Grenade. Some ships were damaged.

Guadeloupe suffered some damage in its plantations. The sea did much damage in the southern part of the island...Marie Galante was saved to a great extent...it was not the same in St. Eustace. The sea caused a great damage there; it rose to a considerable height and covered a great part of the store-houses.

At St. Lucia, only two houses were left standing in the town. At St. Vincent the 'Experiment'... and the Juno, a French forty-gun frigate, were entirely destroyed...At Grenada nineteen sail of loaded Dutch ships were stranded and beat to pieces...In Antigua the wind blew in squalls at first coming from the east-northeast, then it changed by the east to the southeast."[29]

Here is what another historian Atwood (1791, 11-12) wrote about the damages in Dominica:

"In the hurricane season, the damage received in Dominica is principally occasioned by the very heavy rains, or by the sea, which sometimes in those seasons tumbles into the bays, especially that of Roseau...A particular circumstance of this kind, which happened there the last day of September, 1780(Julian calendar, the 11th of October, Gregorian calendar), was the most remarkable that has occurred in this island, in the memory of the oldest inhabitant, and did the most mischief. It did considerable damage among the plantations, and in Roseau destroyed several houses on the bay, and several vessels in the road."[30]

Ships and ship building were vital for transportation, trade and security throughout the 18th and early 19th centuries. At the time *"Ontario"* was built, regiments of British soldiers were moving through the Lake Ontario region to meet the threat of Washington's armies. Loyalists were fleeing the revolutionary colonies and establishing new roots in the Florida Peninsula, the Bahamas, and other Caribbean Islands. Sea transportation was vital because farmers, merchants and fur traders needed to move their goods and products throughout the region in spite of the many wars occurring at the time. The following excerpt was taken from *Legend of the Lake: The 22-Gun Brig-Sloop Ontario, 1780* by Arthur Britton Smith:

"The Great Hurricane of October 1780, the most devastating in a hundred years, had arisen 3,000 miles away in the Caribbean. On October 10th it sank a Royal Navy vessel the size of "Ontario" off the island of St. Lucia, the HMS 'Beaver's Prize' formerly 'Oliver Cromwell.' The same day HMS Cornwall (74 guns) and the HMS 'Vengeance' (32 guns) sank nearby, while at St. Vincent the Experiment (50 Guns) was lost. It was a very black month for the Royal Navy. As well, over one hundred merchant ships foundered or were driven ashore at great cost to Lloyd's of London, the insurers. The hurricane continued northward, striking Bermuda on October 18th and taking a toll of a further fifty ships. Veering a little to the west, it crossed the New England coast and struck Lake Ontario a few days later. The northeast wind mentioned by Brigadier Powell would be the westerly part of the counter-clockwise hurricane, probably with winds upwards of 80 knots, which after dark, would strike without warning."[31]

CHAPTER TEN

THE COMPELLING ACCOUNT OF THE LOSS OF HIS MAJESTY'S SHIP THE 'PHŒNIX'

Lieutenant Archer, of *HMS Phoenix* wrote in his log book with regards to the hurricane's impact at Montego Bay *"Many of the houses, where we had been so merry, were so completely destroyed, that scarcely a vestige remained to mark where they stood."* The *Phoenix* under Sir Hyde Parker, was driven ashore near Cape Cruz in Cuba just as she was about to founder. In addition, the *'Scarborough,' 'Barbadoes,'* and *'Victor'* which were anchored at Montego Bay were lost in the storm. Archer crossed back to Jamaica in a rickety open boat and procured assistance for the survivors. With regards to the storm, it is stated by other authorities that a fearful pestilence broke out shortly after which was due to the putrefaction of the unburied corpses. The best narrative of this great hurricane, was written by the young Lieutenant Archer of the *HMS Phoenix*, which commanded by Sir Hyde Parker, known as *'Old Vinegar,'* who had also experienced typhoons in the Indian Ocean before this voyage in the West Indies. In a letter to his mother in England that was dated November 6, 1780, Archer described his compelling experience with this storm.

The Phœnix of 44 guns, Capt. Sir Hyde Parker was lost in the Great Hurricane of 1780, off Cuba, in the West Indies, in the year 1780. The same hurricane destroyed the Thunderer, 74; Stirling

Castle, 64; La Blanche, 42; Laurel, 28; Andromeda, 28; Deas Castle, 24; Scarborough, 20; Beaver's Prize, 16; Barbadoes, 14; Cameleon, 14; Endeavour, 14; and Victor, 10 guns. Lieut. Archer was first-lieutenant of the Phœnix at the time she was lost. His very descriptive narrative in a letter written to his mother shortly thereafter, contains a most correct and animated account of one of the most awful events in the service. It is so simple and natural as to make the reader feel himself as on board the Phœnix. Every circumstance is detailed with feeling, and powerful appeals are continually made to the heart. It must likewise afford considerable pleasure to observe the devout spirit of a seaman frequently bursting forth, and imparting sublimity to the relation.

At Sea, June 30, 1781.

My dear Mother,

I am now going to give you an account of our last cruise on the Phœnix; and must promise, that should anyone see it besides yourself, they must put this construction on it—that it was originally intended for the eyes of a mother, and a mother only—as, upon that supposition, my feelings may be tolerated. You will also meet with a number of sea-terms, which, if you don't understand, why, I cannot help you, as I am unable to give a sea description in any other words.

To begin then:—On the 2nd of August, 1780, we weighed and sailed for Port Royal, bound for Pensacola, having two store-ships under convoy, and to see safe in; then cruise off the Havana, and in the Gulf of Mexico, for six weeks. In a few days we made the two sandy islands, that look as if they had just risen out of the sea, or fallen from the sky; inhabited, nevertheless, by upwards of three hundred English, who get their bread by catching turtle and parrots, and raising vegetables, which they exchange with ships that pass, for clothing and a few of the luxuries of life, as rum, etc. About the 12th we arrived at Pensacola, without any thing remarkable happening except our catching a vast quantity of fish, sharks, dolphins, and bonettos. On the 13th sailed singly, and on the 14th had a very heavy gale of wind at north, right off the land, so that we soon left the sweet place, Pensacola, at a distance astern. We then looked into the Havana, saw a number of ships there, and knowing that some of them were bound round the bay, we cruised in the track: a fortnight, however, passed, and not a single ship have in sight to cheer our spirits. We then took a turn or two round the gulf, but not near enough to be seen from the shore. Vera Cruz we expected would have made us happy, but the same luck still continued; day followed day, and no sail. The dollar bag began to grow a little bulky, for everyone had lost two or three times, and no one had won: this was a small gambling party entered into by Sir Hyde and ourselves; every one put a dollar into a bag, and fixed on a day when we should see a sail, but no two persons were to name the same day, and whoever guessed right first was to have the bag.

Being now tired of our situation, and glad the cruise was almost out, for we found the navigation very dangerous, owing to unaccountable currents; we shaped our course for Cape Antonio. The next day the man at the mast head, at about one o'clock in the afternoon, called out: "A sail upon the weather bow! Ha! Ha! Mr. Spaniard, I think we have you at last. Turn out all hands! Make sail! All hands give chase!" There was scarcely any occasion for this order, for the sound of a sail being in sight flew like wild fire through the ship and every sail was set in an instant almost before the orders were given. A lieutenant at the mast head, with a spy glass, "What is she?" "A large ship studding athwart right before the wind. P-o-r-t! Keep her away! set the studding sails ready!" Up comes the little doctor, rubbing his hands; "Ha! ha! I have won the bag." "The devil take you and the bag; look, what's ahead will fill all our bags." Mast head again: "Two more sail on the larboard beam!" "Archer, go up, and see what you can make of them." "Upon deck there; I see a whole fleet of twenty sail coming right before the wind." "Confound the luck of it, this is some convoy or other, but we must try if we can pick some of them out." "Haul down the studding-sails! Luff! Bring her to the wind! Let us see what we can make of them."

About five we got pretty near them, and found them to be twenty-six sail of Spanish merchantmen, under convoy of three line of battle ships, one of which chased us; but when she found we were playing with her (for the old Phœnix had heels) she left chase, and joined the convoy; which they drew up into a lump, and placed themselves at the outside; but we still kept smelling about till after dark. O, for the Hector, the Albion, and a frigate, and we should take the whole fleet and convoy, worth some millions! About eight o'clock perceived three sail at some distance from the fleet; dashed in between them, and gave chase, and were happy to find they steered from the fleet. About twelve came up with a large ship of twenty-six guns. "Archer, every man to his quarters! Run the lower deck guns out, and light the ship up; show this fellow our force; it may prevent his firing into us and killing a man or two." No sooner said than done. "Hoa, the ship ahoy, lower all your sails down, and bring to instantly, or I'll sink you." Clatter, clatter, went the blocks, and away flew all their sails in proper confusion. "What ship is that?" "The Polly." "Whence came you?" "From Jamaica." "Where are you bound?" "To New York." "What ship is that?" "The Phœnix." Huzza, three times by the whole ship's company. An old grum fellow of a sailor standing close by me: "O, d—m your three cheers, we took you to be something else." Upon examination we found it to be as he reported, and that they had fallen in with the Spanish fleet that morning, and were chased the whole day, and that nothing saved them but our stepping in between; for the Spaniards took us for three consorts, and the Polly took the Phœnix for a Spanish frigate, till we hailed them. The other vessel in company was likewise bound to New York. Thus was I, from being worth thousands in idea, reduced to the old 4s. 6d. a day again: for the little doctor made the most prize money of us all that day, by winning the bag, which contained between thirty and forty dollars; but this is nothing to what we sailors sometimes undergo.

After parting company, we steered south-south-east, to go round Antonio, and so to Jamaica, (our cruise being out) with our fingers in our mouths, and all of us as green as you please. It happened to be my middle watch, and about three o'clock, when a man upon the forecastle bawls out: "Breakers ahead, and land upon the lee-bow;" I looked out, and it was so sure enough. "Ready about! Put the helm down! Helm a lee!" Sir Hyde hearing me put the ship about, jumped upon deck. "Archer, what's the matter? You are putting the ship about without my orders!" "Sir, 'tis time to go about! The ship is almost ashore, there's the land." "Good God so it is! Will the ship stay?" "Yes, Sir, I believe she will, if we don't make any confusion;

*she's all aback—forward now?"—"Well," says he, "work the ship,
I will not speak a single word." The ship stayed very well. "Then,
heave the lead! See what water we have!" "Three fathom." "Keep
the ship away, west-north-west."—"By the mark three." "This won't
do, Archer." "No, Sir, we had better haul more to the northward;
we came south-south-east, and had better steer north-north-west."
"Steady, and a quarter three." "This may do, as we deepen a little."
"By the deep four." "Very well, my lad, heave quick." "Five Fathom."
"That's a fine fellow! Another cast nimbly." "Quarter less eight."
"That will do, come, we shall get clear by and by."—"Mark under
water five." "What's that?" "Only five fathom, Sir." "Turn all hands
up, bring the ship to an anchor, boy!" "Are the anchors clear!" "In a
moment, Sir." "All clear!" "What water have you in the chains now!"
"Eight, half nine." "Keep fast the anchors till I call you." "Ay, ay, Sir,
all fast!" "I have no ground with this line." "How many fathoms have
you out? Pass along the deep-sea line!" "Ay, ay, Sir." "Come are you
all ready?" "All ready, Sir." "Heave away, watch! Watch! Bear away;
veer away, no ground Sir, with a hundred fathom." "That's clever,
come, Madam Phœnix, there is another squeak in you yet—all down
but the watch; secure the anchors again; heave the main-top-sail to
the mast; luff, and bring her to the wind!"*

*I told you, Madam, you should have a little sea-jargon: if you
can understand half of what is already said, I wonder at it, though it
is nothing to what is to come yet, when the old hurricane begins. As
soon as the ship was a little too rights, and all quiet again, Sir Hyde
came to me in the most friendly manner, the tears almost starting
from his eyes—"Archer, we ought all, to be much obliged to you for
the safety of the ship, and perhaps of ourselves. I am particularly so;
nothing but that instantaneous presence of mind and calmness saved
her; another ship's length and we should have been fast on shore; had
you been the least diffident, or made the least confusion, so as to make
the ship baulk in her stays, she must have been inevitably lost." "Sir,
you are very good, but I have done nothing that I suppose anybody
else would not have done, in the same situation. I did not turn all
the hands up, knowing the watch able to work the ship; besides, had
it spread immediately about the ship, that she was almost ashore, it*

*might have created a confusion that was better avoided." "Well,"
says he, "It is well indeed."*

*At daylight we found that the current had set us between the
Colorado Rocks and Cape Antonio, and that we could not have got
out any other way than we did; there was a chance, but Providence is
the best pilot. We had sunset that day twenty leagues to the south-east
of our reckoning by the current. After getting clear of this scrape,
we thought ourselves fortunate, and made sail for Jamaica, but
misfortune seemed to follow misfortune. The next night, my watch
upon deck too, we were overtaken by a squall, like a hurricane
while it lasted; for though I saw it coming, and prepared for it, yet,
when it took the ship, it roared, and laid her down so, that I thought
she would never get up again. However, by keeping her away, and
chewing up everything, she righted. The remainder of the night we
had very heavy squalls, and in the morning found the mainmast
sprung half the way through: one hundred and twenty-three leagues
to the leeward of Jamaica, the hurricane months coming on, the
head of the mainmast almost off, and at short allowance; well, we
must make the best of it. The mainmast was well fished, but we were
obliged to be very tender of carrying sail.*

*Nothing remarkable happened for ten days afterwards, when we
chased a Yankee man of war for six hours, but could not get near
enough to her before it was dark, to keep sight of her; so that we
lost her because unable to carry any sail on the mainmast. In about
twelve days more made the island of Jamaica, having weathered all
the squalls, and put into Montego Bay for water; so that we had a
strong party for kicking up a dust on shore, having found three men
of war lying there. Dancing, &c. &c. till two o'clock every morning;
little thinking what was to happen in four days' time: for out of the
four men of war that were there, not one was in being at the end of
that time, and not a soul alive but those left of our crew. Many of the
houses, where we had been so merry, were so completely destroyed,
that scarcely a vestige remained to mark where they stood. Thy works
are wonderful, O God! Praised be thy Holy Name!*

*September the 30th weighed; bound for Port Royal, round the
eastward of the island; the Barbados and Victor had sailed the day
before, and the Scarborough was to sail the next. Moderate weather*

greeted us until October the 2nd. Spoke to the Barbados off Port Antonio in the evening. At eleven at night it began to snuffle, with a monstrous heavy appearance from the eastward. Close reefed the top-sails. Sir Hyde sent for me: "What sort of weather have we, Archer!" "It blows a little, and has a very ugly look: if in any other quarter but this, I should say we were going to have a gale of wind." "Ay, it looks so very often here when there is no winds at all; however, don't hoist the top-sails till it clears a little, there is no trusting any country." At twelve I was relieved; the weather had the same rough look: however, they made sail upon her, but had a very dirty night. At eight in the morning I came up again, found it blowing hard from the east-north-east, with close-reefed top-sails upon the ship, and heavy squalls at times. Sir Hyde came upon deck: "Well, Archer, what do you think of it?" "O, Sir, 't is only a touch of the times, we shall have an observation at twelve o'clock; the clouds are beginning to break; it will clear up at noon, or else—blow very hard afterwards." "I wish it would clear up, but I doubt it much. I was once in a hurricane in the East Indies, and the beginning of it had much the same appearance as this. So take in the top-sails, we have plenty of sea-room."

At twelve, the gale still increasing, wore ship, to keep as near mid-channel between Jamaica and Cuba, as possible; at one the gale increasing still; at two, harder yet, it still blows harder! Reefed the courses, and furled them; brought to under a foul mizen stay-sail, head to the northward. In the evening no sign of the weather taking off, but every appearance of the storm increasing, prepared for a proper gale of wind; secured all the sails with spare gaskets; good rolling tackles upon the yards; squared the booms; saw the boats all made fast; new lashed the guns; double breeched the lower deckers; saw that the carpenters had the tarpawlings and battens all ready for hatchways; got the top-gallant-mast down upon the deck; jib-boom and sprit-sail-yard fore and aft; in fact everything we could think of to make a snug ship. The poor devils of birds now began to find the uproar in the elements, for numbers, both of sea and land kinds, came on board of us. I took notice of some, which happening to be to leeward, turned to windward, like a ship, tack and tack; for they could not fly against it. When they came over the ship they dashed themselves down upon the deck, without attempting to stir till picked up, and when let go again, they would not leave the ship, but endeavored to hide themselves from the wind.

At eight o'clock a hurricane; the sea roaring, but the wind still steady to a point; did not ship a spoonful of water. However, got the hatchways all secured, expecting what would be the consequence, should the wind shift; placed the carpenters by the mainmast, with broad axes, knowing, from experience, that at the moment you may want to cut it away to save the ship, an axe may not be found. Went to supper: bread, cheese, and porter. The purser frightened out of his wits about his bread bags; the two marine officers as white as sheets, not understanding the ship's working so much, and the noise of the lower deck guns; which, by this time, made a pretty screeching to people not used to it; it seemed as if the whole ship's side was going at each roll. Wooden, our carpenter, was all this time smoking his pipe and laughing at the doctor; the second lieutenant upon deck, and the third in his hammock.

At ten o'clock I thought to get a little sleep; came to look into my cot; it was full of water; for every seam, by the straining of the ship, had began to leak. Stretched myself, therefore, upon deck between two chests, and left orders to be called, should the least thing happen. At twelve a midshipman came to me: "Mr. Archer, we are just going to wear ship, Sir!" "O, very well, I'll be up directly, what sort of weather have you got?" "It blows a hurricane." Went upon deck, found Sir Hyde there. "It blows damned hard Archer." "It does indeed, Sir." "I don't know that I ever remember its blowing so hard before, but the ship makes a good weather of it upon this tack as she bows the sea; but we must wear her, as the wind has shifted to the south-east, and we were drawing right upon Cuba; so do you go forward, and have some hands stand by; loose the lee yard-arm of the fore-sail, and when she is right before the wind, whip the clue-garnet close up, and roll up the sail." "Sir! There is no canvass can stand against this a moment; if we attempt to lose him he will fly into rainbands in an instant, and we may lose three or four of our people; she'll wear by manning the fore shrouds." "No, I don't think she will." "I'll answer for it, Sir; I have seen it tried several times on the coast of America with success." "Well, try it; if she does not wear, we can only loose the fore-sail afterwards." This was a great

173

condescension from such a man as Sir Hyde. However, by sending about two hundred people into the fore-rigging, after a hard struggle, she wore; found she did not make so good weather on this tack as on the other; for as the sea began to run across, she had not time to rise from one sea before another lashed against her. Began to think we should lose our masts, as the ship lay very much along, by the pressure of the wind constantly upon the yards and masts alone: for the poor mizen-stay-sail had gone in shreds long before, and the sails began to fly from the yards through the gaskets into coach whips. My God! To think that the wind could have such force!

Sir Hyde now sent me to see what was the matter between decks, as there was a good deal of noise. As soon as I was below, one of the Marine officers calls out: "Good God Mr. Archer, we are sinking, the water is up to the bottom of my cot." "Pooh, pooh! as long as it is not over your mouth, you are well off; what the devil do you make this noise for?" I found there was some water between decks, but nothing to be alarmed at; scuttled the deck, and let it run into the well—found she made a good deal of water through the sides and decks; turned the watch below to the pumps, though only two feet of water in the well; but expected to be kept constantly at work now, as the ship labored much, with scarcely a part of her above water but the quarter-deck, and that but seldom "Come, pump away, my boys. Carpenters, get the weather chain-pump rigged." "All ready, Sir." "Then man it and keep both pumps going."

At two o'clock the chain-pump was choked; set the carpenters at work to clear it; the two head pumps at work upon deck; the ship gained on us while our chain-pumps were idle; in a quarter of an hour they were at work again, and we began to gain upon her. While I was standing at the pumps, cheering the people, the carpenter's mate came running to me with a face as long as my arm: "O, Sir! The ship has sprung a leak in the gunner's room." "Go, then, and tell the carpenter to come to me, but don't speak a word to anyone else." "Mr. Goodinoh, I am told there is a leak in the gunner's room; go and see what the matter is, but don't alarm anybody, and come and make your report privately to me." In a short time he returned: "Sir, there's nothing there, 'tis only the water washing up between the timbers that this booby has taken for a leak." "O, very well; go upon deck and see if you can keep any of the water from washing down below." "Sir, I have had four people constantly keeping the hatchways secure, but there is such a weight of water upon the deck that nobody can stand it when the ship rolls." The gunner soon afterwards came to me: "Mr. Archer, I should be glad if you would step this way into the magazine for a moment:" I thought some damned thing was the matter, and ran directly: "Well, what is the matter here?" "The ground-tier of powder is spoiled, and I want to show you that it is not out of carelessness in stowing it, for no powder in the world could be better stowed. Now, Sir, what am I to do? If you don't speak to Sir Hyde, he will be angry with me." I could not forbear smiling to see how easy he took the danger of the ship, and said to him: "Let us shake off this gale of wind first, and talk of the damaged powder afterwards."

At four we had gained upon the ship a little, and I went upon deck, it being my watch. The second lieutenant relieved me at the pumps. Who can attempt to describe the appearance of things upon deck? If I was to write for ever I could not give you an idea of it—a total darkness all above, the sea on fire, running as it were in Alps, or Peaks of Teneriffe; (mountains are too common an idea); the wind roaring louder than thunder, (absolutely no flight of imagination), the whole made more terrible, if possible, by a very uncommon kind of blue lightning; the poor ship very much pressed, yet doing what she could, shaking her sides, and groaning at every stroke. Sir Hyde upon deck lashed to windward! I soon lashed myself alongside of him, and told him the situation of things below, saying the ship did not make more water than might be expected in such weather, and that I was only afraid of a gun breaking loose. "I am not in the least afraid of that; I have commanded her six years, and have had many a gale of wind in her; so that her iron work, which always gives way first, is pretty well tried. Hold fast! That was an ugly sea; we must lower the yards, I believe, Archer; the ship is much pressed." "If we attempt it, Sir, we shall lose them, for a man aloft can do nothing; besides their being down would ease the ship very little; the mainmast is a sprung mast; I wish it was overboard without carrying anything else along with it; but that can soon be done, the gale cannot last forever; 'twill soon be daylight now." Found by the master's watch that it was five o'clock, though but a little after four by ours; glad it was so near daylight, and looked for it with much anxiety. Cuba, thou art much in our way! Another ugly sea: sent a midshipman to bring news from the pumps: the ship was gaining on them very much, for they had broken one of their chains, but it was almost mended again. News from the pump again. "She still gains! A heavy lee!" Back-water from leeward, half-way up the quarter-deck; filled one of the cutters upon the booms, and tore her all to pieces; the ship lying almost on her beam ends, and not attempting to right again. Word from below that the ship still gained on them, as they could not stand to the pumps, she lay so much along. I said to Sir Hyde: "This is no time, Sir, to think of saving the masts, shall we cut the mainmast away?" "Ay! As fast as you can." I accordingly went into the weather chains with a pole-axe, to cut away the lanyards; the boatswain went to leeward, and the carpenters stood by the mast. We were all ready, when a very violent sea broke right on board of us, carried everything upon deck away, filled the ship with water, the main and mizen masts went, the ship righted, but was in the last struggle of sinking under us.

As soon as we could shake our heads above water, Sir Hyde exclaimed: "We are gone, at last, Archer! Foundered at sea!" "Yes, Sir, farewell, and the Lord have mercy upon us!" I then turned about to look forward at the ship; and thought she was struggling to get rid of some of the water; but all in vain, she was almost full below "Almighty God! I thank thee, that now I am leaving this world, which I have always considered as only a passage to a better, I die with a full hope of the mercies, through the merits of Jesus Christ, thy son, our Saviour!" I then felt sorry that I could swim, as by that means I might be a quarter of an hour longer dying than a man who could not, and it is impossible to divest ourselves of a wish to preserve life. At the end of these reflections I thought I heard the ship thump and grinding under our feet; it was so. "Sir, the ship is ashore!" "What do you say?" "The ship is ashore, and we may save ourselves yet!" By this time the quarter-deck was full of men who had come up from below; and 'the Lord have mercy upon us,' flying about from all quarters. The ship now made everybody sensible that she was ashore, for every stroke threatened a total dissolution of her whole frame; found she was stern ashore, and the bow broke the sea a good deal, though it was washing clean over at every stroke. Sir Hyde cried out:

"Keep to the quarter-deck, my lads, when she goes to pieces, it is your best chance!" Providentially got the foremast cut away, that she might not pay round broad-side. Lost five men cutting away the foremast, by the breaking of a sea on board just as the mast went. That was nothing; everyone expected it would be his own fate next; looked for daybreak with the greatest impatience. At last it came; but what a scene did it show us! The ship upon a bed of rocks, mountains of them on one side, and Cordilleras of water on the other; our poor ship grinding and crying out at every stroke between them; going away by piecemeal. However, to show the unaccountable workings of Providence, that which often appears to be the greatest evil, proved to be the greatest good! That unmerciful sea lifted and beat us up so high among the rocks, that at last the ship scarcely moved. She was very strong, and did not go to pieces at the first thumping, though her decks tumbled in. We found afterwards that she had beaten over a ledge of rocks, almost a quarter of a mile in extent beyond us, where, if she had struck, every soul of us must have perished.

I now began to think of getting on shore, so stripped off my coat and shoes for a swim, and looked for a line to carry the end with me. Luckily could not find one, which gave me time for recollection. "This won't do for me, to be the first man out of the ship, and first lieutenant; we may get to England again, and people may think I paid a great deal of attention to myself and did not care for anybody else. No, that won't do; instead of being the first, I'll see every man, sick and well, out of her before me." I now thought there was no probability of the ship's soon going to pieces, therefore had not a thought of instant death: took a look round with a kind of philosophic eye, to see how the same situation affected my companions, and was surprised to find the most swaggering, swearing bullies in fine weather, now the most pitiful wretches on earth, when death appeared before them. However, two got safe; by which means, with a line, we got a hawser on shore, and made fast to the rocks, upon which many ventured and arrived safe. There were some sick and wounded on board, who could not avail themselves of this method; we, therefore, got a spare top-sail-yard from the chains and placed one end ashore and the other on the cabin-window, so that most of the sick got ashore this way.

As I had determined, so I was the last man out of the ship; this was about ten o'clock. The gale now began to break. Sir Hyde came to me, and taking me by the hand was so affected that he was scarcely able to speak "Archer, I am happy beyond expression, to see you on shore, but look at our poor Phœnix!" I turned about, but could not say a single word, being too full: my mind had been too intensely occupied before; but everything now rushed upon me at once, so that I could not contain myself, and I indulged for a full quarter of an hour in tears. By twelve it was pretty moderate; got some nails on shore and made tents; found great quantities of fish driven up by the sea into the holes of the rocks; knocked up a fire, and had a most comfortable dinner. In the afternoon made a stage from the cabin-windows to the rocks, and got out some provisions and water, lest the ship should go to pieces, in which case we must all have perished of hunger and thirst; for we were upon a desolate part of the coast, and under a rocky mountain, that could not supply us with a single drop of water.

Slept comfortably this night and the next day, the idea of death vanishing by degrees, the prospect of being prisoners, during the war, at the Havana, and walking three hundred miles to it through the woods, was rather unpleasant. However, to save life for the present, we employed this day in getting more provisions and water on shore, which was not an easy matter, on account of decks, guns and rubbish, and ten feet water that lay over them. In the evening I proposed to Sir Hyde to repair the remains of the only boat left, and to venture in her to Jamaica myself; and in case I arrived safe, to bring vessels to take them all off; a proposal worthy of consideration. It was, next day, agreed to; therefore got the cutter on shore, and set the carpenters to work on her; in two days she was ready, and at four o'clock in the afternoon I embarked with four volunteers and a fortnight's provision, hoisted English colors as we put off from the shore, and received three cheers from the lads left behind, which we returned, and set sail with a light heart; having not the least doubt, that, with God's assistance, we should come and bring them all off. Had a very squally night, and a very leaky boat, so as to keep two buckets constantly bailing. Steered her myself the whole night by the stars, and in the morning saw the coast of Jamaica distant twelve leagues. At eight in the evening arrived at Montego Bay.

I must now begin to leave off, particularly as I have but half an hour to conclude; else my pretty little short letter will lose its passage, which I should not like, after being ten days, at different times, writing it, beating up with the convoy to the northward, which is a reason that this epistle will never read well; as I never set down with a proper disposition to go on with it; but as I knew something of the kind would please you, I was resolved to finish it; yet it will not bear an overhaul; so don't expose your son's nonsense. But to proceed—I instantly sent off an express to the admiral, another to the Porcupine man of war, and went myself to Martha Bray to get vessels; for all their vessels here, as well as many of their houses, were gone to Moco. Got three small vessels, and set out back again to Cuba, where I arrived the fourth day after leaving my companions. I thought the ship's crew would have devoured me on my landing; they presently whisked me up on their shoulders and carried me to the tent where Sir Hyde was. I must omit many little occurrences that happened on shore, for want of time; but I shall have a number of stories to tell when I get alongside of you; and the next time I visit you I shall not be in such a hurry to quit you as I was the last, for then I hoped my nest would have been pretty well feathered:—But my tale is forgotten.

I found the Porcupine had arrived that day, and the lads had built a boat almost ready for launching, that would hold fifty of them, which was intended for another trial, in case I had foundered. Next day embarked all our people that were left, amounting to two hundred and fifty; for some had died of their wounds they received in getting on shore; others of drinking rum, and others had straggled into the country.—All our vessels were so full of people, that we could not take away the few clothes that were saved from the wreck; but that was a trifle since we had preserved our lives and liberty. To make short of my story, we all arrived safe at Montego Bay, and shortly after at Port Royal, in the Janus, which was sent on purpose for us, and were all honorably acquitted for the loss of the ship. I was made admiral's aide-de-camp, and a little time afterwards sent down to St. Juan's as captain of the Resource, to bring what were left of the poor

179

devils to Blue Fields, on the Mosquito Shore, and then to Jamaica, where they arrived after three month's absence, and without a prize, though I looked out hard off Porto Bello and Carthagena. Found in my absence that I had been appointed captain of the Tobago, where I remain His Majesty's most true and faithful servant, and my dear mother's most dutiful son.[1]

——ARCHER

CHAPTER ELEVEN
THE IMPACT OF THE GREAT HURRICANE OF 1780 ON THE SUGAR INDUSTRY OF THE CARIBBEAN

In the 1700's and 1800's, the English sugar islands: Barbados, St. Kitts, Antigua, Montserrat, Nevis and Jamaica, began to boil over with great excitement as there were suddenly great fortunes to be made. All of Europe including England demanded more of the highly prized West Indian sugar. Many of the European population drank tea on a regular basis and sugar was used exclusively as a sweetener; as such, prices for West Indian sugar increased every year. As a result, every island stripped its slopes of all growing things and replaced it with the highly prized crop of sugarcane. Plantation owners, dizzy with this new found wealth, left the island plantation homes, their fields, their hordes of slaves, to overseers and agents, and squandered their money away on the extravagances of Paris, Bath and London. The only real menace to all this was the ferocity of these powerful West Indian hurricanes. Hurricanes made kindling of plantation houses and slave huts, tore off the roofs of sugar works, even leveled masonry walls. Hurricanes waves undermined wharfs, warehouses and waterside streets, cut great gullies in fertile slopes and washed the good soil into the sea. Hurricanes overturned sugar ships in these harbours, leaching the sugar out of the hogsheads barrels. Hurricanes sank ships carrying sugar to England or bringing needed supplies to the islanders: New England salt herring and Carolina rice for slave food, cheap Osnaburg cloth for slave clothing, navy cutlasses for cane knives, sugar mill equipment, even the oxen for the carts and the mules for turning the grinding mills, windmill parts, copper boilers, sugar mill machinery, barrel starves, building material, shingles, bricks, lime for the fields, and all the luxuries demanded by the planters and their families.

The sugarcane plant was the main crop produced on the numerous plantations throughout the Caribbean through the 18th, 19th and 20th centuries. Almost every island was covered with sugar plantations and mills for refining the cane for its plantation properties. The main source of labour was African slaves. These plantations produced eighty to ninety percent of the sugar consumed in Western Europe. In the 1700's and 1800's sugar dominated Martinique, Grenada, Saint Croix, Jamaica, Barbados, the Leeward Islands, Dominica, Santo Domingo (modern day Haiti and the Dominican Republic), Cuba, Guyana and many other islands that were run by French or British land owners. On the British islands, sugar was the only crop grown, and on the French Islands (Martinique and Guadeloupe), sugar was their most important crop. The sugar was best grown on land that was near the coast where the soil was naturally yellow and fertile. In the mid 1600's, sugarcane was brought into British West Indies by the Dutch from Brazil. Upon landing in Barbados and other islands, they immediately urged local farmers to change their main crops from cotton and tobacco to sugarcane. With depressed prices of cotton and tobacco due mainly to stiff competition from the North American colonies, the farmers switched, leading to an instant boom in the Caribbean economies. Sugar was quickly snapped up by the British which used the sugar for cakes, and sweetener in teas.

During the colonial period, the arrival of the sugar culture in the Caribbean significantly changed the society by not only dramatically increasing the ratio of slaves to free men, but also the average size of the slave plantation. Early sugar plantations had an extensive use of slaves because sugar was considered a cash crop that exhibits economies of scale in cultivation, and it was most efficiently grown on large plantations with a large number of workers. As a result, slaves were imported from Africa to work on the sugar plantations.

For example, before 1650, more than three-quarters of the island's population was white. In 1680, the median size of a plantation in Barbados had increased to about 60% slaves. Over the decades, the sugar plantations became larger and larger. In 1832, the median plantation in Jamaica had about 150 slaves, and nearly one of every four bondsmen lived on units that had at least 250 slaves.

For about the next one hundred years Barbados remained the richest of all the European colonies in the Caribbean region due in part by its rich fertile soil and abundant supply of rainfall. The prosperity in the colony remained regionally unmatched until sugar cane production grew in geographically larger countries such as Hispaniola, Jamaica and elsewhere. As part of the mass sugar production, the process gave rise to other related commodities such as rum, molasses, and Falernum. The West India Interest was formed in the 1740s when the British merchants joined with the West Indian sugar planters. The British and West Indies shared profits and needs. This organization was the first sugar trading organization which had a large voice in parliament. In the 1740s, Jamaica and Haiti became the world's main sugar producers. They increased the production by using an irrigation system that the French engineers built and an abundant supply of African slave labour. The engineers also built reservoirs, diversion dams, levees, aqueducts and canals. In addition, they improved their mills and used varieties of cane and grasses.

Boiling houses in the 17th through 19th centuries converted sugarcane juice into raw sugar. These houses were attached to sugar plantations in the colonies of the Caribbean. Slaves often ran the boiling process normally under very poor conditions. Made of cut stone, rectangular boxes of brick or stone served as furnaces with an opening at the bottom to stoke the fire and remove ashes. At the top of each furnace were up to seven copper kettles or boilers, each one smaller and hotter than the previous one. The process of extracting the cane juice began in the largest kettle. The juice was then heated and lime added to remove the impurities from it. The juice was then skimmed and then channeled to successively smaller kettles. The last kettle, which was called the 'teache', was where the cane juice became syrup. The next step was a cooling trough, where the sugar crystals hardened around a sticky core of molasses. As it dried, molasses dripped out, which slaves collected for distilling it into rum. Therefore, sugar planters profited from both the sale of sugar and its by-product molasses. This raw sugar was then shoveled from the cooling trough into hogsheads (wooden barrels), and from there into the curing house.

Christopher Columbus first brought sugarcane plant during his second voyage to the Americas, initially to the island of Hispaniola. In the early colonial times, sugar formed one side of the triangular trade of the New World, raw materials, European manufactures, and African slaves. France found its sugarcane islands so valuable that it effectively traded its portion of Canada, famously dubbed "a few acres of snow," to Britain for their return of Guadeloupe, Martinique and St. Lucia at the end of the *"Seven Years War."* The Dutch similarly kept Suriname, a sugar colony in South America, instead of seeking the return of the New Netherlands (New York). Cuban sugarcane produced sugar that received price supports from and a guaranteed market in Russia; the dissolution of that country forced the closure of most of Cuba's sugar industry. Today, sugarcane remains an important part of the economies of Belize, Barbados, Haiti, the Dominican Republic, Guadeloupe, Jamaica, and other islands.

Hurricanes also caused extensive damage to the elaborate infrastructure needed to grow and process the crops in the Caribbean. Sugar plantations, with their windmills, boiling houses, and other buildings were particularly vulnerable. For example, a hurricane in 1733 on the island of Montserrat destroyed thirty of the thirty six windmills used in the production of sugar on that island. Hurricanes routinely caused significant damage to the sugar plantations of the Caribbean by significantly reducing production while requiring additional expenditures to purchase provisions and supplies, rebuild damaged buildings, and replace equipment and possibly slave labourers killed during the storm. Most planters often survived these economic shocks, often with the help of credit provided by English merchants or local lenders, but at times, particularly in the sugar islands, hurricanes were the breaking point for marginal or heavily indebted planters, forcing them to give up their properties. Such bankruptcies, in turn, helped consolidate sugar estates into the hands of the richest planters or later in the eighteenth century, resulted in the transfer of estates to the English merchant creditors.

Planters took what steps they could to reduce the risk from hurricanes, but their efforts provided only minimal protection. Nevertheless, despite the risks associated with the storms and the possibility of having the entire plantation devastated by the storm, the potential profits from sugar production kept the West Indian planter rebuilding in the wake of the storms. Hurricanes did not transform the plantation economy of the Caribbean, but they did shape the experience of plantership throughout the seventeenth and eighteenth centuries. The economic consequences of hurricanes in the Greater Caribbean varied over time. Storms in the early years of settlement terrified colonists and devastated their homes and crops, but the relative lack of physical development limited the overall economic damage.

In addition, hurricanes also destroyed ships and port facilities, both essential for shipping crops to markets throughout the Atlantic. For example, in the 1675 hurricane on the island of Barbados, twelve ships in Bridgetown's harbour some of which were laden with sugar were driven ashore and broken to pieces. Similarly, a hurricane in 1712 sank numerous vessels in Kingston's harbour laden with sugar and other supplies. Some hurricanes even claimed the lives of slaves held on ships before they were unloaded and sold. Some two hundred slaves perished in 1722 when a hurricane sank the slave ship *Kingston* that had only recently arrived in Jamaica. Planters' letters, officials' correspondence, and published travel narratives all provide vivid descriptions of the destruction bought on by hurricanes in the seventeenth and eighteenth centuries, but they reveal few specifics about their effects on the plantation production and the planters' profits.

Assessing the economic consequences of hurricanes is difficult, especially for the seventeenth century, when systematic record keeping was less developed and hurricanes often destroyed plantation accounts and official documents. The Governor of the Leeward Islands, for example, informed London officials in 1676 that he could not furnish good statistics on Nevis's economic and demographic situation because only a few records remained after several hurricanes and other calamities. More reliable and complete records exist for the eighteenth century, and aggregate production statistics provide some evidence of the effects of hurricanes on the sugar plantation operations. Export figures for the sugar colonies in 1698-1775 indicated significant drops in production in the year after a major storm struck a particular island. Exports of muscovado sugar from Jamaica, for example, declined from 257,422 cwt to 138,424 cwt of the 1722 hurricane. It then rose slightly to 207,841 cwt in 1724 before regaining pre-hurricane levels in 1725. The 1733 hurricane affected all of the Leeward Islands, but production appeared most disrupted in Nevis and Antigua. In the former, production fell by almost 50 percent, from 70,132 cwt to 37,709 cwt, and exports remained low for several years. Antiguan exports fell from 208,977 cwt in 1733 to 96,172 cwt in 1734, although planters there rebounded by 1735. Jamaica and Barbados struggled for several years to recover from the hurricanes in early October 1780. Sugar production, already starting to significantly decrease as a result of the American Revolution, dropped even further in 1781, and sugar imports into England from the islands did not return to pre-hurricane levels until 1783. Furthermore, rum exports provided additional proof for the loss of agricultural productivity. Barbados shipped 3,315 hogsheads to England.[1]

Economic losses from hurricanes increased as colonists made more permanent and more valuable agricultural investments. The development of sugar production in the West Indies created new economic and material conditions that generated great wealth but also made the colonists' fortunes increasingly vulnerable to hurricanes. Sugar was not the only crop grown in the colonies. Some islands, notably Jamaica, produced coffee, ginger, and cotton for export, but it was sugar which significantly dominated the economy and accounted for a disproportionate amount of the planters' wealth. For example, in one Jamaican parish in the middle of the eighteenth century, sugar and rum generated about 85% of the total revenue earned from exports. However, after these devastating hurricanes in 1780, planters were also encouraged to plant provisional root crops such as, yams, cassava and potatoes, which were less likely to be damaged or destroyed during a hurricane. The reliance on plantains proved to be very disastrous to the plantation economies of the West

Indies during these storms in 1780, and after 1780, many planters; especially in Jamaica and Barbados were determined not to repeat that mistake.

Hurricanes sank slave ships, reducing the supply from Africa of the slave labour necessary for every detail of sugar production, and increasing the profits in slave dealing made by the English Royal African Company and its noble shareholders. In fact, everything about the production of sugar was dependent on hurricanes. Hurricanes set the schedule for the entire year. Planting began after October at the end of the hurricane season and continued until Christmas. Then the slaves were allowed their brief riotous holiday. The fourteen months the sugarcane was ripe for cutting in January. It was carried to heavy rollers of the mill, turned by oxen or mules, waterpower or windmills as in Barbados. The clear juice ran along a wooden trough to the coppers of the boiling house, over fires hot with cane trash. Boiling went on day and night until the tense moment when the skilled Negro sugar boiler thrust his finger and thumb into the seething mass. If it threaded right, the sugar was made. The cooled raw crystals, bright yellow or straw coloured, gray or low brown, were shoveled into hogsheads, tierces or small barrels to be shipped to England.

The sugar markets at Bristol and London were highly risky and were quite a gamble. The very rumors of wars, earthquakes, slave insurrections, hurricanes in one island or another, set the prices see-sawing. This was because the prices varied as the quality of sugar varied from year to year, according to the demands of grocers for Christmas, of refiners, and of the raw-sugar dealers who sold great stocks to northern Europe. The British Government grew rich on heavy sugar duties. The first sugar shipped in spring, when the English ships raced out and back for the first sales, got the best prices. But the best sugars might be deteriorated by the rough voyage on the edge of an early July hurricane. Sugars that were left standing too long in Bristol warehouses, as the molasses drained off, fetched inferior prices. As a general rule, prices were high for fine sugars, less for middling or low sugars. But gluts or shortages made a big difference. The long green fields of Barbados, crawled over by oxcarts, made very fine sugars, and excellent prices, if a hurricane did not ruin them or there were too many Demerara sugars unloaded at Bristol. St Kitts from the sea halfway up the wooded ridge of Mt. Misery produced good muscovado sugars but so did other islands. If one island was impacted by a hurricane then the other unaffected islands were made rich by their sugar crop.

The loss of valuable crops to hurricanes often had significant short-term consequences for the supply and price of sugar in the British Atlantic marketplace, depending on the extent of damage to individual colonies and the number of colonies struck during any given year. The potential disruption from a hurricane and its effects on prices meant that correspondents in England anxiously awaited word from the colonies each fall. The London sugar market fluctuated widely upon news of a hurricane in the Leeward Islands or Jamaica (the largest producers of muscovado sugar), often producing a sudden rise of between two and ten shillings per hundredweight, and timely information could mean significant profits for merchants selling sugar to the metropolitan grocers and refiners. Even rumors of a hurricane, and the corresponding threat of a small crop, could influence European markets and prices. News of a hurricane in Carolina spread around London in the fall of 1743, prompting anxious merchants to prepare for shortages and high prices. The rumor soon proved false.

High prices for crops, however, did not always offset the losses caused by the storms. In spite of high prices, individual West Indian planters often found themselves unable to salvage enough sugar from a storm-damaged crop to provide much income. The managers of the Codrington College plantations in Barbados reported that in 1781 that the hurricane the previous year had resulted in a much smaller sugar crop that was very inadequate to pay for the wages of the workers and the expenses of the plantation. One significant reason was that the costs for plantation supplies rose enormously along with the prices for staple goods, since the storms destroyed not only the sugar crop but also the essential food supply and building materials. Furthermore, this storm in 1780 destroyed provision crops as readily as they laid waste to the sugar fields, creating widespread food shortages. Plantains, a major source of food for slaves in Barbados and other islands were especially hard hit by this storm. The delicate trees and their fruits suffered significant damage or uprooted them completely in the storm. Provisions were very scarce and expensive on Barbados in the aftermath of the 1780 storm. This was true throughout the Caribbean and North America after a major hurricane had passed. For example, in effort to keep prices of essential goods down after the 1752 hurricane, the South Carolina Assembly passed a law forbidding the export of corn, peas, and other foods from the colony, and officials sought provisions from northern merchants to help keep supplies plentiful and prices reasonable.

Although the effect of hurricanes differed from plantation to plantation and from storm to storm, a case study approach provides insights on the losses caused by the storms and the specific issues planters encountered as they went about rebuilding and reestablishing their operations. Excellent documentation exists for the 'Great Hurricane of 1780' which struck Barbados in October 1780, which allows for this kind of analysis. As it name indicates, the 1780 storm was very intense, but the issues confronting planters were common in the wake of storms throughout the period. The Great Hurricane struck on Tuesday, October 10, 1780, and inflicted widespread and horrifying destruction on the island. The *Barbados Mercury* reported that "in most plantations all the buildings, the sugar mills excepted, are level with the earth, and that there is not a single estate in the island which has entirely escaped the violence of the tempest." In the after effects of the storm, officials ordered a survey of individual parishes to determine losses. The findings were amazing: the hurricane killed over two thousand slaves and six thousand head of cattle and caused total property damage of more than £1,300,000 currency.

Wayne Neely

Record of Losses Sustained in Barbados from the Great Hurricane of 1780 on a Parish by Parish Basis:

Parish:	Slaves Killed:	Cattle Killed:	Total Damages Sustained:
St. George's	128	934	£102,282
St. James's	108	514	£100,765
St. Thomas's	84	650	£104,115
St. Andrew's	47	325	£66,656
St. Joseph's	63	343	£61,0171
St. Peter's	48	614	£74,671
St. Lucy's	33	335	£28,784
St. John's	49	260	£61,522
St. Philip's	180	463	£116,011
St. Michael's	916	834	£412,284
Christ Church	377	1,334	£192,398
Total	2,033	6,606	£1,320,564

Sources: Hurricanes and Society in the British Greater Caribbean, 1624-1783-Matthew Mulcahy Pg 77...Sheila Lambert, ed., House of Commons Sessional Papers of the Eighteenth Century: Report of the Lords of Trade on the Slave Trade, 1789, Wilmington, DE, 1975, pgs 69:296...Barbados Department of Archives.

Only one parish report, from St. Georges's has survived, but it provides a significant view of the losses planters suffered. Two hundred and seventy-six individuals filed claims for damages totaling £99,864. Planters with large operations sustained the greatest losses. Francis Bell lost three slaves and thirty head of cattle (worth £540), had £110 worth of furniture and clothing destroyed, and reported damages of £3,585 to his buildings and crops. John Prettejohn claimed losses of £7,000, including twelve slaves. Benjamin Gittens lost one slave, several cattle, and almost £3,000 worth of buildings and crops. The enumerator grouped together the largest planters with the greatest losses, and these thirty estates (11 percent of the total 276 claims) reported damages of £76,150, 76 percent of the total losses in the parish. The average loss for these larger planters was £2,538. Among the remaining 246 residents, the average loss was smaller, only £96. Thirty-eight individuals (15 %) in this group reported the death of slaves, as opposed to sixteen (53%) of the first group. Many smaller planters reported the death of one or more slaves, but they may have represented the planter's entire workforce. Others lost cattle, equipment, and houses that otherwise may have constituted their entire estates and these losses contributed significantly to the island's great debt after the storm. Without inventories or tax lists, which do not exist for the parish, it is difficult to measure the extent of the losses compared to the overall estates of these individuals, but many colonists may have lost their most valuable property or had it severely damaged, and it is certain that most of them encountered great difficulties in the aftermath of the storm.

Records from individual plantations in Barbados give an even clearer picture of the hurricane's economic consequences. For example, Turners Hall plantation, in St. Andrew's parish on the island's windward coast, was owned by an absentee planter, William FitzHerbert (later Sir William) of Derbyshire. The estate suffered considerable damage from the 1780 disaster. When a new plantation overseer, Richard Gill, arrived in 1781, the effects of the storm still remained quite noticeable. Richard Gill wrote to FitzHerbert, that the sad appearance of the citizens after the storm made it quite difficult to describe. Almost every building on this estate suffered significant damage. The hurricane destroyed the curing house, rum house, liquor house, and the trash house beyond repair and reduced other structures to their foundations. The boiling house was severely damaged, and its roof was blown away. The sugar mill sustained the most serious structural damage. Furthermore, the plantation 'sick house' and mule pen were badly damaged.

The storm destroyed several hundred pots of clayed sugar stored in the curing house, valued at £300, but of greater concern was the state of canes in the fields. Richard Gill reported that in many of the fields many of the first and second generation of canes were greatly affected by the storm. In addition, he reported that no slaves died during the storm but many of them died in the ensuing months from food shortages and disease caused by the storm's lingering effects. He estimated that the overall loss on the plantation by the storm was well over £4,000.(see table below)

Wayne Neely

DAMAGES AND LOSSES SUSTAINED BY THE GREAT HURRICANE OF 1780 ON THE TURNER HALL PLANTATION:

Item:	Value:
Old curing house	£200.00
Rum house	£100.00
Liquor house	£150.00
Trash house	£100.00
Dwelling house(repairs)	£50.00
Mason's work	£60.00
House carpenter and cooper	£75.00
Nails	£55.00
Timber(cut from woods)	£200.00
Timber and arm bought for mill	£22.10
Mill carpenter	£80.00
Plumber	£10.00
Braisare	£20.00
Blacksmith's account	£40.00
Cattle (number =7)	£54.00
Sheep (number =3)	£10.05
Mules (number =2)	£50.00
Corn	£68.15
Yams	£30.00
Plantains	£100.00
Peas	£80.00
Canes	£1,500.00
Labour (workmen)	£115.00
Food, rum, sugar for workmen	£50.00
Sugar lost	£300.00
Sugar pots destroyed (number = 400)	£67.10
Drips (number = 300)	£28.7.6
Tiles	£250.00
New curing house repairs	£250.00
Rum and molasses lost	£50.00
Wood injured	£200.00
Total:	£4,306.7.6*

Sources: Hurricanes and Society in the British Greater Caribbean, 1624-1783-Matthew Mulcahy Pg 79, FitzHerbert Papers, ME 20755…Barbados Department of Archives.

*Actual amount adds up to £4364.

Gill's assessment of the situation proved to be very accurate because sugar and rum production on the plantation decreased significantly for two years after the passage of the storm in 1780. While production dropped, expenses on the other hand rose significantly in 1780 and 1781 for timber and skilled labourers to repair buildings and extra food for slaves, among other things. The cost for these essentials increased dramatically after the storm. Well over £150 was used to buy food for the slaves and over £500 was used to repair the buildings on the plantation. Overall, the impact of the hurricane and the costs associated with rebuilding resulted in two back to back years of losses for the plantation.

TURNERS HALL PLANTATION ACCOUNT ABSTRACTS, 1778-1783:

Year:	Provisions:	Real Expenses*:	Income:	Profit(+)/Loss(-):
1778	263.16.2	£1,337.5.8	£3,713.19.10	+£2,376.14.2
1779	255.13.2	£1,329.18.3	£3,284.3.5	+£1,954.5.2
1780	353.0.4	£1,817.17.11[oo]	£2,691.9.5	+873.11.6
1781[a]	317.2.7	£1,787.10.11	£657.4.10	-£1,130.6.1
1782 [a]	224.6.5	£961.19.9	£956.18.8	-£5.1
1783	320.5.11	£1,364.6.5	£4,393.13.8	+£3,029.7.3

Sources: *Hurricanes and Society in the British Greater Caribbean, 1624-1783*-Matthew Mulcahy Pg 80...*Abstract of Accounts, FitzHerbert Papers*, ME 20688-20693.
* Includes provisions.

[oo]Includes purchase of seven slaves (£224) and loss of £300 worth of sugar.

+Notice the significant losses sustained after the Great Hurricane of 1780 in the following years of 1781 and 1782.

It is important to note here that other planters sustained similar losses. For example, William Senhouse was a relative newcomer to Barbados in 1780. He arrived on the island only a few years earlier with a commission as a Surveyor-General for Barbados and the Leeward Islands. In 1774 he bought the Grove Plantation in St. Philip's Parish and its 109 slaves for £18,000. Senhouse found the plantation in St. Philip's to be in a deplorable state. As a result, he spent a large sum repairing, improving and bringing it up to an expectable standard so as to make a worthwhile profit. Some of the problems he encountered were drought, excessive amounts of sugar ants, low productivity, and high plantation maintenance. Senhouse experienced a significant production drop in 1780 and this was due almost exclusively to the October hurricane but it must be noted here to that this drop was also associated to the occurrence of the sugar ants which also ate the cane. As the hurricane was devastating the island on October 10, Senhouse and his family fled from the falling debris of their residence and took up shelter in the buttery where they rode out the remainder of the storm.

Emerging the next morning to take a look at the damage, William Senhouse reported that the storm devastated the dwelling house, boiling house, curing house, corn house, and slaves' houses, along with most other structures on the plantation. Two horses, nineteen sheep, and three more would die in the coming weeks after this storm. Senhouse estimated that the total damage sustained to the plantation was £2,448, with £100 for slaves, £418 for animals, £500 for corn and canes, £770 for plantation buildings, and £660 for the dwelling house and furnishings. However, after the shock of the hurricane had passed, Senhouse and his slaves began the huge rebuilding efforts. These slaves on William Senhouse's Barbados plantation had a massive amount of work to do after this Great Hurricane of 1780. They were engaged in the work of burying the dead human bodies and dead animals, salvaging what provisions they could, and planting a new crop of corn and plantain. William Senhouse reported that on his plantation after the corns were planted, heavy rains washed away the seeds in both November and December so he was forced to replant the corn seeds at least four times. Even if the weather had cooperated, it took several months for these crops to mature and in the case of plantains it took several years. The next thing they did was to rebuild the sugar compound. Senhouse reported only £130 in income in 1781; on the other hand, his expenses skyrocketed to well over £1000. Sugar production levels increased in 1781, but his profits remained low, and the plantation lost money for more than three years. However, it was only in 1785 that the plantation made a significant profit, which it continued to do for the next fifteen years.

WILLIAM SENHOUSE'S GROVE PLANTATION ACCOUNTS, 1774-1786:

Year:	Expenses:	Production:	Loss:	Cleared:
1774	£503.10.2	£25.19.3	-£477.10.11	
1775	£1,197.6.7	£149.7.3	-£1,001.19.10*	
1776	£1,460.11.11	£2,517.0.7		£1,056.8.8
1777	£769.1.5	£1,002.6.5		£233.5
1778	£881.8.6	£708.3.10	-£173.4.7	
1779	£828.18	£1,293.9.3		£464.11.3
1780	£990.3.8	£990.3.8	£386.3.1	-£604.0.7
1781	£1,023.0.2	£130.6.3	-£892.13.11	
1782	£868.2.8	£795.13.10	-£72.8.10	
1783	£521.5	£219.7.4	-£301.17.7	
1784	£973.3.4	£676.66.11	-£296.16.5	
1785	£1298.6.4	£2363.3.8		£1,064.17.3
1786	£678.9.9	£999.2.1		£320.12.4

Sources: Hurricanes and Society in the British Greater Caribbean, 1624-1783-Matthew Mulcahy Pg 82...Autobiographical Manuscript of William Senhouse, JBMHS 3 (February 1936), pg 90....Barbados Department of Archives.
* Numbers do not add up.

CHAPTER TWELVE
The Impact of the Great Hurricane of 1780 and Other Historic Hurricanes on the Life and Times of People in the Caribbean and the Americas.

The American Revolution is the political upheaval during the last half of the eighteenth century in which thirteen of Great Britain's colonies in North America at first rejected the style of governance of the Parliament of Great Britain, and later the British monarchy itself, to become the sovereign United States of America. In this period the colonies first rejected the authority of the British Parliament to govern them without representation, expelling all royal officials and setting up thirteen Provincial Congress or equivalent to form individual self-governing states. Through representatives sent to the Second Continental Congress, they originally joined together to defend their respective self-governance and manage the armed conflict against the British known as the American Revolutionary War (1775-1783, also called the *American War of Independence*). The states ultimately determined collectively that the British monarchy, by acts of tyranny, could no longer legitimately claim their allegiance. They then united to form one nation, breaking away from the British Empire in July

1776 when the Congress issued the Declaration of Independence, rejecting the monarchy on behalf of the United States of America. The war ended with effective American victory in October 1781, followed by formal British abandonment of any claims to the United States with the Treaty of Paris in 1783.

The Revolutionary War was not going well for General George Washington in 1780. By August of that year, the British had captured South Carolina, and in September, traitor Benedict Arnold gave the British the plans for the fort at West Point, New York. But the winds of fortune drastically shifted in October when the most powerful North Atlantic hurricane in recorded history struck and decimated the British warships in the Caribbean. Even though the Great Hurricane of 1780 didn't strike the continental United States or any of the American colonies vying for America's Independence, the storm did change the course of history and was the tipping point of this war in their favor. The extraordinarily powerful British Navy had hoped to blockade the rebellious colonies, and it was the rival French forces that worked to counter the tactic on behalf of the Americans. Both fleets suffered heavy damage from the storm, resulting in a notable impact on the progress of the war. The October storms scuttled much of the British and Spanish navies and aided the colonies in the American Revolution. In fact, the British Navy suffered more losses from these hurricanes than it did from entire battle in the Revolutionary War. Furthermore, scarcities existed to some degree after all of the major hurricanes during the seventeenth and eighteenth centuries, but the worst crisis emerged during the American Revolution, when the combination of several major hurricanes and the elimination of trade with North American suppliers brought widespread suffering and death to thousands of slaves in Jamaica and Barbados.

The presence of hurricanes made the colonists question their ability to transform the hostile environment of the Caribbean and North America and by extension their ability to establish successful and stable societies in this region. When the Europeans first arrived in the Caribbean, hurricanes were new to them even though they experienced great storms in Europe, they did not begin to compare with the frequency or ferocity with which hurricanes struck the Caribbean. The storms regularly swept across the colonies, destroying fields and crops, leveling plantations, cites, and towns, disrupting shipping and trade, and causing widespread devastation and death among the colonists and slaves. Hurricanes quickly entered the collective histories of the colonies and they became blights on the lives of the colonists. Almanacs listed the dates of major hurricanes alongside the birthdays of monarchs and major public holidays. Additionally, special fast-day services commemorated particularly devastating disasters. Although other catastrophes including, earthquakes, droughts, and epidemics threatened colonial settlements in the region at various times, hurricanes definitely generated the most fear and respect among the colonists.

For some, perhaps a significant majority of the colonists during the first several decades of the seventeenth century believed that these storms came directly from the hands of God. They interpreted hurricanes as 'wondrous events,' divine judgments for iniquity of human sins. While others linked the storms to various natural processes, including shifting wind patterns, the explosion of various chemicals in the atmosphere, and the celestial movement of the planets and stars. Explanations for hurricanes remained diverse throughout the seventeenth and eighteenth centuries, and colonists continued to debate their possible causes and the meaning of the destruction that accompanied them. Hurricanes remained *'Acts of God,'* but unlike early interpretations of the storms as special providences sent by God in response to some specific human transgressions. By the turn of the century, colonists increasingly saw hurricanes as part of God's general providence, arising from fixed natural processes observable to humans. Furthermore, the nature and geography of hurricanes challenged the perception of these storms as 'national judgments' by which God spoke directly to a specific group of people about these hurricanes or sent them to harm one particular country or race of people. This became quite obvious over time because individual storms routinely struck various islands colonized by different European powers. For example, a hurricane in 1707 devastated the English Leeward Islands, the Dutch islands of Saba and St. Eustatius, and the French island of Guadeloupe. In 1674, a Dutch attack on the French islands was prevented by a hurricane, which also caused significant damage in the English Leeward Islands and also in Barbados.

Providential interpretations, however, did not come to an end during the eighteenth century. Some colonists continued to see hurricanes, or at least particular storms, as special providences under the immediate and direct control of God. For example, the *South Carolina Gazette* reported that the shift in wind direction during the peak of the September 15, 1752, hurricane, which saved the city from total destruction by flooding, was "as signal an instance of the immediate interposition of the Divine Providence, as ever appeared."[1] Others remained certain that the storms signaled divine wrath and judgment. In addition, some evidence suggests that some slaves may have viewed the storms as divine punishment while others saw them as hazards created by a devil figure. However, it seems probable that African attitudes about hurricanes evolved along with European ones over the seventeenth and eighteenth centuries, although what form that progression took is not entirely clear.

By the 1680's, many of the colonists began to describe 'fast days' and 'thanksgiving days' ceremonies to these storms and had become prescribed events in several colonies to give God thanks for sparing them during the passage of a hurricane or thanking Him for not sending any hurricanes during that particular season. In fact, alternate Fridays during the months of August, September, and October were specifically designated as fast days in St. Christopher in 1683. That tradition continued in the Leeward Islands into the eighteenth century. The Governor of the Leeward Islands called for a general fast in the wake of the devastating 1772 hurricane. Jamaican officials instituted a perpetual fast after the hurricane of August 28, 1722, which struck ten years to the day after an earlier storm. In St. Croix in the US Virgin Islands from the late 1600's after a powerful and deadly hurricane struck this island, every July 26th, the islanders take the day off to attend church services on what they call '*Hurricane Supplication Day,*' to pray for protection from hurricanes and that is a tradition that is still practiced even to this day. Eventually, colonists in the Caribbean gradually learned that hurricanes struck within a well-defined season and saw them less as acts of God. Early colonists believed that hurricanes could strike at any time, but by the middle of the seventeenth century most of them came to realize that there was a distinct hurricane season. This was because hurricanes simply occurred too often during the summer months for them to remain unusual or divine events in most of the colonists' eyes.

Increased experiences with these storms did not make them any less terrifying or fearful, but it did make them less as divine judgments and more as a part of the natural world. Actually, several letters and reports from officials in the Caribbean, specifically noted that the period between July and October in the Caribbean as the 'time of hurricanes.' By the middle decades of the eighteenth century, some even argued that the storms were even beneficial, increasing rainfall and clearing the air. These shifting interpretations of hurricanes and the operations of the natural world more generally, mirrored intellectual changes in England during this period, but the colonists' ideas about hurricanes remained grounded in their specific experiences. By the end of the seventeenth century, hurricanes had become expected and, at least among a few colonists, occasionally even welcomed. Colonists continued to view the storms as divinely ordained, as 'acts of God,' but their emphasis shifted from linking hurricanes to an interventionist creator punishing sin and portending future judgments to offering more general acknowledgments of God's providence and the natural world he had created.

The effects of the storms in the 1700's and 1800's were extended beyond the colonies themselves and in the Caribbean, slavery, plantation agriculture, and British mercantilism were important in defining the effects of hurricanes and shaping the colonists' response to them. The plantation colonies of the Caribbean formed the 'brightest jewels' in the crown of the British, French, Dutch and Spanish Empires. Hurricanes, of course, did not respect international political boundaries. Major storms routinely struck Spanish Florida and Spanish, French, Dutch, and Danish colonies in the West Indies. Although most shared basic characteristics with their British neighbors-notably slavery and plantation agriculture-important differences in cultural, political, legal, and religious systems distinguished the colonies, which influenced both the impact of the storms and how colonists recovered from them. These Caribbean islands produced exotic staple crops that fed the appetites of consumers on both sides of the Atlantic and generated tremendous wealth not only for colonial planters but for the empire as a whole. The West Indian islands in particular served as the hub of the British Empire, connecting Britain, Africa, and the mainland colonies in an elaborate trading network. The devastation caused by hurricanes in the Caribbean thus reverberated throughout North America and Europe.

The loss of crops by hurricanes often drove up the cost of sugar for coffee and tea drinkers and raised the price of rice in Britain and elsewhere in Europe. The physical damage caused by the storms increased the demand in the colonies for everything from provisions to building supplies to finished crafts and furniture, and North American and British merchants and artisans rushed to supply this need. However, merchants and ship captains tried to schedule voyages to the region before or after the hurricane season to avoid this threat. Furthermore, as planters learned about the seasonality of these storms and the signs associated with an approaching hurricane, they took what steps they could to lessen the risks to their plantations. Canes in the fields remained particularly susceptible, but sugar planters did their best to ensure that the previous year's crop was milled, processed, and shipped before the start of the hurricane season. Some farmers even went as far as to take down sections of their mills to protect them from the damage from the storm. The widespread destruction accompanying hurricanes required major capital expenditure for rebuilding efforts.

West Indian farmers faced with increased expenses and little prospect of income from their hurricane mangled crops, turned to outside creditors for financial assistance. The British merchants served as the main lending source for the large planters in the Greater Caribbean. In some cases, many of these local planters became highly indebted to these British Merchants forcing many of them to declare bankruptcy or go into default. When hurricanes left these planters unable to pay the expenses and loan payments, they were forced to transfer ownership to the British merchants. The reverberations from bankruptcies and defaults after hurricanes helped reshape the economic landscape of the colonies at various points during the seventeenth and eighteenth centuries, especially in the sugar islands. During the mid-seventeenth century, many of the smaller planters in

Barbados and the Leeward Islands grew small amounts of sugar on their own as tenants for larger planters. Eventually, however, credit arrangements that put them in debt to their neighbors forced many of them off their lands. At times hurricanes further exacerbated this forced possession of the land. Without access to credit after a major devastating hurricane such as the one in 1780, smaller farmers were forced to sell their lands to wealthier and more secure planters, who therefore expanded their landholdings and production capabilities. By and large, hurricanes aided the progression by which, during the seventeenth and early eighteenth centuries, land in many of the sugar colonies came to be dominated by wealthier planters and larger plantations.

Hurricanes also influenced another important aspect of the business of sugar production and that was shipping. Everyone involved in the production and sale of the sugar crop had an interest in getting them safely to the various markets in North America and Europe. This meant taking account of the threat to vessels transporting the sugar crop. Merchants and ship captains tried to avoid arriving or departing during the peak of the hurricane season. However, it is important to note here that shipping in the region never came to a complete halt, but it did slow down significantly during the dangerous late summer months, as captains attempted to fill their cargo holds and leave for Europe and North America before the peak of the hurricane season. Furthermore, some captains avoided certain ports during the hurricane season because they were particularly vulnerable. Bridgetown, for example, was completely exposed to the sea, and ships caught there during even minor tropical storms were often blown ashore and destroyed. On the other hand, many of them believed that the harbour at St. Johns, Antigua, with a ring of hills surrounding it was relatively secure, and ships often anchored there during the hurricane prone months. In fact, other captains moved south for the entire hurricane season, believing that the waters off the coast of South America were much safer. Planters could not insure their crops while they were in the field, but they could insure them on ships, and many did so in an effort to secure that year's output and profit. This insurance offered some protection to planters who otherwise had little means of countering the threat from hurricanes.

However, the cost of insurance doubled for ships that sailed during the hurricane season. As a result, anxious planters and merchants tried to load their ships with sugar and depart before the beginning of August and September the peak of the hurricane season.

Throughout the seventeenth and eighteenth centuries, hurricanes repeatedly devastated the sugar plantations of the Greater Caribbean. The storms ruined crops, destroyed buildings and infrastructure, sank ships, and took the lives of the highly prized African slaves. The combined effects of such destruction resulted in serious short-term physical and economic hardships for most planters, and complete financial ruin for some. Even though hurricanes drove some planters from the region, most absorbed their losses and rebuilt, often with the help of outside creditors. What kept these planters rebuilding despite the risk of future hurricanes was the simple fact of money earned from sugar. The demand for this plantation staple and it's by product of rum, and the protected market for sugar in Great Britain meant that the potential profits from this crop was great enough to ensure that the colonists absorb the risks involved in the production. Despite repeated destruction from hurricanes, diseases and other natural disasters, this crop brought tremendous rewards, and successful sugar planters became among the wealthiest of all the colonists in the Caribbean.

The hurricanes which devastated the Caribbean in 1780 contributed to calls for increased local production of provisions and diversification of crops on some islands. Some planters experimented with new food sources such as, the breadfruit tree, which was brought into the region in the 1780s by William Bligh, or attempted to increase production on secondary crops like cotton. Overall, planters in the Caribbean remained dedicated to sugar throughout the seventeenth and eighteenth centuries and beyond. Hurricanes did play some role in the shift away from sugar on some islands in the region, but only at the end of the nineteenth century. Likewise, hurricanes also contributed to the decline of rice production in the coastal low country of South Carolina, but not until 1890s. This was when a series of storms struck the final blows to an industry already shaken by the physical devastation and societal changes brought about by the Civil War. However, if hurricanes did not transform the economic structure of the

Greater Caribbean during the seventeenth and eighteenth centuries, they did shape the experience of plantership. Colonists everywhere in the overwhelmingly agricultural colonies of the Caribbean worried about the weather and its effects on their crops, but no others faced such regular threats to the larger economic infrastructure as those in the Greater Caribbean did from hurricanes.

During the 1700s in the Caribbean, very few colonists made use of the barometer to predict storms. The barometer was a fairly new instrument and was developed in the middle of the seventeenth century. Members of the Royal Society began sending the instruments to correspondents in the West Indies by the 1670's which was much earlier than the instruments appeared in North America. This was done with the sole purpose of gathering information on hurricanes with a view of obtaining some kind of advanced warnings from these instruments. Sir Peter Colleton sent several baroscopes (barometers) to Barbados in 1677 in order *"to examine whether they would be of any use for the foretelling the seasons and mutations of the weather as they are found to do here, especially concerning hurricanes."* Ralph Bohun speculated in 1671 that *"There might be excellent use made of the Barometer for predicting of Hurricanes,"* based on accounts of its use by *"a person of Quality"* who lived near the sea and who had observed movement in the instrument before storms. Some early accounts indicated that this might indeed be the case. A report to the Royal Society in the 1680s stated that 'Quick Silver' (Mercury) in barometers in Barbados did not react "unless in a violent storm or Hurricane." The use of barometers and other meteorological instruments, nonetheless, were not widespread, nor were their results viewed as trustworthy. Barometers were expensive, and the select few who had these instruments, the majority of them didn't know how to use them. In fact, one frustrated correspondent to the Royal Society wrote that no one in Barbados made use of either a barometer or a thermometer before, during, or after the Great Hurricane of 1780. Uncertainty about the barometer's accuracy during the Great Hurricane of 1780 meant the older native traditions of forecasting this storm was based on observing the natural elements such as, clouds, rainfall and watching the behaviour of animals and birds just before the onset of this storm.[2]

Hurricanes also caused extensive damage to elaborate infrastructures needed to grow and process the crops. Sugar plantations, with their windmills, boiling houses, curing houses, and other buildings were particularly vulnerable and were often the first victims of these storms. For example, losses from a 1733 hurricane in Montserrat included thirty of the thirty-six mills on the island, *"the other six...much shatter'd, having lost their Veins and Round Houses,"* along with significant damage to "most of the Boiling-Houses, and the Sugar in them, which was considerable." Another planter, Henry Laurens estimated that on one of his plantations, one-third of the rice lands *"suffer'd by Salt Water breaking over the Banks,"* damaging fields during a 1769 storm. In Carolina, the storms often damaged or destroyed the complex series of gates and embankments used to control the flow of water onto rice fields.[3]

In addition, hurricanes destroyed ships and port facilities, both essential for shipping crops to markets throughout the Caribbean, North American and Europe. During the Great Hurricane of 1675 in Barbados, twelve ships in Bridgetown's Harbour, *"some of them laden with sugar were driven ashore and broken to pieces."* The Great Hurricane of 1712 sank numerous vessels in Kingston Harbour, which afterward appeared *"full of Wrecks...and great quantities of goods and dead bodies floated from place to place, as the wind blew."* A powerful 1728 storm destroyed or damaged twenty three ships in Charleston Harbour and ruined over two thousand barrels of rice on ships or in city warehouses. The 1752 hurricanes in South Carolina destroyed the wharves and warehouses along the Cooper River that functioned as the colony's hub of trade and commerce. Damage and debris on Bridgetown's docks after the Great Hurricane of 1780 greatly obstructed and restricted the shipping business. Some hurricanes also claimed the lives of slaves held on ships before they were unloaded and sold. Some two hundred slaves perished in 1722 when a hurricane sank the slave ship Kingston that had recently arrived in Jamaica. Henry Laurens warned one correspondent in July 1755 to avoid having cargoes arrive in the late summer. "We would not choose them (slaves) sent in the Hurricane Season," he wrote to one, because the risk of loss was simply too great. Furthermore, major hurricanes often killed dozens, sometimes hundreds, and occasionally thousands of slaves on plantations throughout the Caribbean during the seventeenth and eighteenth centuries. Planters' letters, officials' correspondence, and published travel narratives all provide vivid description brought on by hurricanes in the seventeenth and eighteenth centuries, but they reveal few specifics about their experiences with these storm from a firsthand point of view.[4]

Major hurricanes of the Caribbean not only devastated infrastructures but they routinely damaged or destroyed the fortifications that colonists had erected during the seventeenth and eighteenth centuries to guard against outside attacks. Damage to guns and fortifications by these hurricanes weakened colonial defenses, and the history of warfare in the region gave more than enough evidence of the dangers posed by foreign foes. The medieval walls surrounding the fortifications in Jamaica suffered significantly from the 1722 hurricane. The east end of Fort Charles in Port Royal sank several feet, and most of the cannons were washed into the sea. These storms often rendered useless in a matter of hours fortifications that had taken years to build. In many of the forts throughout the Caribbean, the cannons were often dismounted and their carriages swept away. The colonists were often amazed and horrified of the power of the winds and storm surge that moved heavy cannons as if they were mere toys. Colonial officials often feared that such destruction left the particularly vulnerable to what many officials called 'insults of our envious neighbors' as well as 'intestine rebels.' Contemporaries often referred to hurricanes as 'enemies,' and many colonists worried about the potential alliance between their human and natural foes.

African slaves, like the European colonists, had little experience with hurricanes, although tornadoes are frequent in West Africa, and it seems likely that slaves made some connection between the two. Charles Leslie suggested that eighteenth-century slaves in Jamaica worshipped "two gods, a good one and a bad one." According to Leslie, "The evil god sends storms, Earthquakes, and all kinds of mischief." The Jamaican penkeeper Thomas Thistlewood noted that slaves in Westmoreland Parish connected the "bad weather" and ensuing 1780 hurricanes to the burial of a local merchant named Cholman: "The negroes say him (Cholman) and the devil were playing cards together, which occasioned the storm." Such evidence suggests that some slaves viewed the storms which descended on the West Indies as divine punishments, while others simply saw them as hazards caused by some wicked or devil figure. It seems probable that African attitudes about hurricanes evolved along with Europeans ones over the seventeenth and eighteenth centuries, although what form that evolution took is not entirely clear. Slaves almost certainly learned to search the skies for signs of coming hurricanes and shared with English colonists a general sense of the hurricane season, but few colonists commented on African attitudes or knowledge about the storms. When they did, such comments were often negative. One visitor to Jamaica in the early nineteenth century, for example, wrote that slaves believed that hurricanes were "indicators of the divine wrath, as punishments inflicted by heaven on the human race for their crimes and impiety; they have no idea of their arising from natural causes; the necessary war elements is to them an incomprehensible doctrine." The slaves, he claimed, "did not look much to natural causes and remote causes."[5]

Providential interpretations, however, did not cease during the eighteenth century. Some colonists continued to view hurricanes, or at least particular storms, as special providences under the immediate and direct control of God. For example, the South Carolina Gazette reported that the shift in wind direction during the peak of the September 15, 1752 hurricane, which saved the city from total destruction by flooding, was "as signal an instance of the immediate interposition of the Divine Providence, as ever appeared." Others remained certain that the storms signaled divine wrath and judgment. Shifting through the debris on his Barbados plantation after the devastating Great Hurricane of 1780, one of William Senhouse's slaves uncovered a collection of sermons by the English minister John Tillotson. Senhouse read Tillotson's comments that "if the hand of God be severe, and heavy upon us, in any affliction, we may be assured that it is not without great cause that so much goodness is highly offended and displeased with us." Senhouse wondered rhetorically whether the terrible destruction was "directed by chance or by the immediate Providence of God, which suffers not a sparrow to fall to the ground without its knowledge, and numbers the very hairs of our head!"[6]

CHAPTER THIRTEEN
WARS, POLITICS, SLAVES AND THE GREAT HURRICANE OF 1780.

Although famine may have been averted, hurricanes caused widespread suffering and malnutrition in slave communities throughout the seventeenth and eighteenth centuries. Slaves often got by on a reduced and increasingly monotonous diet of one or two foods as they waited for outside supplies to arrive or local provisions to mature. Slaves routinely suffered provision shortages in the wake of major hurricanes, but they faced their biggest challenges in 1780 after the Great Hurricanes in 1780. The political crisis of the American Revolution left Jamaica and Barbados with little food and a few options for relief. The war severed relations between the rebellious mainland and the loyal West Indies colonies, eliminating the islands' closet and best source of provisions. The consequences of that separation proved disastrous when two hurricanes struck Jamaica and Barbados less than a week apart in early October 1780. Thousands of slaves died during the storms, most crushed beneath falling buildings or drowned in storm surges, but others perished in the following weeks and months from starvation due to inadequate food and disease, and all faced shortages and difficult conditions for a long time.

The Caribbean Islands were caught up in the strained political crisis between Britain and the North American colonies during the 1770s. This was done to force West Indian colonists to support their cause; the Continental Congress enacted a non-exportation agreement or act in 1774-75 known as 'The Association,' stopping trade with England, Ireland, and the British Caribbean. After the outbreak of hostilities in 1775, Parliament passed its own Prohibitory Act suspending all trade between the British Empire, including the loyal West Indies, and the rebellious colonies of America. Planters and other colonists' vehemently opposed this new law arguing that the trade embargo threatened would result in serious food shortages in the region or even outright famine or even death. The Barbados Assembly claimed in 1776 that the cost of goods had skyrocketed and that the planters could not afford to buy provisions for themselves or, more importantly, for their slaves. Governor William Burt of St. Kitts reported to London in March 1778 that the Leeward Islands suffered significantly because of the lack of provisions. He reported that the Island of Antigua lost well over one thousand black slaves, Montserrat approximately twelve hundred and some whites; Nevis three to four hundred slaves-all due to food shortages on these islands because of this blockade in trade. A few months later his desperation started to set in because he pleaded with those English officials to send ships loaded with relief supplies right away or face the consequences of more than half of the population going hungry and it would be further exacerbated if there was a powerful hurricane.

The storms in 1780 destroyed the islands main locally grown food, plantains, while the American Revolution eliminated their closet source of imported supplies. The war ended in 1783, but trade between the islands of the Caribbean and the new United States remained restricted. After the signing of the Treaty of Paris in July 1783, the British Government issued two orders-in-council reinscribing the basic principles of the Navigation Acts that had presided over trade within the British Empire since the middle of the seventeenth century. This order maintained the regulations limited trade between the islands and the mainland implemented at the beginning of the war. This prohibited importing any American beef, pork, dairy products, and fish, reserving the trade in those items to Canada, Ireland, or England. However, they were able to import flour, grain, lumber, and vegetables from the United States, but only in British ships. Smuggling and illegal trade from neutral islands ensured that the islands received some supplies from North America in the years after 1783. It must be noted that the new laws did authorize local officials to lift restrictions to import goods from North America but only with pre-approval from the Governor and the King of England and under extreme emergency conditions.

Slaves on these plantations were considered very valuable commodity and many of them perished in these storms. Colonist during the era of the 1700s in Jamaica and Barbados soon found this out the hard way. Two hurricanes in October 1780 devastated the colonies. At least two thousand slaves perished in Barbados during the Great Hurricane of 1780, and perhaps an equal number of whites. Many slaves died during this storm, but others died in the following days and weeks from injuries sustained during the hurricane, inadequate food, contaminated water, disease, or the combination of all of these factors. One account from early January 1781 reported that four thousand persons died in the storm, and an additional one thousand from their wounds. On William Senhouse's plantation, three slaves died during the storm, but three more died in the following weeks as a result of the storm. Senhouse also lost his youngest son two weeks after the storm due to a severe cold which he caught on the night of the hurricane. William Dickson, who served as secretary to Barbados's Governor in the 1770s, noted that tax returns showed five thousand fewer slaves in Barbados in 1781 than in 1780, and he contended that the significant majority of them were killed by the Great Hurricane of 1780. The slave population of Barbados remained consistently steady from the late 1770s through the mid-1780s, rising or falling by at most 1,600 persons, not including the 1780 hurricane season. It is fair to speculate that even taking into account slave imports and normal slave mortality, many more slaves perished in 1780 than the 2,033 reported in parish returns, and many of these deaths were likely caused by the hurricane or the aftermath of the storm.[1]

Many other historical accounts suggested that food shortages persisted on the island for weeks and months after the storm and that hunger and diseases likely contributed significantly to the increased mortality rate. The British military commander Major General John

Vaughan wrote that the conditions after the storm gave "too much reason to fear that a famine must inevitably ensue unless some effectual means are used to prevent it." A letter written from a planter in early November warned of famine and stated that "100 Negroes have perished...since the hurricane for want of food." Besides from supplies from England, along with newly planted ground provisions, relieved the crisis somewhat by the beginning of 1781, however, shortages still persisted. Richard Gill informed the absentee owner William FitzHerbert in April 1781 that he had already spent £150 on food and that in addition to the two hundred bushels of beans FitzHerbert had sent out from London, "many more will be required." He also noted that fish, a major source of protein in the slaves' diet, was extremely expensive and he requested ten or twelve barrels of herring. One traveler who arrived on the island in July 1781 found Bridgetown still in the devastated condition from the storm and noted that "every article of produce is very scarce, particularly fruit, all the trees in the Island having been blown up by the Roots." Senhouse reported in the summer of 1781 that corn was so scarce that it could not be purchased except at a very expensive price. He quit trying to buy food for some of his slaves and gave the "best and most provident of our Negroes money in lieu of corn that they might purchase food for themselves." The food supply in Barbados in 1781 remained in extremely short supply throughout much of 1781, and quite a number of slaves perished because of these shortages and other post-hurricane conditions.[2]

The hurricane that struck western Jamaica one week earlier on October 3, the Savanna-la-Mar Hurricane resulted in similar death and misery. Jamaican officials did not file an official report of losses like their counterparts in Barbados, but various accounts indicated that hundreds of slaves, and perhaps as much as a thousand, perished during the storm. The Kingston Gazette reported that over two hundred slaves died on the Blue Castle plantation when a boiling house in which they sought refuge collapsed. Four hundred people "white and black" perished in Lucea, and a similar amount at Savanna-la-Mar. Although blacks and whites were grouped together in many figures, several reports indicated that more slaves than whites died. In fact, one report from Westmoreland noted that "several white people and some hundreds of negroes" died in the storm. According to a report in the Jamaican's Annual Register, "a great number of white inhabitants, and of necessity, a much greater of the negroes, perished during the course of the hurricane." Thomas Thistlewood reported that the best account of the deaths at Savanna-la-Mar indicated that seventy whites and at least five hundred slaves died in the storm.[3]

It is important to note here that food shortages were less pronounced in Jamaica than in Barbados and this was attributed to the fact that the storm struck only the western parishes of the island. However, the Governor wrote that the residents of those parishes were in a truly "wretched situation," with no shelter, clothes and worst of all, "Famine staring them full in the face." Colonial officials and Kingston merchants coordinated relief efforts and rushed food to the region in the weeks after the storm, and the timely arrival of several ships from England helped eased the crisis somewhat. Nevertheless, provisions remained scarce in the hurricane-ravaged parishes of Hanover and Westmoreland, and slaves struggled to obtain adequate food. Thomas Thistlewood sent his slaves into nearby marshes in the days following the storm to pick up whatever "flower, rum, beef, pork, butter, and cloth" could be saved. Furthermore, he also allowed them to eat several sheep killed during the storm.

In addition to the lack of provisions, Thistlewood's slaves faced a number of other difficulties. The hurricane flooded his property, leaving many slaves without shelter for days. Clean drinking water was also a problem and Dysentery, common on many West Indian plantations even in good times, flourished in these conditions, further adding to the high death toll. He also reported that several slaves were gravely ill in the weeks following the hurricane. He did not specifically connect their illness to the storm, but it seems probable that they were connected. Another account written by a planter several years later reported that "negroes on different properties throughout the island were every day perishing in large numbers, mainly from diseases (mostly from dysentery) brought on by unhealthy food, and partly from absolute starvation!" Exactly how many slaves and colonists died in the parish in the weeks after the storm is unclear, but slaves clearly suffered great material and physical hardships, and some likely lost their lives as a result of the lingering effects of the storm. A committee from the Jamaican Assembly conducted an official investigation and found out that at least 15,000 slaves (out of a population of 256,000) perished as a result of the five hurricanes in the 1780s. This number, the committee reported, "may be fairly attributed to these repeated calamities, and the unfortunate measure of interdicting foreign supplies." Clearly, some slaves died from causes unrelated to these hurricanes in the West Indies, but numerous accounts, public and private, suggested that hundreds if not thousands perished from hardships caused by the storms and by the loss of trade with North America. For West Indian slaves who encountered seasonal hunger and malnutrition in the best of times, conditions in the 1780s were truly disastrous.

CHAPTER FOURTEEN
THE ROLE, PURPOSE AND IMPACT OF CHARITY AFTER THE GREAT HURRICANE OF 1780

Throughout the seventeenth and eighteenth centuries, the widespread devastation accompanying hurricanes created both immediate and long-term hardships for the colonists in the Caribbean, and charitable donations from persons in Europe often provided important assistance to the victims in the West Indian colonies. Disaster relief came from two major sources. Local donors provided the most immediate aid throughout this period. Local parish churches were often the main source of donations because they often organized relief efforts and collected funds and supplies for the sufferers within the colony. Colonial governments sometimes supplemented these efforts by distributing direct monetary grants to sufferers, by purchasing essential supplies, or by reimbursing private individuals for large donations of supplies. Beginning in the 1740s, disaster relief expanded in size and scope but it took off significantly after the Great hurricane of 1780 devastated the Caribbean. Donors in Britain and in distant colonies increasingly offered help to victims of fires, hurricanes, and other disasters in the Caribbean and elsewhere. The amount of money raised, moreover, often exceeded the previous efforts.

In addition to local charities, colonists also sought assistance from England and from other British colonies in America. Such assistance played only a minimal role in aiding disaster victims during the seventh and early eighteenth centuries, but by the second half of the eighteenth century relief campaigns in Britain and in the colonies routinely raised significant sums for colonists in the Caribbean and elsewhere in British America. The greatest of these campaigns followed the 1780 hurricanes and raised tens of thousands of pounds from donors throughout Britain to aid the victims in Barbados and Jamaica. However, sometimes it took weeks, sometimes months, and occasionally years before this outside aid was collected, sent to the colonies, and distributed among the victims and humanitarian relief played a growing role in post-disaster recovery efforts.

The growth in the number of newspapers and periodicals in Britain and the colonies, the increased economic connections among the colonies and between the colonies and Britain, the emergence of a humanitarian sensibility among residents on both sides of the Atlantic, and an expanded sense of British nationalism and patriotism that considered far-off colonists as fellow subjects rather than strangers made certain that news of disasters spread widely and quickly and that more and more people felt duty-bound to help alleviate the pain and suffering. Not every hurricane or major disaster resulted in a formal relief campaign but their frequency after 1780 represented a major new way that colonists recovered from hurricanes and other disasters. Colonists also often look for disaster relief from the British government and the occasionally received it, most notably after the 1780 hurricanes when Parliament allocated £120,000 sterling to victims in Barbados and Jamaica. The British Parliament's action in 1780 was extraordinary as were the hurricanes which impacted these countries.

Floods, epidemics, earthquakes, and fires routinely brought damage and despair to towns and villages throughout England and the rest of Europe. In the aftermath of such disasters and calamities, donors often came to the victims' aid. Charity briefs (also called *king's brief*, *church briefs*, and *letters patent*) had their origin in the medieval church briefs that the Pope issued to raise funds for specific projects, often to repair churches destroyed by fires or to ransom Christian captives in the Holy Land. In the aftermath of the Great Hurricane of 1780 and the other 1780 hurricanes, local officials in Barbados, Jamaica and other devastated islands requested the permission to make an appeal on behalf of the victims. If the request was approved, then notices were sent to parishes calling on ministers to read a description of the disaster or issue to their congregations. Clerks often read out loud "Please remember the brief" collected donations at the end of the service, and church wardens often followed this up with door-to-door collections in the parish. The money was then sent to vestrymen or other local officials for distribution to victims.

Briefs often raised funds for a variety of reasons during the sixteenth, seventeenth, and eighteenth centuries, including church repairs or construction, aid for persecuted Protestants in France and Ireland, the redemption of English sailors captured by Barbary pirates. However, the most important cause was for devastating hurricanes or other natural disasters relief. It is important to note here that briefs proved most effective in raising money from neighboring communities, where donors had firsthand knowledge of the disaster and the victims. Successful national appeals existed in the seventeenth and early eighteenth centuries, but charity briefs were most effective in collecting funds in local communities rather than far away ones. Colonists brought the system of charity briefs with them to the New World. The governor replaced the king as the granter of the briefs, but the system operated along similar lines. As in England, briefs raised money for various purposes, including disaster relief. However, charity briefs provided a structured means of raising money, but individual parishes at times solicited funds without the official authorization of a brief.

Turning to transatlantic relief became so regular that after the Great Hurricane of 1780, members of the vestry of St. Michael's, Barbados, wrote to London officials suggesting that "a proper application for a Brief thro' the Churches in England, is not only usual on such occasion, but the most probable means to procure us sufficient relief in our great necessity." The campaigns to support victims of the two hurricanes which struck Jamaica, Barbados, St. Vincent, and Dominica in October 1780 represented the largest and most significant relief effort of the eighteenth century. Week after week throughout the spring of 1781, British and Irish newspapers carried list of donors and the amount they gave, ranging from one shilling to over one thousand pounds. The Society of the West India Merchants and Planters in London raised at least £15,000. A special committee in Dublin led by the lord mayor collected over £20,000, led by a £1,000 contribution from the merchant house of Latouche and Sons. A special benefit theater performance in early March raised an additional £48. Donations to a separate campaign to help rebuild churches in Barbados totaled £1,362 by 1782.[1]

On at least one occasion during the eighteenth century, local officials sponsored a lottery to raise funds for recovery efforts after the Great Hurricane of 1780. Barbados officials passed a new law in 1783 authorizing a lottery to raise £5,000 for rebuilding St. Michael's Church in Bridgetown after this hurricane had devastated it. The king rejected the initial plan, arguing that the lottery had to help all of the churches on the island. Officials on the island responded with a new revised bill creating two lotteries, one for St. Michael's and another for the remaining churches. The sale of the tickets went on sale in February of 1785, but sales were slow and to counteract these slow sales, the governor tried selling tickets in the neighboring Leeward Islands. In May of 1786, local officials discovered that many unsold tickets had disappeared, and they immediately halted the lottery. Although unsuccessful, the lottery represented another means of raising money for recovery efforts.

It is important to note here that not all donations were monetary because some individuals or groups gave clothing or manufactured goods. The islands even received some sort of assistance from the rebellious North Americans. Writing from Paris, Benjamin Franklin ordered all American ships to allow safe passage of any vessels from Ireland transporting cargoes of relief supplies to the islands. "Principles of common humanity," Franklin later wrote, required him to take such an action. The size of donations and the geographic scope of donors distinguished these eighteenth century aid campaigns, but so too did the form of appeal. Charity briefs preached in local parishes throughout England and the colonies continued to be important in disaster relief, but a new method arose alongside it and that was the act of private subscriptions.

Subscriptions were different from briefs in the sense that briefs were public instruments-they had to be approved by officials and were administered through local parishes but on the other hand, private individuals or groups organized in campaigns. The New England Merchants, the Committee for the Affairs of Canada, and the Society of West India Merchants and Planters, along with other groups, coordinated private subscription campaigns for disaster victims in the aftermath of the Great Hurricane of 1780. Meeting in coffeehouses and taverns, they publicized their causes in newspapers, periodicals, and broadsides rather than from the altar. In an effort to encourage donations in 1780, for example, the west India Merchants and Planters placed advertisements in newspapers and financed publication of an eighty page pamphlet containing accounts from the islands that detailed the devastation shaped by the storms. Instead of church collections, subscription campaigns employed local bankers throughout Britain who used subscription books to register and collect funds.

Subscription campaigns also emerged in the sugar islands of the Caribbean in the mid to late 1700s. For example, Governor John Dalling's £2,000 donation headed the subscription organized in Spanish Town to support victims in the western parishes of Jamaica after the Savanna-la-Mar Hurricane in 1780. After the Great Hurricane of 1780 in Barbados, merchants in Bridgetown "formed an association, and appointed committees for the interment of the dead, and the distribution of provisions for the relief of their indigent fellow sufferers." Private subscriptions also saved time because they did not require formal government approval and had the potential to reach a broader audience than just the church going population. They also signified a growing middle-class distrust of government-sponsored briefs, whose high administrative costs reduced the amount of money that reached the storm ravaged victims. In some cases, at least a third or more of the total amount of money went to the overhead administrative fees rather than to the victims. Other donors grew tired of scandals that overwhelmed the brief system, especially the practice of farming briefs, in which middlemen coordinated relief efforts in return for a percentage of the money. By the middle of the eighteenth century, even many churchgoers turned away from briefs and embraced the new system of committees and causes.

Organizers of these relief campaigns used the funds to buy food, building supplies, and other necessities for victims or sent the money directly to the colonies with the sole purpose of distributing it to the victims. Much of the relief dispatched from Ireland after the 1780 hurricane arrived in Barbados in the form of food and supplies. The Dublin committee shipped caps, linens, and men's and women's shoes. Once the supplies or funds arrived in the colony, a committee of local officials, often parish vestrymen, oversaw their distribution to the victims. Most committees ordered an inquiry of some form to determine the losses suffered by individual colonists and to serve as a basis for allocating supplies and money. After the Great Hurricane of 1780, the Barbados Council divided the £1,000 raised by residents of Cork with some attention to the relative population and losses of each parish. Council officials then divided the food and supplies shipped from Ireland among the parishes, leaving local vestrymen to determine the specific amount individuals would be allocated in proportion to their losses.

Given the speed of travel in the late eighteenth century, it took weeks and sometimes months for the news of a devastating hurricane in the Caribbean to reach Britain or the northern colonies. Often months, and sometimes even years passed before victims received supplies or money. Private donations raised for the victims of the Great Hurricane of 1780, including significant amounts of money, were still arriving in Barbados four years after the disaster. For example, when relief supplies from Ireland arrived in Barbados in 1781, months after the hurricane, residents of St. George's parish wrote to the island officials urged them not to delay in distributing the food, clothing, and building materials. "Our poor are numerous, needy, and distressed," they pleaded. Parish officials even offered to send wagons to Bridgetown to speed things up. Regardless of when it arrived, food was especially welcomed after major hurricanes in the islands, in which the residents had become very reliant on these imported supplies.

It is difficult to trace exactly what happened to the disaster relief funds once they were distributed in the colonies, but the money definitely provided a significant boost to the local economy. Much of the relief money was used to help with the rebuilding efforts, thus stimulating the local building trades and the economy. Tradesmen such as carpenters, plumbers, and bricklayers generally made large sums of money or became overnight success after the passage of the Great Hurricane of 1780 on the island of Barbados. White craftsmen profited from the relief funds spent on rebuilding the plantations and homes, but some slaves-those who hired themselves out may have also benefited as well. In either case, individual victims welcomed the funds as they struggled to rebuild their lives, and the colonial economy more broadly benefited from the demand for services and from the circulation of money throughout the local economy. The success of these disaster relief efforts in 1780, and more specifically, the raising of money in Britain, highlighted the important shift in attitudes among the Englishmen about their fellow subjects in the West Indian colonies. Throughout the seventeenth and into the eighteenth centuries only a few residents of Great Britain concerned themselves with the colonies and colonists. But that all changed after the Great Hurricane of 1780. Certainly whatever thoughts Englishmen had about colonists in the sugar islands, it simply did not translate into any significant financial assistance to these disaster victims until this hurricane in 1780. After this hurricane, colonial affairs occupied an increasingly prominent place in the minds of many British Citizens.

One newspaper writer laid out the complex economic connections between the colonies and Britain in even greater detail after the Great Hurricane of 1780 in Barbados. When he had described the economic damage that a 'typical' five hundred acre plantation on Barbados suffered from a major hurricane, the author turned to the effect such losses had on people in Great Britain. He estimated that an average plantation would have produced two hundred hogsheads of sugar, each with a value of £15, along with two hundred hogsheads of rum, each with a value of £5 each. The loss of tax revenue, he wrote, including the 4% paid in the islands and a £4 duty on each hogshead, represented a loss "to his majesty and the Publick" of roughly £1,000. Furthermore, the author argued that such a figure did not include the "Loss of Freight to the Ship-Owner, Commission to the Merchant, Employment for the Manufacturer, the Consumption of British Manufactures being considerable in a Sugar Plantation." It was an "undoubted Truth," he continued, "that the publick, in various Ways, receives much greater Profits from the Produce of a Sugar Plantation than its Owner does." He concluded by stating that while some might think "some Interested West-Indian is the Penner hereof; there is no Briton who is not interested herein, and the Writer glories in being a Briton who is not interested herein, and the Writer glories in being a Briton, but more particularly in being a Citizen of the World." Whatever, the merits of the author's economic analysis, his argument recognized the importance of the colonies, and the empire generally, to the economic well-being of the British Citizens at home. Such awareness extended beyond the merchants, traders, and absentee planters who organized and coordinated relief campaigns and donated the largest sums. However, thousands of ordinary men and women also donated to various relief efforts.

Colonists continued to rely on local fund-raising after many hurricanes and other disasters, but relief from Britain and from other colonies provided an increasingly significant source of aid. Even though it often took weeks or even months for the funds or supplies to arrive, humanitarian assistance assisted greatly recovery efforts, and colonists came to expect such assistance as they struggled to rebuild their homes, plantations, and societies. The campaign to aid victims of the 1780 hurricane in Barbados embodied the high point of the eighteenth-century relief efforts. Drawing on images of distress and despair, highlighting the wealth the sugar colonies created an incredible response from individuals across Britain, who contributed tens of thousands of pounds to aid their fellow subjects.

CHAPTER FIFTEEN
THE ROLE, PURPOSE AND IMPACT OF AID DISTRIBUTION AND BARBADOS POLITICS AFTER THE GREAT HURRICANE OF 1780

In the immediate aftermath of the *Great Hurricane of 1780* and the *Savanna-la-Mar Hurricane*, colonists in Jamaica and Barbados and their allies in London drafted petitions to the King of England and the British Parliament appealing for aid. After a short debate in 1781, the British Parliament appropriated £120,000 sterling for the two islands. Parliament's action was definitely an unusual one. This was because disaster-stricken colonists often sought aid from the British Government during the seventeenth and eighteenth centuries, but never before had they ever received such a massive amount of public funds. British officials in government often sent military supplies or building materials to the colonies in the aftermath of major hurricanes to help strengthen defenses, and sometimes they gave small amounts of money to the colonies themselves.

What circumstances pushed these officials to allocate such extraordinarily large sums of public funds to the colonists in Jamaica and Barbados? Before these two hurricanes, these islands never had to deal with such widespread devastation and far reaching consequences. Certainly these powerful hurricanes in 1780 caused significant misery and suffering, but so too had other hurricanes. Speakers in Parliament stressed their desire to ease the hardships and suffering caused by these storms, but humanitarian concerns were not the main reasons for this massive amount of assistance in the minds of many British officials. Political factors also acted as a significant 'pull factor' in the influence for their decisions to help these British colonies. It just so happened that these two hurricanes struck during the midst of the American War of Revolution. Island colonists remained loyal, but they often complained about British policies affecting the islands, especially the decision to halt trade with the American mainland. Criticism grew louder after France entered the war in 1778 and the West Indies became a major battleground of military operations. By 1780 many island colonists had become frustrated with what they saw as inadequate attention to their needs and their defense. As a result of this frustration, many British officials saw this massive amount of disaster relief as a means of silencing growing criticism by many West Indian planters and merchants of Britain's handling of the war effort and of reaffirming their concern for the welfare of the loyal colonists in the islands.

Politics also played a significant role in the distribution of aid in the colonies after these hurricanes. The parliamentary bounty became a major bone of contention between political leaders and institutions in Barbados and between social and economic groups in Jamaica and Barbados. Fierce debates emerged in both colonies about how to distribute and use the money and which colonists should receive financial assistance. The debates about the distribution of the parliamentary aid suggest that major economic divisions also characterized white society after these storms in these islands. The politics of disaster relief therefore offers a window both on the relationship between the colonies and Britain and on relationships within the white colonial society in the islands. As they struggled to assess their losses and rebuild, colonists in Jamaica and Barbados also drafted petitions to the king and Parliament seeking financial assistance. "We now throw ourselves at your Majesty's feet to implore your royal favour, and the nation's bounty," Barbados leaders wrote in late October, "to enable us to bear up under this dreadful shock to our finances, and assist us to repair the uncommon damage we have sustained." Without such aid, "your Majesty's most ancient and ever loyal colony of Barbados may be lost in every point of valuable consideration to the crown and parent state, and sink themselves into an abyss of indigence and despair." The Barbados absentee planters and merchants reported that distressed colonists now looked to the "humanity, liberality, and policy of this honourable house, from whence they most humbly hope to receive speedy and effectual relief; such relief as will not only secure them from impending want, but by assisting them to erect a new their buildings, and to procure other necessaries, enable them to cultivate again their estates."[1]

The petitions appealed to many of the same themes of nationalism and sentimentality used in subscription campaigns and charity sermons. The Barbados merchants and planters described the suffering and despair brought on by the storm as 'shocking,' writing that "above 20,000 whites, were left almost destitute of habitations, food, and raiment." They also noted Barbados's position as "the most ancient English colony in the West Indies" and emphasized that the island was "ever actuated by the principles of loyalty to the crown, and love of the British constitution," stressing their patriotism during the current military conflict. The committee also incorporated economic arguments: "Should the unhappy sufferers be so fortunate as to receive from parliament such generous aid, they entertain a sanguine hope, and think it not ill-founded, that...the island will soon see its ancient fertility revive, again flourish, and in proportion to its own wealth and affluence to the parent state."[2]

The House of Commons debated the question of relief funds in late January of 1781. Speaking for the committee responding to the petitions, Lord North remarked that the hurricane had reduced the colonists "to the lowest state of wretchedness, and well entitled them to some assistance from the parent state." North believed that the British Parliament should offer some kind of relief to the poorer class of the colonists who were least able to afford to rebuild after the storm. He further advocated separate grants for Jamaica and Barbados but believed that the lion's share of the aid should go to Barbados because in Jamaica only part of the island was devastated, whereas, in Barbados the entire country was devastated. Furthermore, he noted that Barbados has fewer internal resources to rebuild and recover so they should receive the larger portion of the grant. Based on this notion, North proposed granting £80,000 sterling to Barbados and £40,000 to Jamaica, and after some debate, the House passed the measure. North recommended that the best means of distributing this aid was to turn it over to the various parish vestries in the colonies and allow them with the assistance and oversight of the governors and council to determine the needs of the individual victims. However, several other members suggested that the absentee planters and merchants in London should advise the Treasury on the distribution of the funds, and that was agreed to and the amendment was approved unanimously. Parliament's action in 1781 represented an extraordinary response to the sufferings of disaster victims in the West Indian colonies.

In reality, Britain did not need to appease the West Indians; there was little chance that they would join the rebellion. Nonetheless, disaster relief made good political and economic sense. It demonstrated Britain's concern for the welfare of its far-flung colonies and demonstrated the benefits of British subject hood at a time when many colonists in America were revolting against that very same idea. Parliament made no specific mention of protecting the colonies in its January 1781 resolution providing aid to Jamaica and Barbados, although France's entry into the American War of Revolution made the Caribbean a theater of war and heightened issues of defense. The resolution spoke mainly of humanitarian aid. The language of the debates, however, masked key political concerns. As Lord North emphasized, concerns by the mother country for its West Indian colonies, along with broader humanitarian motives encouraged Parliament to act. Such acts of concern were important in the 1780s in the aftermath of these storms. It must be noted here that most historians agree that there was very little chance that Jamaica and Barbados would ever join with the rebellious states of North America in open revolt. This was because the island colonists were simply too afraid of a slave revolt, too dependent on the British Army and Navy for security reasons, and too dependent on the protected home markets for the sale of their sugar crop. Nevertheless, many colonists had grown increasingly disillusioned with British policies and policy makers during the revolutionary years. Political disagreements between the locally elected assemblies and the London-appointed governors, the restriction on trade with the mainland, and complaints that Britain was not providing enough security to the islands, especially after France entered the war, created tensions between the colonies and Britain.

In Barbados, political disagreements between the Assembly and the governor escalated steadily after the Stamp Act crisis. Matters came to a head in the mid-1770s, sparked by London's 1775 prohibition of trade with the rebellious American colonies. This Law enacted by the British Parliament prohibited American beef, pork, dairy products, and fish and stipulated that all flour, grain, lumber, and vegetables arrive in British vessels. Colonists argued that trade restrictions would result in severe shortages of provisions and economic ruin but in the long run these trade restrictions proved less disruptive than many had initially feared. Governor Edward Hay created an uproar among the Assembly leaders by refusing to support a planter's petition to the king asking for relief from the trade embargo. Additionally, Hay reported to London in 1776 that the island had a large surplus of food and to make matters worse, he allowed a British naval squadron that arrived on the island to purchase as many provisions as they could find, creating even greater scarcity for residents. Hay's lack of concern, and at times outright hostility, to the planters' anxieties generated bureaucratic retaliation from the Barbados Assembly leaders. In some cases they refused to approve spending measures that Hay proposed to strengthen Barbados fortifications and militia after France joined the war. The island's economy was too unstable to afford such measures, they claimed. Furthermore, it was England's duty to defend the West Indian colonies because England had provoked the hostilities with the American colonies that now had threatened them. Discontent on the island grew considerably after 1778 when France, and later Spain, entered the war and the Caribbean colonies appeared more vulnerable to attack. Petitions from West Indian merchants and planters in London supported complaints from colonists in Jamaica and Barbados. The West Indian lobbyists, which increased in both organization and effectiveness after the Seven Years War, bombarded Parliament with requests for greater military support for the islands.

Calls for aid and protection grew louder after the fall of Grenada and St. Vincent in 1779.

Parliament therefore faced mounting criticism from London lobbyists and absentees and festering discontent on the islands when news of the hurricanes in 1780 and pleas for help arrived in late 1780. Definitely humanitarian motives influenced Parliament's action, but disaster relief also made good political sense. It tempered the criticisms from West Indian lobbyists that the government was not doing enough for the troubled Caribbean colonies, and it provided substantial support to colonists just when they were complaining about the lack of such aid from England. Secretary of State Germain vehemently voiced such concerns in a letter to Cunningham: the relief funds provided "a striking proof of the warm affection borne by the people of England to their fellow subjects in the West Indies, and the unbounded benevolence of Parliament, and ought to remove every jealously of their good will and produce the most sincere Petition of Gratitude and Affection." He echoed such themes in another letter to Cunningham later that year: "The late munificence of Parliament must convince the people how ready this country is to attend to their Interest, and relieve their distresses." That British leaders allocated the money during an expensive war, Germain wrote to Dalling in Jamaica, provided further "testimony of the tender regard of government, for the faithful subjects of the King, in all parts of his majesty's dominions, and of the good will borne them by the people of this country, and ought to remove every ground of jealousy or distrust." Therefore, the British Parliament used disaster relief to reaffirm the connection between Britain and the West Indian colonies and to deflect the criticisms that the British officials were inattentive to the needs of colonists. After the Great Hurricane of 1780, it became apparently clear that British officials soon embraced disaster relief as a political tool for the good of the country and for themselves.[3]

Major General James Cunningham replaced Hay as governor in 1779. The change in administration did little to soften the strained relations. Things started poorly when the Assembly greeted Cunningham with a message stating that "impoverished state of the island" meant that he would receive only £2,000 in addition to his pay from London, £1,000 less than his predecessor. They added an incentive clause, however, stating that if Cunningham managed to eliminate the much despised 4.5 percent duty, which was a tax going as far back as the early seventeenth century; they would grant him the additional £1,000. In a highly unusual move, the Council, which was duty bound not to amend money bills, added a statement to go along with what they were saying by stating that the bill was an "indignity to government" and a "discredit to the island." Cunningham in a surprising move as the newly appointed governor agreed. Annoyed and insulted, he responded by trying to impose a system of fees intended to supplement his salary, a plan that gained some support from the Council. But the attempt triggered indignation among members of the Assembly, who believed only they had the right or the authority to impose taxes. When the petitions for hurricane relief arrived in London, the Secretary of State, Lord George Germain, informed Cunningham that "the late behavior of the Assembly of Barbados has not been such as to give the Island a claim to the benevolence either of his Majesty or of Parliament."

The decision to distribute relief funds in January 1781 generated little debate among members of Parliament, but decisions about how best to use the money triggered intense controversy in both islands. In Barbados, debate over the parliamentary bounty quickly became entangled with the ongoing disputes between the governor and the Assembly. Political differences first delayed distribution of the supplies and money and ultimately redirected much of it away from the island's poorest inhabitants and to Barbados's planter class. Barbados received its first shipments of disaster relief in early 1781, not from Parliament but from private donations raised in Ireland. Residents of Cork circumvented the relief campaign organized by officials in Dublin and sent £1,000 sterling directly to hurricane victims. In May, several cargo ships from Dublin arrived in Bridgetown harbour bringing barrels of herring, beans, and flour along with linens, caps, and shoes. The donors gave the aid to the Governor for distribution, and he then turned to the Council for help in distributing these funds and provisions to the neediest on the island. They distributed the money among the eleven parishes, with each getting between £100 and £160 currency to distribute to the victims. In addition, they also requested the local leaders in each parish to conduct interviews to determine the substantive losses and to determine who should receive provisions and supplies. It remains unclear if this census ever took place, but by mid-May the Council began distributing the relief fund to the individual parishes. When more Irish cargo ships arrived with aid in August, officials distributed the supplies in the same manner.

Cunningham excluded the Assembly leaders from the decision making with regards to the Irish relief supplies, but he had to include them in any decisions made about the Parliamentary bounty. Parliament had turned over the control of the funds to the Treasury but suggested they seek advice from the Barbados Planters and Merchants in London. The committee suggested, and the Treasury approved a plan calling for the Governor, Council, and Assembly to determine the most adequate means of determining individual losses and distributing this aid on the island. Cunningham therefore had to deal with the Assembly leaders, and the bounty quickly became caught up in political turmoil between the two branches. Cunningham wanted to use the funds to repair the island's fortifications. Annoyed by the Assembly's continued reluctance to allocate money for defense, he saw the money as a major occasion to advance his plans and believed that Parliament's generosity would overcome any lingering opposition. The bounty, "provided for the relief of your Distress," he wrote to the Assembly in May 1781, "cannot fail to excite your Zeal, Ardor, and Exertion in rebelling...his Majesties Enemies." But Assembly leaders refused to go along, and by November Cunningham informed Germain that "had Parliament the smallest idea of the Assembly here acting so Undutiful a Part of Great Britain, they would have appropriated a Part of the Donation to the Repairing of the Fortifications and Public Buildings." He later advocated that the king should get involved to ensure that some funds were used for these purposes.[4]

Assembly leaders wanted to use the funds to aid the poorest residents who had suffered the most during the storm. The initial bill emerged out of a joint committee of the Assembly and Council called for a general distribution of the money and provisions among all victims of the hurricane, but when the plan reached the Assembly for debate in early October 1781, opposition emerged, led by the Speaker of the Assembly, Sir John Gay Alleyne. Alleyne believed that if passed the bill would challenge the wishes of Parliament; indeed, it was "so flagrant a Breach of Trust" that if passed it would result in a public "censure." British officials allocated funds to help "such of them as have been reduced to Distress and Necessity by the dreadful Calamity." Instead of aiding those most in need, Alleyne charged that this plan assisted "all the sufferers alike, altho' many of the, great as their Losses had been, remained with comfortable Fortunes, and some even possessed of ample ones." Alleyne and the Assembly drafted an revised bill at the end of October that called for a committee in each parish to examine the losses of individual colonists, to determine their present situation and whether they had received any aid from the Irish donation, and then to allocate the aid in accordance with Parliament's directive, namely to the poor and others facing real "distress and necessity."[5]

When the Assembly Bill arrived for debate on November 27, the Council immediately rejected it without even a second reading believing that it was essentially flawed in its principles. Among other issues, the Council alleged that the Assembly was playing politics by not giving Cunningham enough executive power in the proceedings. Specifically they condemned the plan to remove Cunningham's veto power, "which the Lords of the Treasury intended he should have," and transferred effective control of the bounty to the Speaker and "his party in the Assembly." In response, Councilman Henry Frere introduced a new plan. Frere suggested using the bounty to pay off the island's debt, which stood at £34,000 in 1781 and was growing. He estimated the annual government operating costs during the war at roughly £10,000 and argued that these bills had to be paid "or we must submit to the ignominy of being a bankrupt Government, with numerous, clamorous improvised creditors." Frere believed it was unlikely that residents would give in to new taxes to reduce the debt. This was because no one was in a position to do so because of the significant losses they sustained during the hurricane. However, Frere contended that "by putting this Money into the Treasury everything may be made Easy. We must pay off the Country's debt; we shall also have additional year's expenses, and the burthen of taxation will, for a time, be done away." Regarding the motives of the British

Government, Frere said it was plain to see that the Parliament had given the legislature "discretionary power" over the aid.[6]

The competing plans resulted in a legislative stalemate, and in early December Cunningham informed Germain that no action had been taken with regards to the allocation of the funds and provisions. Officials on the island decided to write to England for specific instructions on what to do with the money. In the meantime, a Council bill for distribution of supplies and provisions that arrived in November failed because Cunningham frustrated with Assembly leaders over fortifications, fees, and other issues, dismissed them for two months at the end of November 1781. The Assembly later passed a resolution denouncing Cunningham's actions, stating that he had purposefully suspended the Assembly even though relief supplies had recently arrived and, by "repeated adjournments" during January, had kept them from meeting, thereby "rendering ineffectual the Bounty and benevolent Intention of Parliament."[7]

These heated conflicts and debates had serious repercussions for many island residents. As officials awaited instructions from London on how to proceed on the distribution of funds and provisions, food and supplies sat in Bridgetown warehouses costing roughly £200 a month for storage. When Cunningham finally recalled the Assembly in February, one member emphasized the need for quick action, because the food supplies of beans, peas, bread and flour were extremely perishable and the more time they took debating this issue the quicker the food items would spoil and be unfit for use. Furthermore, the food items sitting on the warehouse would benefit no one he declared. Although much of the debris from the destroyed buildings and on the plantations had been cleared away, reconstruction remained incomplete as the colonists waited for building supplies and money to pay for them. Finally, one Council member Samuel Husbands said that the money and provisions were gifts from the British people to the needy citizens of Barbados and all of the needy sufferers. Another member, James Straker suggested that all classes of victims should benefit from the aid including the rich plantation owners. Another member, Alleyne mounted a vigorous attack against those ideas. He repeated the language of the parliamentary resolution about aiding those in "distress and necessity" and quoted an advertisement in a

London newspaper stating that the private donations were going to the poor and most "distressed" in the colony, not to wealthy sugar planters. He rigorously opposed the idea of using hurricane aid to pay the public debt as some had suggested. Alleyne's defense of the poor and "distressed" mixed humanitarian concern for the poor with larger political motives some contended. Alleyne himself was a wealthy planter whose family had been in Barbados and in Barbadian politics for generations and some simply suggested he was playing politics with hurricane aid distribution.

Such humanitarian and political motivations were also mixed in the debate on the Council bill whether to distribute the provisions separately. Straker, concerned about the cost of delay and the possibility of the provisions' spoiling wanted to get supplies into the hands of those who needed it, but he also worried that any further delay might give Cunningham greater control over the relief process. By distributing the funds and provisions immediately, Straker argued, the House would display their "good sense and moderation" and could at least control part of the process while they continued to fight Cunningham, "our rapacious Plunderer," over distribution of the funds. Alleyne and several other members, however, worried that separate bills might imply that the funds could be used for purposes other than the relief of the victims. The motion to separate the money and provisions passed by one vote, but Alleyne managed to secure the backing of the Assembly, and the impasse between the two branches continued throughout the month of March and into April.

Instructions from London finally arrived in late April 1782, more than eighteen months after the Great Hurricane of 1780. Replying with some bureaucratic understatement that the "mode formerly proposed of disposing of the (bounty) by the Legislature of the Country" had been found "so difficult as to render the prosecution thereof unadvisable if not impractical," the Barbados Committee ordered that an equal number of members of the Council and the Assembly form a special committee, excluding the governor, with the power to allocate the bounty as they saw fit. Each house then selected members, and the new committee met in early May. It immediately passed a motion by William Bishop of the Council to use half of the remaining funds for retiring the public debt, and held back the other half for direct allocation to victims of the hurricane. Alleyne again opposed the idea, but other members of the committee, including his fellow assemblyman Samuel Husbands, supported it, and the plan passed. Officials also agreed to divide the supplies and provisions equally among the parishes, although Cunningham recommended that some of the stores were sold and the money shared between sufferers.

The actual distribution of the parliamentary money was delayed for many months due to bureaucratic red tape, and that didn't help the situation because many small expenses continued to eat into the principal. The London Committee shipped £20,000 sterling in specie to Barbados in December 1782-in two boxes conveniently labeled "Barbados Sufferers No. 1 and Barbados Sufferers No. 2" another £20,000 in January and a final £3,500 in April 1783. Transporting actual coins rather than employing bills of exchange created additional expenses and deductions for freight and insurance. The Committee in charge of dispensing the money finally approved a resolution in August 1783 calling for commissioners to allocate £1,800 in each parish, among colonists whose losses did not exceed £1,500, although in some cases advertisements of meetings where victims could claim losses did not appear until November. In the meantime, the commissioners distributed funds for a number of public projects, including several thousand pounds for rebuilding the town hall in Bridgetown and £1,900 for repairing several churches destroyed in the hurricane. They also paid the salary of the island's agent located in London. Some of the money allocated by Parliament eventually did end up in the hands of the poorest and neediest colonists, but political disputes in Barbados delayed distribution of the funds and diverted a large amount to the island's wealthiest colonists in the form of tax relief. In fact, much of the hurricane relief designated to the poorer class of sufferers actually ended up in the hands of sugar planters.[7]

CONCLUSION

This great hurricane helped define life in the colonies impacted by this great storm. Initially hurricanes were entirely new to European migrants, and they immediately became a defining feature of the region's physical environment. The frequency of hurricanes challenged efforts to establish permanent settlements, and forced these colonists to re-evaluate many of their basic perceptions of the natural world and their economic expectations. This storm caused great physical and economic devastation in 1780, leveling houses, towns, farms, plantations and sinking ships. The valuable sugar crop lay ruined in the fields in the aftermath of this major storm, as did plantation infrastructure. For the slaves on these plantations in the West Indies, it brought a greater workload and significant hardships. This storm totally destroyed provisional crops as readily as staple crops, and along with the powerful winds and storm surge, hunger and disease claimed the lives of many slaves throughout this dry and barren time. Colonists took what steps they could to lessen the devastation, such as, harvesting the crops or shipping them out before the hurricane season but in most cases they could ultimately do little to tame the wrath of Mother Nature. Eventually, colonists in the Caribbean came to realize that living in this region meant living with great risks over their heads and living with destructive hurricanes. The storm for many years to follow, continued to terrify and amaze all who had experienced this storm, and this was the case since the inception of colonization in the early 1620s. Although it can be argued that residents, over time gained insightful experiences with these storms that would benefit them later on down the road.

Even after the Great Hurricane of 1780, these storms still damaged and destroyed both crops and infrastructure used to process them but never in the magnitude as this one in 1780. They also caused significant financial losses to the farmers, but this storm also provided the guideline or threshold level that many other great storms of this magnitude came to follow. The end of the American War of Revolution in 1783 was an important dividing point in the history of hurricanes in this region. The signing of the Treaty of Paris in 1783 signaled the end of the first British Empire in America because South Carolina and Georgia joined the new United States of America, while the West Indian colonies remained loyal to Great Britain. Changes in the political geography of the region had important repercussions for residents of the old colonies and new states as they battled hurricanes in the years prior to 1780. Planters argued that the regulations cost the lives of thousands of slaves who perished in the aftermath of this great storm in 1780, so they continued to lobby the British Parliament to repel these orders. Changing social, political, and economic conditions helped shape the history of hurricanes in the Caribbean during the seventeenth and eighteenth centuries and beyond. However what remained constant over time were the storms themselves. Each summer brought a renewed threat from hurricanes, and rarely did a year passed when a storm did not strike somewhere, giving heartache to some residents in the region.

Although the exact strength of this storm is unknown, anecdotal evidence of its destruction leads modern researchers to conclude that the Great Hurricane of 1780 was a Category 5 storm, possibly with winds in excess of 200 miles per hour. With ferocious hurricanes, they can change the course of our lives in the blink on an eye. Amid the chaos that follows, survivors are left to work through the disaster and grief and try to search for answers, which in most cases they may never find. This great storm in 1780 made this year in many ways the worst year in the North Atlantic hurricane history. News of this great storm travelled far and wide and sealed the reputation of the Caribbean as a dangerous place for habitation and trade. This year was a turning point in the history of the Caribbean, marking the end of a long period of prosperity and the beginning of an episode of economic and cultural decline.

Our planet, earth, is surrounded by an 'envelope' of air called the atmosphere. Weather is the state of the atmosphere at any particular time and location. It is probably mankind's most widely discussed subject, and its effects are all-pervasive, ranging from the trivial to the tragic. Weather believe it or not dictates the kind of life we lead, our homes, our clothes, and our leisure pursuits. The weather in any one region can vary from place to place and from day to day, or even hour to hour. Climate, on the other hand, is the typical weather for a location and takes into account long-term averages and extremes. Minimally, accurate weather records for periods of 30 years or more are needed in order to construct a worthwhile profile of the climate of any given area. While meteorological records have been kept for only a couple of centuries, they can be supplemented by historical data and a growing body of evidence from the natural world to provide information about the earth's changing climate. One of the main reasons why we as humans study the weather is simply because we are highly inquisitive and wish to classify and explain atmospheric phenomena, such as, deadly hurricanes in simple terms. More important, however, is the need to anticipate the weather, so that we can prepare for extreme weather conditions such as, these devastating hurricanes, or simply take advantage of favorable conditions. Meteorology-the scientific study of weather is a relatively new discipline but thankfully, today, our understanding of the science of weather is reinforced with the help of modern technology. Sadly, that didn't exist in 1780 when the region experienced the wrath of a hurricane of mega proportions.

There is nothing like hurricanes in the atmosphere. Even seen by sensors on satellites thousands of miles above the earth, the uniqueness and destructibility of these powerful, tightly coiled storms are clear. Hurricanes believe it or not are not the largest storm systems, nor are they the most violent-but they combine those qualities as no other phenomenon does, as if they were designed to be engines of death and destruction. In the Northern Hemisphere, these storms are called hurricanes, a term that echoes early colonial Spanish and Caribbean Indian words for evil spirits and big winds. These storms are products of the tropical oceans and atmosphere: powered by heat from the sea, steered by the easterly trade winds and temperate westerlies, and driven by their own fierce energy. Around their tranquil core, winds blow with lethal velocity and the ocean develops an inundating surge. Furthermore, as they move ashore, tornadoes may descend from the advancing bands of thunderclouds. Hurricanes, as poorly understood as they are today, seem to have one single major benefit-they are a major source of rain for those continental corners over which their unpredictable tracks carry them. Mostly they are seen as heat engines of tragedy, which still leave death and destruction in their paths, even though the effectiveness of warning systems have doubled and redoubled in recent decades.

In a hurricane, wind speeds can reach over 155 mph, because the wind's impact increases exponentially with its speed, it can tear off roofs and totally flatten buildings. This destructive power can be made worse because within the hurricane the wind blows in the opposite directions on either side of the hurricane's center or eye. Violent as it is, wind is the secondary cause of damage and the storm surge accounts for most of the damages and death in the storm. Such surges are a hazard for most hurricanes occurring in the Caribbean, where they often play a deadly role in the hurricanes that hit many of the islands of the Caribbean. Hurricanes form best in hot conditions, and form in regions where the sea's surface temperature exceeds 26.5°C. In the North Atlantic, heat stored during the summer produces a peak hurricane season from early August to mid September, while off northern Australia the cyclone season reaches its height between January and March. However, once the sea starts to cool, violent tropical cyclones are rare, but with an increase in Global Warming, meteorologists speculate that zones of warm water will become larger and more persistent. As a result, the threat from hurricanes and typhoons is almost certain to increase. With more of this oceanic heat available to create rising air, cyclonic hurricanes are likely to become more frequent, and the strength of each storm may increase. The vast amounts of moisture that it carries into the atmosphere will more than likely increase. In addition, hurricanes may also move further north from the tropics than they do now, threatening areas as far north as New England in the United States relatively often. At present, this danger is still hypothetical but the next few decades will definitely show whether or not it is real.

Although scientists have not yet completely understood the complex nature and conditions of hurricanes within the earth's atmosphere, nonetheless they have made incredible strides in hurricane forecasting. By keeping close tabs on developing tropical storms and using advanced computer models, they have made these remarkable strides in forecasting hurricanes in recent years with the help of modern equipment and advanced technology. Today, there is a steady increase in actual storm damage but fortunately, the death toll has significantly decreased. This should come as no surprise, since there has been a tremendous increase in persons wanting to build on or near the coast. The day of the multi-billion dollar hurricane is now here. This is due in part to the abundance of major developments on or along the hurricane prone coast. Most meteorologists attribute this low death toll to better and more comprehensive warning systems throughout the region. However, the improvements in our warning service are not keeping pace with the high demands imposed by the increasing coastal population. It is time to launch a grassroots community and individual public awareness program about hurricanes in general and about their potential dangers.

There are ways in which humans can defend themselves against nature's fury. Maintaining the natural ecosystem helps to mitigate floods, hurricanes and drought. Scientists have made great strides in predicting all kinds of disasters, and societies, chastened by recurring tragedy, have begun to fortify against the inevitable. However, a hurricane in a remote area is not considered a natural disaster. From Bridgetown, Barbados to New Orleans, the media has provided chilling images that show the potential for destruction when a cataclysm hurricane like the Great Hurricane of 1780 strikes cities and villages. The extent of the carnage depends on both the force of the storm and its location. If aimed directly at a populated city center, even a small storm can prove lethal. A 50-mile dogleg in the path of a hurricane can mean the difference between nuisance and tragedy. Unfortunately, humans tend to hug the vulnerable hurricane prone coasts, where the sea and sky conspire to brew monster storms. In an even crueler twist, hurricanes tend to punish those least capable of putting up a fight especially here in the Caribbean. Over and over, the earth pummels people who are already starving and homeless and who possess only meager resources with which to recover or rebuild. Sadly, disasters such as, hurricanes never occur in a vacuum. They demolish towns, divide families, sink ships, and bankrupt governments. Victims suffer lingering effects-social, political, economic, and cultural-long after the skies clear and the flood waters recedes.

So why do people continue to live in hurricane prone volatile regions? In some places, such as the Mississippi Delta, a catastrophe can deliver benefits, as flood waters from these storms can deposit fertile soils. In other cases, denial reigns. People instinctively expect the world to continue to behave as it has during their lifetime. If a hurricane has not struck a particular area for many years people believe that they are immune from future storms. In fact, even when a disaster is imminent and residents may see the sure signs of this impending storm they often refuse to flee or they might wait until the last minute to evacuate. Sadly, variations on those kinds of stories weave throughout this region, almost always with tragic endings. This book provides gripping accounts of these terrible events, along with stories of nick-of-time escapes, heroic rescues, and triumphant discoveries. Sometimes the earth plays the villain and sometimes the reacting victim, but its gestures are invariably awe-inspiring. Could another 1780 disaster happen again? The easy answer is no. Now, in the twenty-first century, we receive advanced warnings days ahead of the impending storm so that we can either brace our homes or run like hell. The present generation should pay close attention because these tales are not only of our past but also our future as well, so it is so important that we always remain vigilant and prepared for when a future storm strikes any location within this region.

FOOTNOTES:

PREFACE

1. J.D. Jarrell, Max Mayfield, Edward Rappaport, & Chris Landsea *NOAA Technical Memorandum NWS TPC-1 The Deadliest, Costliest, and Most Intense United States Hurricanes from 1900 to 2000(And Other Frequently Requested Hurricane Facts).*
2. *Mitch: The Deadliest Atlantic Hurricane Since 1780-* National Climatic Data Center-U.S. Department of Commerce.

CHAPTER ONE

Prelude to a 'Great' Hurricane

1. Sir Robert Schomburgk' *The History of Barbados: Comprising a Geographical and Statistical Description of the Island, a Sketch of the Historical Events Since the Settlement, and an Account of Its Geology and Natural Productions.* Pg 11, pgs 642-43, pgs 206-7.
2. The Sun-Sentinel-June 01, 2010-*Hurricane timeline: 1495 to 1800....1495 -- Columbus encounters a hurricane near Hispaniola. Hurricane Section Pg 1.*

CHAPTER THREE

The History behind the word 'Hurricane' and other Tropical Cyclone Names

1. Emanuel, K.(2005) *Divine Wind-The History and Science of Hurricanes*, Oxford University Press, pgs 3-5.
2. Emanuel, K.(2005) *Divine Wind-The History and Science of Hurricanes*, Oxford University Press, pgs 18-21.
3. Emanuel, K.(2005) *Divine Wind-The History and Science of Hurricanes*, Oxford University Press, pg 21.
4. Barratt, P. (2006) *Bahama Saga-The Epic Story of the Bahama Islands*, AuthorHouse pg 51.
5. Saunders, A.(2006) *History of Bimini Volume 2*, New World Press, pgs 5-9.
6. Saunders, A.(2006) *History of Bimini Volume 2*, New World Press, pgs 6-9.
7. Barratt, P. (2006) *Bahama Saga-The Epic Story of the Bahama Islands*, AuthorHouse pg 51.
8. Saunders, A.(2006) *History of Bimini Volume 2*, New World Press, pg 14.
9. Mulcahy, M. (2006) *Hurricanes and Society in the British Greater Caribbean, 1624-1783*, The John Hopkins University Press, pg 35.
10. *An Early Colonial Historian: John Oldmixon and "The British Empire in America-Journal of American Studies Vol.3, No. 2*(Aug.,1973), pgs 113-123...Cambridge University Press.
11. http://hrsbstaff.ednet.ns.ca/primetl/school/juan/hurricanesheets.htm.
12. http://www.fascinatingearth.com/node/311.
13. Millas C.J. (1968) *Hurricanes of The Caribbean and Adjacent Regions 1492-1800*, Edward Brothers Inc/ Academy of the Arts and Sciences of the Americas Miami, Florida. Pg xi.
14. Millas C.J. (1968) *Hurricanes of The Caribbean and Adjacent Regions 1492-1800*, Edward Brothers Inc/

Academy of the Arts and Sciences of the Americas Miami, Florida. Pg xi.

15. Benzon, G. (1837) *History of the New World Vol. 21*, Hakluyt Society.

16. Tannehill, I.(1950) *Hurricanes-Their Nature and History*, *Princeton University Press, pg 141.*

17. National Geographic Magazine, November 1986-*A Columbus Casebook-A Supplement to "Where Columbus Found the New World."*

18. *Neely, W.(2011) The Great Bahamas Hurricane of 1866*, *Iuniverse, Inc. pg 28.*

CHAPTER FOUR

The Naming of Hurricanes

1. http://www.william-shakespeare.info/shakespeare-play-the-tempest.html.

2. Stewart, George R.(1941) *STORM.* University of Nebraska Press.

3. www.nhc.noaa.gov/archive/2003/dis/al172003.discus.016. shtml.

CHAPTER FIVE

The New Classification of Hurricanes in the North Atlantic Basin

1. www.nhc.noaa.gov/aboutsshws.php.

2. www.nhc.noaa.gov/aboutsshws.php.

3. www.nhc.noaa.gov/pdf/nws-nhc-6.pdf.

4. Duedall, I., Williams, J. (2002) *Florida Hurricanes and Tropical Storms 1871-2001,*USA, University Press Of Florida. Pgs xii,5.

5. www.aoml.noaa.gov/hrd/tcfaq/D2.html.

6. www.aoml.noaa.gov/hrd/tcfaq/A3.html.

7. www.nws.noaa.gov/os/hurricane/resources/ TropicalCyclones11.pdf.

8. *www.aoml.noaa.gov/hrd/tcfaq/.*

CHAPTER SIX

The 1780 North Atlantic Hurricane Season

1. *harvardforest.fas.harvard.edu/data/p01/hf012/hf012-05-reports.html.*
2. http://www.archive.org/stream/attempttodevelop00reiduoft/ attempttodevelop00reiduoft_djvu.txt. THE LAW OF STORMS-Lieut.Colonel W.Reid, C.B. Published by John Weale, London.
3. Mulcahy, M. (2006) *Hurricanes and Society in the British Greater Caribbean, 1624-1783*, The John Hopkins University Press, pg 98.
4. Mulcahy, M. (2006) *Hurricanes and Society in the British Greater Caribbean, 1624-1783*, The John Hopkins University Press, pg 165.
5. http://jamaica-gleaner.com/pages/history/story008.html.
6. Emanuel, K.(2005) *Divine Wind-The History and Science of Hurricanes*, Oxford University Press, pgs 63-64.
7. http://jamaica-gleaner.com/pages/history/story008.html.
8. www.archive.org/stream/.../attempttodevelop00reiduoft_ djvu.txt.
9. *Southey, T.(1827) The Chronological History of the West Indies Vol. 2. Longman, Rees, Orme, Brown, and Green, Pg 471.*
10. Millas C.J. (1968) *Hurricanes of The Caribbean and Adjacent Regions 1492-1800*, Edward Brothers Inc/ Academy of the Arts and Sciences of the Americas Miami, Florida. Pg 253.
11. *Thrilling Narratives of Mutiny, Murder and Piracy-A Weird Series of Tales of Shipwreck and Disaster...With Accounts of Providential Escapes and Heart-Rending Fatalities*-Hurst & Co Publishers, New York. Pgs 1-49.
12. Bolton, H. & Marshall, T.(1920) *The Colonization of North America-1493-1783* by MacMillian & Co.
13. Bolton, H. & Marshall, T.(1920) *The Colonization of North America-1493-1783* by MacMillian & Co.

CHAPTER SEVEN
NEMO Remembers the Great Hurricane of 1780

1. Friday, October 7, 2005-National Emergency Management Organization (NEMO)-Celebrates the 225th Anniversary of *The Great Hurricane of 1780*. Written by Dr. Colin Depradine-Principal of the Caribbean Institute of Meteorology and Hydrology (CIMH). The article was originally published in *The Barbados Advisory*, 35th Anniversary Edition of the CIMH in 2002.

CHAPTER EIGHT
Impact of the Great Hurricane of 1780

1. J.D. Jarrell, Max Mayfield, Edward Rappaport, & Chris Landsea *NOAA Technical Memorandum NWS TPC-1 The Deadliest, Costliest, and Most Intense United States Hurricanes from 1900 to 2000(And Other Frequently Requested Hurricane Facts)*.
2. http://dpcaptain.blogspot.com/.
3. Mulcahy, M. (2006) *Hurricanes and Society in the British Greater Caribbean, 1624-1783*, The John Hopkins University Press, pg 24.
4. L'Art de Terifier les Dates ou *Chronologie Historique de l'Amerique*, par M.D.B. Warden, Vol. viii. Pg 516.
5. Mulcahy, M. (2006) *Hurricanes and Society in the British Greater Caribbean, 1624-1783*, The John Hopkins University Press, pg 57.
6. L'Art de Terifier les Dates ou *Chronologie Historique de l'Amerique*, par M.D.B. Warden, Vol. viii. Pg 516.

CHAPTER NINE
Personal Recollections of the Great Hurricane of 1780

1. www.hum.leiden.edu/research/.../monthly-letter-october-2009.html.

2. www.hum.leiden.edu/research/.../monthly-letter-october-2009.html.
3. www.hum.leiden.edu/research/.../monthly-letter-october-2009.html.
4. *Piddington, H. (1848) The sailor's horn-book for the law of storms, John Wiley, New York.*
5. www.hum.leiden.edu/research/.../monthly-letter-october-2009.html.
6. www.hum.leiden.edu/research/.../monthly-letter-october-2009.html.
7. www.hum.leiden.edu/research/.../monthly-letter-october-2009.html.
8. *Extract from the ship's log book of the H.M.S. Albermarle(1780).*
9. www.hum.leiden.edu/research/.../monthly-letter-october-2009.html.
10. Reclus, E. (1873) *The Ocean*, Harper and Brothers.
11. Kimber, I & Kimber, E. (1780) *The London Magazine, or Gentlemen's Monthly Intelligencer, Vol. 49*, pgs 622-623.
12. *The Barbados Mercury*, Dated October 28th 1780, CO 28/57/214-Barbados National Archives.
13. Maury, M & Fontaine, M.(1806)-*The Physical Geography of the Sea.*: By M. F. Maury.
14. Milner, T.(1857) *The Gallery of Nature or Wonders of the Earth and the Heavens Vol. 2.*-Caleb Wright-Boston, pgs 674-675.
15. Milner, T.(1857) *The Gallery of Nature or Wonders of the Earth and the Heavens Vol. 2.*-Caleb Wright-Boston, pgs 674-675.
16. Smith, A.(1997) *Legend of the Lake: The 22-Gun Brig-Sloop Ontario, 1780*, Kingston, ON: Quarry Press, pg 159.
17. Hyde, S.(1831) *Account of the Fatal Hurricane by which Barbados Suffered & Genealogy of Barbados Families,- The Journal of Barbados Museum and Historical Society*, pg 57.

18. *Materials relating to the West Indies from the Senhouse Papers 1762-1831*-The Journal of the Barbados Museum and Historical Society in August, 1935.
19. Stoute, E. *Peeps into Barbados History-The Hurricane of 1780*-The Barbados National Trust, pg 2.
20. Stoute, E. *Peeps into Barbados History-The Hurricane of 1780*-The Barbados National Trust, pg 2.
21. Stoute, E. *Dreadful Rampage of the 1780 Storm*-The Barbados National Trust, pgs 1 & 2.
22. Schomburgk, R.(1848) *The History of Barbados: comprising geographical and statistical description of the island: a sketch of the historical events since the settlement: and an account of its geology and natural productions,* Great Britain, Longman, Brown, Green and Longmans Publishers, Pgs 48-50.
23. Friday, October 7, 2005-National Emergency Management Organization (NEMO)-Celebrates the 225th Anniversary of *The Great Hurricane of 1780.* Written by Dr. Colin Depradine-Principal of the Caribbean Institute of Meteorology and Hydrology (CIMH). The article was originally published in *The Barbados Advisory,* 35th Anniversary Edition of the CIMH in 2002.
24. Friday, October 7, 2005-National Emergency Management Organization (NEMO)-Celebrates the 225th Anniversary of *The Great Hurricane of 1780.* Written by Dr. Colin Depradine-Principal of the Caribbean Institute of Meteorology and Hydrology (CIMH). The article was originally published in *The Barbados Advisory,* 35th Anniversary Edition of the CIMH in 2002.
25. Schomburgk, R. (1848) *The History of Barbados: comprising geographical and statistical description of the island: a sketch of the historical events since the settlement: and an account of its geology and natural productions,* Great Britain, Longman, Brown, Green and Longmans Publishers, Pgs 46-50.
26. Schomburgk, R.(1848) *The History of Barbados: comprising geographical and statistical description of*

the island: a sketch of the historical events since the settlement: and an account of its geology and natural productions, Great Britain, Longman, Brown, Green and Longmans Publishers, Pgs 46-50.

27. Schomburgk, R.(1848) *The History of Barbados: comprising geographical and statistical description of the island: a sketch of the historical events since the settlement: and an account of its geology and natural productions,* Great Britain, Longman, Brown, Green and Longmans Publishers, Pgs 48-50.

28. Schomburgk, R.(1848) *The History of Barbados: comprising geographical and statistical description of the island: a sketch of the historical events since the settlement: and an account of its geology and natural productions,* Great Britain, Longman, Brown, Green and Longmans Publishers, Pgs 48-50.

29. L'Art de Terifier les Dates ou *Chronologie Historique de l'Amerique,* par M.D.B. Warden, Vol. viii. Pg 516.

30. Millas C.J. (1968) *Hurricanes of The Caribbean and Adjacent Regions 1492-1800,* Edward Brothers Inc/ Academy of the Arts and Sciences of the Americas Miami, Florida. Pg 258.

31. Smith, A.(1997) *Legend of the Lake: The 22-Gun Brig-Sloop Ontario, 1780,* Kingston, ON: Quarry Press, pg 159.

CHAPTER TEN

The Compelling Account of the Loss of His Majesty's Ship the 'PHŒNIX'

1. *Account of the Loss of His Majesty's Ship Phoenix-_ Thrilling Narratives of Mutiny, Murder and Piracy-A Weird Series of Tales of Shipwreck and Disaster,-1781* by Hurst & Co. Publisher./*The Loss of His Majesty's Ship Phoenix off the island of Cuba, In the Year 1780* by Lieutenant Archer. Hartford-Andrus and Starr-1813 pgs-276-294.

CHAPTER ELEVEN

The Impact of the Great Hurricane of 1780 on the Sugar Industry of the Caribbean

1. McCusker, J. (1989) *Rum and the American Revolution: The Rum Trade and the Balance of Payments of the Thirteen Continental Colonies*, Garland Publishers-New York, pgs 905-19./Account of sugar imported to England is found in the *Proceedings of the Honourable House of Assembly of Jamaica on the Sugar and Slave Trade*(St. Jago de Vega, Jamaica, 1792)./ Mulcahy, M. (2006) *Hurricanes and Society in the British Greater Caribbean, 1624-1783*, The John Hopkins University Press, pg 74.

CHAPTER TWELVE

The Impact of the Great Hurricane of 1780 and Other Historic Hurricanes on the Life and Times of People in the Caribbean and the Americas.

1. *The South Carolina Gazette 1732-1780*-Thomas Whitemarsh Publishers-Charles Town. Part 5.
2. Mulcahy, M. (2006) *Hurricanes and Society in the British Greater Caribbean, 1624-1783*, The John Hopkins University Press, pg 53./Weather and *Weather Forecasting in Colonial America*-Eisenstadt, pg 207. Clark, W., Golinski & Schafer, S(1999) *"Barometers of Change: Meteorological Instruments as Machines of Enlightenment," in The Sciences in Enlightened Europe.* University of Chicago Press Chapter 3.
3. Mulcahy, M. (2006) *Hurricanes and Society in the British Greater Caribbean, 1624-1783*, The John Hopkins University Press, pg 72/ Robertson, R.(2010) *A short Account of the Hurricane that pass'd thro' the English Leeward Caribbee Islands*, London-Gale ECCO-Print Edition.
4. Ludlum, D.(1963) Early American Hurricanes 1492-1870, American Meteorological Society, pg 43-44./ Mulcahy, M. (2006) *Hurricanes and Society in the British Greater*

Caribbean, 1624-1783, The John Hopkins University Press, pg 72./*Minutes of the Vestry of St. Michael's, March 30, 1781*-Barbados National Archives.

5. Mulcahy, M. (2006) *Hurricanes and Society in the British Greater Caribbean, 1624-1783*, The John Hopkins University Press, pg 54./Wood, P.(1974) *Black Majority: Negroes in Colonial South Carolina from 1670 through the Stono Rebellion*, New York, WW Norton and Company, pg 60.

6. *The Works of the Most Reverend Dr. John Tillotson containing two hundred sermons and discourses, on several occasions*, 2nd Edition, Ralph Baker Pub. pg 700.

CHAPTER THIRTEEN
Wars, Politics, Slaves and the Great Hurricane of 1780

1. Dickerson, W.(1814) *The Mitigation of Slavery in Two Parts-London*/Lambert S. *House of Commons Sessional Papers of the Eighteenth Century*-Wilmington) pgs 69, 296.

2. *Vaughan to War Office, October 30, 1780-CO 5/238/133/ Copy of a Letter from a Planter at Barbados*, Carlisle Bay, November 4, 1780.

3. *Burke, E.(1782) Dodsley's Annual Register or a view of the History, Politics and Literature, for the Year 1781.* Pgs 35/36.

CHAPTER FOURTEEN
The Role, Purpose and Impact of Charity after The Great Hurricane of 1780

1. *St James Chronicle*, July 27, 1781/ Schomburgk, R.(1848) *The History of Barbados: comprising geographical and statistical description of the island: a sketch of the historical events since the settlement: and an account of its geology and natural productions*, Great Britain,

Longman, Brown, Green and Longmans Publishers, Pgs 344.

CHAPTER FIFTEEN

The Role, Purpose and Impact of Aid Distribution and Barbados Politics after the Great Hurricane of 1780

1. *A general account of the calamities occasioned by the late tremendous Hurricanes and Earthquakes in the West India Islands...With petitions to, and resolution of, the House of Commons, on behalf of the sufferers at Jamaica and Barbados*-John Gay Alleyne(Speaker of the House of Assembly, October 31, 1780. J. Stockdale Publisher. Pgs 41-43.

2. *A general account of the calamities occasioned by the late tremendous Hurricanes and Earthquakes in the West India Islands...With petitions to, and resolution of, the House of Commons, on behalf of the sufferers at Jamaica and Barbados*-John Gay Alleyne(Speaker of the House of Assembly, October 31, 1780. J. Stockdale Publisher. Pgs 41-54.

3. Germain to Cunningham, *February 7, 1781, CO 28/58/47-58 Barbados National Archives.*

4. Cunningham to Assembly, May 1, 1781, Cunningham to Germain, January 1, 1782, *CO28/59/145-Barbados National Archives./Mulcahy, M. (2006)* Hurricanes and Society in the British Greater Caribbean, 1624-1783, *The John Hopkins University Press, pg 175.*

5. The New Annual Register or General Repository of History, Politics, and Literature for the year 1781, -*G. Robinson, pg 202.*

6. Assembly Minutes, *February 27, CO 31/41/179;* Cunningham to Germain, *December 1, 1781, CO 28/59/114/*Council Records, November 28, 1781, *CO 31/42/143-45.*

7. The Barbados Mercury, July 12, 1783/ The Barbados Mercury July 12, 1783/ The Barbados Mercury, December 6, 1783-The Barbados National Archives.

REFERENCES:

- *"HURRICANE!"*A Familiarization Booklet by NOAA, April, 1993.
- *Mitch: The Deadliest Atlantic Hurricane Since 1780*-National Climatic Data Center-U.S. Department of Commerce.
- *The Royal Almanack and Register for the Island of Jamaica for the Year 1760,* Kingston, Jamaica, 1759.
- *The Royal Almanack and Register for the Island of Jamaica for the Year 1787,* Kingston, Jamaica, 1786.
- *Thistlewood Diaries, October 3-December 31, 1780-Slaves ill & Slaves and whites.*
- *The St. James Chronicle, January 4 & 30 1781.*
- *Barbados Council Minutes, April 20, 1767, CO 28/50/188; February 2, 1781, CO 31/42/36-42; May 15, 1781, CO 31/42/52; May 21, 1781, CO 31/42/61; August 8, 1781, CO 31/42/103; August 21, 1781, CO 31/42/106; August 28, 1781, CO 31/42/106; December 20, 1781, CO 31/41/154-55; March 19, 1782 CO 31/42/182-83; April 11, 1782, CO 31/42/186-87, April 23, 1782, CO 31/42/190-99.*
- *Barbados Council Records, November 28, 1781, CO 31/42/143-45.*
- *Barbados Assembly Minutes Meetings, April 18, 1781, CO 31/41/90-92/176-79; February 27, 1782, CO 31/41/173-75/180-90/193; April 23, 1782, CO 31/41/194-99.*

- *The House of Assembly Bill, October 30, 1781 CO 28/59/100-113.*
- *A Copy of a Letter from a Planter at Barbados, dated Carlisle Bay, November 4th, 1780, reprinted in Fowler, General Account of the Calamities,* pg 42.
- *The Barbados Annual Register, 1781, pg 35.*
- *Letter from Germain to Cunningham, January 3, 1781, CO 28/58/1-2; 28/59/114/188-89.*
- *Cunningham to Assembly, May 1, 1781.*
- *Cunningham to Earl of Shelburne, May 25, 1782, CO 28/59/308.*
- *Cunningham to Germain June 20, 1781, CO 28/58/176-86; November 26, 1781, CO 28/59/90;December 1, 1781 CO 28/59/92-93; January 1, 1782, CO 28/59/145.*
- *Fowler, General Account of the Calamities, 40-41, 74-78,& 80-83.*
- *Carrington, West Indian Opposition to British Policy, pgs 39-41.*
- *Dublin Journal, January 27, 1781 & February 3, 1781.*
- *House of Commons Sessional Papers of the Eighteenth Century(Wilmington, DE)* pgs 69 & 296.
- *Minutes of the Vestry of St. Michaels with regards to Transatlantic Relief, November 2, 1780, Barbados National Archives.*
- *Minutes of the Vestry of St. Michaels with regards to a Lottery, October 7, 1783, February 15, 1785, September 22, 1785, December 20, 1785, January 4, 1786, April 26, 1786, May 23, 1786, Barbados National Archives.*
- *Return of the losses in the Parish of St. George by the late Hurricane on the 10th day of October, 1780, RB 9/3/9, Barbados National Archives.*
- *The Senhouse Manuscript JBMHS 2* (May 1935) pgs 115-34.
- *Vaughan to War Office, October 30, 1780, CO 5/238/133.*
- *A copy of Benjamin Franklin's letter dated February 7, 1781-PRO, CO 28/58/214.*

- Friday, October 7, 2005-National Emergency Management Organization (NEMO)-Celebrates the 225th Anniversary of *The Great Hurricane of 1780*. Written by Dr. Colin Depradine-Principal of the Caribbean Institute of Meteorology and Hydrology (CIMH). The article was originally published in *The Barbados Advisory*, 35th Anniversary Edition of the CIMH in 2002.

- Sheridan, *Crisis of Slave Subsistence*, pgs 615-41.

- *Peeps into Barbados History-The Hurricane of 1780* by Edward Stoute-A series published by the Barbadian Heritage Publications Trust.

- *Glimpse of Old Barbados-Deadly Rampage of 1780 Storm* by Edward Stoute-A series published by the Barbadian Heritage Publications Trust.

- L'Art de Terifier les Dates ou *Chronologie Historique de l'Amerique*, par M.D.B. Warden, Vol. viii. Pg 516.

- Extract from George Wilson Bridges (1827), *The Annals of Jamaica*, London, pg 28.

- Extract from Herbert Bell, *British Commercial Policy in the West Indies, 1783-1793*.

- *Extract from the ship's log book of the H.M.S. Albermarle(1780)*.

- *The Barbados Mercury, October 28th 1780, CO 28/57/21, pgs 207-210.*

- *The Barbados Mercury, October 28, 1780-Official Account of the Losses in Barbados from the 1780 Hurricane.*

- *The Barbados Mercury, October 28, 1780-Official Account of the Losses in Barbados from the 1780 Hurricane, enclosed in CO 28/4. pgs 208-15.*

- *The Barbados Mercury, July 12, 1783, August 2, 1783, November 29, 1783.*

- *The Barbados Advocate, Wednesday, October 9, 1985-Anniversary of dreadful 1780 Hurricane*-By Edward Stoute.

- *The Barbados Sun, Sunday, November 1, 1998, It so Happened-October a rare time for a hurricane*-By Warren Alleyne.

- A Reassessment of Historical Atlantic Basin Tropical Cyclone Activity, 1700-1855-Michael Chenoweth. *Climatic Change* 76 (1–2): 169–240.
- *Florida Historical Society: The Florida Historical Quarterly Volume 65 issue 3.*
- *Weathering the Storms: Hurricanes and Risk in the British Greater Caribbean.* Business History Review, Vol. 78, No. 4, Winter 2004.
- Ahrens, D. (2000) *Meteorology Today, An Introduction to Weather, Climate, and the Environment,* USA, Brooks/ Cole Publishing.
- Beckford, W. A(1790) *A Descriptive Account of the Island of Jamaica* (London), pgs 1 & 116.
- Black, C.V. (1965) *The Story of Jamaica*, London, Collins Publishers, pg 109.
- Buckley, B., Hopkins, E., Whitaker R. (2004) *Weather-A Visual Guide*, Sidney, Australia, Firefly Books.
- Burroughs, Crowder, Robertson, et al. (1996) *The Nature Company Guides to Weather,* Singapore, Time-Life Publishing Inc.
- Burton, H., Burton, S. (2000) *The Impact of Tropical Cyclones*, Barbados, CIMH.
- Butler, E. (1980) *Natural Disasters,* Australia, Heinemann Educational Books Ltd.
- Calderon, M.E. *The Tainos of Puerto Rico: Rediscovering Borinquen,* USA, Yale University.
- Challoner, J. (2000) *Hurricane and Tornado,* Great Britain, Dorling Kindersley.
- Clarke, P., Smith, A. (2001) *Usborne Spotter's Guide To Weather,* England, Usborne Publishing Ltd.
- Clark, W., Golinski, J., & Schaffer (1999) *Barometers of Change: Meteorological Instruments as Machines of Enlightenment,* in the Sciences in Enlightened Europe, Chicago, pgs 69-93.
- Craton, M.(2001) *A History of the Bahamas (3rd Ed)* Canada, San Salvador Press.

- Davis, K.(2005) *Don't Know Much About World Myths*, USA, HarperCollins Publishers.
- Day, F., Downs, R. et al. (2005) *National Geographic Almanac of Geography*, National Geographic, Washington, D.C.
- Dickson, W. (1969) *The Mitigation of Slavery, in Two Parts*, (London) reprint in 1969 pgs 431-32.
- Dove, E.C. Reid. C. et al, (1862) *The Law of the Storms*, London, Spottiswoode and Company Publishers, pgs 210-215.
- Douglas.S.M. (1958) *Hurricane,* USA, Rinehart and Company Inc, pgs 164-174.
- Duedall, I., Williams, J. (2002) *Florida Hurricanes and Tropical Storms 1871-2001,* USA, University Press Of Florida.
- Durschmied, E. (2001) *The Weather Factor-How Nature has changed History,* New York, Arcade Publishing, Inc.
- Emanuel, K. (2005) *Divine Wind-The History and Science of Hurricanes,* New York, Oxford University Press, pgs 63-66.
- Fitzpatrick, J.P. (1999), *Natural Disasters-Hurricanes,* USA, ABC-CLIO, Inc, pgs 10, 23,154 & 155.
- Gardner, W.J. (1971) *A History of Jamaica,* London, Frank Cass and Co.
- Gibson, C. (2007) *Extreme Natural Disasters,* New York, Hydra Publishing.
- Gore, A.(2006), *An Inconvenient Truth,* New York, USA, Rodale Books.
- J.D. Jarrell, Max Mayfield, Edward Rappaport, & Chris Landsea *NOAA Technical Memorandum NWS TPC-1 The Deadliest, Costliest, and Most Intense United States Hurricanes from 1900 to 2000(And Other Frequently Requested Hurricane Facts).*
- Jones W. (2005) *Hurricane-A Force of Nature,* Bahamas, Jones Communications Intl Ltd. Publication.

- Hall, M. (1916) *No. 455 Notes of Hurricanes, Earthquakes, and other Physical Occurrences in Jamaica up to the commencement of the Weather Service, 1880.* Jamaican Meteorological Service Publication. Pg 4.
- Hook, P. (2006) *Weather Watching,* London, HarperCollins Publishers Ltd.
- Kahl, J. (1998) *National Audubon Society First Field Guide To Weather,* Hong Kong, Scholastic Inc.
- Keith, A. (1948) *Relaxations in the British Restrictions on American Trade with the British West Indies, Journal of Modern History-March, 1948* pgs 1-17.
- Kindersley, D. (2002) *Eyewitness Weather,* London, Dorling Kindersley Ltd.
- Lauber, P. (1996) *Hurricanes: Earth's Mightiest Storms,* Singapore, Scholastic Press.
- Ludlum, D. M. (1989) *Early American Hurricanes 1492-1870.* Boston, MA: American Meteorological Society, pg 198.
- Lyons, A.W. (1997) *The Handy Science Weather Answer Book,* Detroit, Visible Ink Press.
- MacPherson, J. (1967) *Caribbean Lands-A Geography of the West Indies, 2nd Edition,* London, Longmans, Green and Co. Ltd.
- McCusker, J, Menard, R. (1989) *The Economy of British America, 1607-1789,* 2nd ed. Chapel Hill, NC.
- Millas C.J. (1968) *Hurricanes of the Caribbean and Adjacent Regions 1492-1800,* Edward Brothers Inc/ Academy of the Arts and Sciences of the Americas Miami, Florida pgs 249-262.
- Moore, W. and Oliver, L. (1913) *Hurricanes of the West Indies, U.S. Dept. of Agriculture, Weather Bureau Bulletin,* U.S.G.P.O. Washington, D.C. pg 28.
- Mulcahy, M. (2006) *Hurricanes and Society in the British Greater Caribbean, 1624-1783,* Baltimore, The John Hopkins University Press, pgs 2-194.
- Pearce, A.E., Smith G.C. (1998) *The Hutchinson World Weather Guide,* Great Britain, Helicon Publishing Ltd.

- Perez, L. (2001) *Winds of Change: Hurricanes and the Transformation of Nineteenth Century Cuba*, Chapel Hill, NC, pgs 83-108.
- Poyer, J. (1808) *History of Barbados,* pgs 44-45, 414-421, 441-446, 449-455, 457-459 & 493-516.
- Reid, W. (1850) *The Law of Storms by means of facts arranged according to place and time; and hence to point out a cause for the variable winds with the view to practical use in navigation-3rd Ed.* John Weale, Library of Civil, Military, and Mechanical Engineering.
- Redfield; W.C., (1846), *On Three Several Hurricanes of the Atlantic and their Relations To the Northers of Mexico and Central America,* New Haven.
- Reynolds, R. (2000) *Philip's Guide To Weather,* London, Octopus Publishing Group Ltd.
- Robertson, C. (1987) *Fight for Freedom,* Kingston, Kingston Publishers Ltd.
- Saunders, G, and Craton, M. (1998*) Islanders in the Stream: A History of the Bahamian People Volume 2,* USA, University of Georgia Press.
- Schomburgk, R.(1848) *The History of Barbados: comprising geographical and statistical description of the island: a sketch of the historical events since the settlement: and an account of its geology and natural productions,* Great Britain, Longman, Brown, Green and Longmans Publishers, Pgs 46-51 & 339-341.
- Sheets, B., Williams, J.(2001) *Hurricane Watch-Forecasting the Deadliest Storms on Earth,* USA, Vintage Books.
- Smith, A (1997) *Legend of the Lake: The 22-Gun Brig-Sloop Ontario,* 1780., Ontario, Quarry Press.
- Stevens, W.(1999) *The Change in the Weather-People, Weather, and the Science of Climate,* USA, Dell Publishing Inc.
- Stewart, J. (1808) *An Account of Jamaica and Its Inhabitants by a Gentleman Long Resident in the West Indies,* London, pgs 31-32.

- Tannehill, I.(1950) *Hurricanes-Their Nature and History-Particularly those of the West Indies and the Southern Coasts of the United States*, USA, Princeton University Press, pgs 1-5 & 146.
- Treaster, J.(2007) *Hurricane Force-In the Path of America's Deadliest Storms,* USA, Kingfisher.
- Walford, C. (1882) *King's Brief: Their Purposes and History, Transactions of the Royal Historical Society* Great Britain, pgs 1-74.
- Williams, E. (1944) *Capitalism and Slavery* USA, Chapel Hill, pg 52.
- Williams, J. (1997) *The Weather Book*, USA, Vintage Books Ltd.
- Williams, I. (2006) *Rum: A Social and Sociable History of the Real Spirit of 1776*, USA, Nation Books.
- www.enchantedlearning.com
- www.aoml.noaa.gov
- www.noaa.gov
- www.nasa.gov
- www.nhc.noaa.gov
- www.wmo.ch
- www.hurricanecity.com
- www.hum.leiden.edu
- www.nytimes.com
- www.weather.unisys.com
- www.jamaica-gleaner.com
- www.weathernotebook.org
- www.hurricaneville.com
- www.deadlystorms.com
- www.bom.gov.au
- www.stormcarib.com
- www.bbc.co.uk
- www.answers.com
- www.weather.com
- www.wxresearch.org
- www.heldref.org
- www.history.com

- www.bermuda-online.org
- www.weathernotebook.org
- www.wunderground.com
- www.usatoday.com
- www.keyshistory.org
- www.palmbeachpost.com
- www.wikipedia.org
- www.colorado.edu
- www.iri.columbia.edu
- www.nationalgeographic.com
- www.weathersavvy.com
- www.usaid.gov
- www.caribbeannetnews.com

ACKNOWLEDGEMENTS

The writing of a book is a lot of work and you need help from many great persons and organizations to get the job done. The writing and development of this book has been a highly satisfying project, made so by the subject itself but also by the people who have helped and assisted me in some way or the other. To these vast array of individuals-scientists, corporations, researchers, authors, readers, meteorologists, friends, and moral supporters-I owe a great debt of appreciation. To list them all would fill another book, but I especially wish to express my sincere thanks and gratitude to several outstanding people below in no particular order:-

Mr. Lofton and Francita Neely
Ms. Deatrice Adderley
Dr. Steve Lyons
Mr. Andrew McKinney
The late Mr. William Holowesko
The Hon. Glenny's Hanna-Martin
Mr. Murrio Ducille
Mr. Charles & Eddie Carter
Mr. Bryan Norcross
Mr. Max Mayfield
Mr. Christopher Landsea
The late Mr. Herbert Saffir
Mrs. Pleasant McCreary
Rev. Theo and Blooming Neely and family

Mr. Coleman and Diana Andrews and family
Mr. Joshua Taylor and family
Dr. Myles Munroe
Dr. Timothy Barrett
Mr. Rupert Roberts Jr.
Mrs. Lindsey Peterson
Ms. Kristina McNeil
Mr. Ethric Bowe
The late Mrs. Macushla Hazelwood
Mr. Ray Duncombe
Ms. Stephanie Hanna
Mr. Leroy Lowe
Mrs. Shavaughn Moss
Mr. Orson Nixon
Mr. Michael and Philip Stubbs
Mr. Neil Sealey
Mrs. Carole Balla
Ms. Elisa Montalvo
Ms. Sherrine Thompson
Staff and Management of the Nassau Guardian Newspaper
Staff and Management of Media Enterprises
Staff and Management of the Tribune Newspaper
Staff and Management of IslandFM Radio Station
Staff and Management of the Exuma Breeze Radio Station and Newspaper
Staff of the Broadcasting Corporation of the Bahamas (ZNS)
Staff of the Department of Archives
Staff of the Department of Meteorology
Staff of the Barbados Museum and Archives
Staff of the Caribbean Meteorological Institute
Staff of NOAA and the National Hurricane Center in Miami
Mr. Jim Williams and staff of Hurricane City
Mr. Jack and Karen Andrews
Mrs. Margaret Jeffers
Ms. Kathy-Ann Caesar
Mr. Horace & Selvin Burton
Mr. Nigel Atherly

Mrs. Joan Braithwaite

FOR BOOKING AND SPEAKING ARRANGEMENTS HERE
IS MY CONTACT INFORMATION: -

Mr. Wayne Neely
P.O. Box EE-16637
Nassau, Bahamas

E-Mail: wayneneely@hotmail.com
  or wayneneely@yahoo.com

I would like to sincerely thank each one of these sponsors both individual and corporate below who assisted me financially and in many other ways in making this book project a reality. Without them this book would have not been possible, so from the bottom of my heart I thank each and every one you:

Mr. Andrew McKinney
Mr. William Holowesko
Mr. Charles Carter-IslandFm
Mrs. Patricia Beardsley Roker-IslandFm
Mrs. Macushla Hazelwood-Johnbull
Mr. Raymond E. Duncombe-Bobcat Bahamas
Mrs. Darnell Osborne-Insurance Company of the Bahamas.
Ms. Janett Jackson-Insurance Company of the West Indies
Mr. Neil Williams-Security & General Insurance Co.
Mr. Jim Williams-Hurricanecity
Mrs. Joan Braithwaite-Barbados National Archives.
Mr. Christopher Landsea-National Hurricane Center
Mr. Ethric Bowe-Advance Technical Enterprises
Mrs. Patrice Wells-Cole Thompson Pharmacy
Mrs. Jan Roberts-Logos Bookstore
Mrs. Stephanie Hanna-JS-Johnson & Co.
Mr. Dwight Hart-The BreezeFm.
Mr. Rupert Roberts Jr-Super Value Ltd.

Mr. Leroy Lowe-Bahama Divers Co.

Since I first started writing these books on notable Bahamian and Caribbean hurricanes, there have been several companies who stood with me side by side in seeing that these books are not only published, but also placed in our local schools here in the Bahamas. My and their goal is a simple one, and that is to see that future generations of Caribbean residents can read about these great storms and the significant impact that they had on the region as a whole. If you can, please support these companies because your support of these companies helps make this book possible. I would like to sincerely thank each one of these sponsors below, both individual and corporate who assisted me financially and in other ways in making this book project a reality. Without them, this book would have not been possible, so from the bottom of my heart I thank each and every one of them.

B**obcat**
ahamas

dive paradise with

SUPER VALUE FOOD STORES LTD.

#432 East Bay Street
P.O. Box CR-54288 | Nassau, N.P. Bahamas
Tel: 242-322-6735 | 242-322-6736 | Fax: 242-322-6793
Email: admin@afsbahamas.com| Facebook: AFSBahamas | Twitter@AFSBahamas

#120 Mermaid Blvd. West
P.O. Box CR-54288 | Nassau, N.P. Bahamas
Tel: 242-341-7575 | 242-341-3670 | Fax: 242-341-2018
Email: admin@atelbahamas.com

269

Cole-Thompson Pharmacy
P.O. Box SS-5366
Bay & Charlotte Streets
Nassau, Bahamas
Tel: 242-322-2062 or 242-322-2301
Fax: 242-356-3140
Email: colethompsonpharmacy@gmail.com

WEATHER DEFINITIONS:

Air
This is considered the mixture of gases that make up the earth's atmosphere. The principal gases that compose dry air are Nitrogen at 78.09%, Oxygen at 20.95%, Argon at 0.93, and Carbon Dioxide at 0.033%. One of the most important constituents of air and most important gases in meteorology is water vapour.

All Clear
All Clear simply means that the hurricane has left the affected area and all the warnings, and watches are lifted but the residents in that area should exercise extreme caution for downed power lines, debris fallen trees, flooding etc.

Anemograph
An instrument used to measure the wind speed and direction.

Atmosphere
The envelope of gases that surround a planet and are held to it by the planet's gravitational attraction. The earth's atmosphere is mainly nitrogen and oxygen.

Atmospheric Pressure
The pressure exerted by the atmosphere at a given point. It measurements can be expressed in several ways. One is Millibars,

another is Hector Pascal's and another is in inches or millimeters of Mercury.

Barometer
A weather instrument used for measuring the pressure of the atmosphere. The two principle types are aneroid and mercurial.

Bermuda High
A semi-permanent, subtropical area of high pressure in the North Atlantic Ocean that migrates east and west with varying central pressure. Depending on the season, it has different names. When it is displaced westward, during the Northern Hemispheric summer and fall, the center is located in western North Atlantic, near Bermuda. In the winter and early spring, it is primarily centered near the Azores Islands.

Best Track
A subjectively-smoothed representation of a tropical cyclone's location and intensity over its lifetime. The best track contains the cyclone's latitude, longitude, maximum sustained surface winds, and minimum sea-level pressure at 6-hourly intervals. Best track positions and intensities, which are based on a post-storm assessment of all available data, may differ from values contained in storm advisories. They also generally will not reflect the erratic motion implied by connecting individual center fix positions.

Calm
Atmospheric conditions devoid of wind or any other air in motion and where smoke rises vertically. In oceanic terms, it is the apparent absence of the water surface when there is no wind.

Cape Verde Islands
A group of volcanic islands in the eastern Atlantic Ocean off the coast of West Africa. A Cape Verde hurricane originates near here.

Cape Verde Type Hurricane
A hurricane system that originated near the Cape Verde Islands just west of the west coast of Africa.

Center
Generally speaking, the vertical axis of a tropical cyclone, usually defined by the location of the minimum wind or minimum pressure. The cyclone center position can vary with altitude.

Central Pressure
The central Pressure is sometimes referred to as the Minimum Central Pressure is the atmospheric pressure at the center of a high or low. It is the highest pressure in a high and lowest pressure in a low, referring to the sea level pressure of the system on a surface chart.

Climate
The historical record and description of average daily and in seasonal weather events that help describe a region. Statistics are generally drawn over several decades. The word is derived from the Greek klima, meaning inclination, and reflects the importance early scholars attributed to the sun's influence.

Cold Front
The boundary created when a cold air mass collides with a warm air mass.

Convergence
Wind movement that results in a horizontal net inflow of air into a particular region. Convergent winds at lower levels are associated with upward motion.

Coriolis Force
This is an apparent force observed on any free-moving objects in a rotating system. On the earth, this deflective force results from the earth's rotation and causes moving particles (including the wind) to be deflected to the right in the Northern Hemisphere and to the left in the Southern Hemisphere. It was first described in 1835 by French scientist Gustave-Gaspard Coriolis.

Cyclone
An area of low atmospheric pressure, which has a closed circulation, that is cyclonic (counterclockwise in northern hemisphere and

clockwise in southern hemisphere). It is a particularly severe type of tropical storm with very low atmospheric pressure at the centre and strong winds blowing around it. Violent winds and heavy rain may affect an area of some hundreds of miles. The name applies to such storms in the Indian Ocean. 'Typhoons' and 'hurricanes' are other names applied to the same phenomena in the Pacific and Atlantic Oceans respectively.

Depression
It is a region where the surface atmospheric pressure is low. A distinctive feature on a weather map and the opposite of an anticyclone. Usually associated with clouds and rain and sometimes-strong winds. A less severe weather disturbance than a tropical cyclone.

Disturbance
This has several applications. It can apply to a low or cyclone that is small in size and influence. It can also apply to an area that is exhibiting signs of cyclonic development. It may also apply to a stage of tropical cyclone development and is known as a tropical disturbance to distinguish it from other synoptic features.

Doppler radar
An advanced kind of radar that measures wind speed and locates areas of precipitation. It is like conventional radar in that it can detect areas of precipitation and measure rainfall intensity. But a Doppler radar can do more-it can actually measure the speed at which precipitation is moving horizontally toward or away from the radar antenna. Because precipitation particles are carried by the wind, Doppler radar can peer into a severe storm and reveal its winds.

El Niño
A Spanish term given to a warm ocean current, and to the unusually warm and rainy weather associated with it, which sometimes occurs for a few weeks off the coast of Peru (which is otherwise an extremely dry and cool region of the tropics). Several years may pass without this current appearing.

Equator
The ideal or conceptual circle at 0 degrees latitude around the Earth that divides the planet into the northern and southern hemispheres.

Evacuate
To leave an area, usually to escape some impending danger.

Extratropical
A term used in advisories and tropical summaries to indicate that a cyclone has lost its "tropical" characteristics. The term implies both pole ward displacement of the cyclone and the conversion of the cyclone's primary energy source from the release of latent heat of condensation to baroclinic (the temperature contrast between warm and cold air masses) processes. It is important to note that cyclones can become extratropical and still retain winds of hurricane or tropical storm force.

Eye
A region in the center of a hurricane (tropical storm) where the winds are light and skies are clear to partly cloudy.

Eyewall
This is a wall of dense thunderstorms that surrounds the eye of a hurricane.

Feeder Bands
These are the lines or bands of thunderstorms that spiral into and around the center of a tropical system. Also known as outer convective bands or spiral Rainbands, a typical hurricane may have several of these bands surrounding it. They occur in advance of the main rain shield and are usually 40 to 80 miles apart. In thunderstorm development, they are the lines or bands of low level clouds that move or feed into the updraft region of a thunderstorm.

Flash Flood
A localized flood caused by heavy rain falling in a short period of time.

Flood
Overflowing by water of the normal confines of a stream or other body of water, or accumulation of water by drainage over areas that are not normally submerged.

Front
The transition or boundary between two air masses of different densities, which usually means different temperatures. The several types of fronts bring distinct weather patterns.

Funnel Cloud
A violent, rotating column of air visibly extending from the base of a towering cumulus of cumulonimbus toward the ground, but not in contact with it.

Gust
A sudden brief increase in the speed of the wind, followed by a lull or slackening.

Hemisphere
The top and bottom halves of the earth are called the Northern and Southern Hemisphere.

High
The center of an area of high atmospheric pressure, usually accompanied by anticyclonic and outward wind flow. This is an area where the atmospheric pressure is high in contrast to the areas surrounding it forming a distinctive pattern on a weather map. The weather is usually calm and settled at or near the centre of the high. Also known as an anticyclone.

Hurricane
This the term used in the North Atlantic Ocean, Caribbean Sea, Gulf of Mexico, and in the eastern North Pacific Ocean to describe a severe tropical cyclone having winds in excess of 64 knots (74mph) and capable of producing widespread wind damage and heavy flooding; Beaufort scale numbers 12 through 17. The same tropical cyclone is

known as a typhoon in the western Pacific and cyclone in the Indian Ocean.

Hurricane Season
The part of the year having a relatively high incidence of hurricanes. The hurricane season in the Atlantic, Caribbean and Gulf of Mexico runs from June 1 to November 30.

Hurricane Warning
A formal advisory issued by hurricane forecasters when they have determined that hurricane conditions are expected in a coastal area or group of islands within a 24 hour period. A warning is used to inform the public and marine interests of the storm's location, intensity, and movement. At this point residents should have completed the necessary preparations for the storm.

Hurricane Watch
A formal advisory issued by forecasters when they have determined that hurricane conditions are a potential threat to a coastal area or group of islands within 24 to 36 hour period. A watch is used to inform the public and marine interest of the storm's location, intensity, and movement and residents of the area should be prepared.

Knot
The unit of speed in the nautical system; one nautical mile per hour. It is equal to 1.1508 statute miles per hour or 0.5144 meters per second.

Landfall
The intersection of the surface center of a tropical cyclone with a coastline. Because the strongest winds in a tropical cyclone are not located precisely at the center. It is possible for a cyclone's strongest winds to be experienced over land even if landfall does not occur. Similarly, it is possible for a tropical cyclone to make landfall and have its strongest winds remain over the water.

Latent Heat
The energy released or absorbed during a change of state or quite simply, the energy stored when water evaporates into vapor or ice melts into liquid. It is released as heat when water vapor condenses or water freezes.

Lightning
A sudden and visible discharge of electricity produced in response to the build up of electrical potential between cloud and ground, between clouds, within a single cloud, or between a cloud and surrounding air within a cumulo-nimbus cloud.

Low
An area of low barometric pressure, with its attendant system of winds. Also called a depression or cyclone.

Meteorologist
A scientist who studies and predicts the weather by looking at what is happening in the atmosphere.

Meteorology
The study of the atmosphere and the atmospheric phenomena as well as the atmosphere's interaction with the earth's surface, oceans, and life in general.

Millibar
A unit of pressure, which directly expresses the force exerted by the atmosphere. Equal to 1000 dynes/cm^2 or 100Pascals.

National Hurricane Center
The National Weather Service office in Coral Gables, Florida, that tracks and forecasts hurricanes and other weather in the Atlantic, Gulf of Mexico, Caribbean Sea, and parts of the Pacific.

National Weather Service
The federal agency that observes and forecasts weather. Formerly the U.S. Weather Bureau, it is part of the National Oceanic and

Atmospheric Administration, which is part of the Department of Commerce.

NOAA
National Oceanic and Atmospheric Administration.

Precipitation
Any and all forms of water particles, liquid or solid, that falls from the atmosphere and reach the ground.

Radar
Acronym for RAdio Detection And Ranging. An electronic instrument used to detect objects (such as falling precipitation) by their ability to reflect and scatter microwaves back to a receiver.

Rain
This is the amount of precipitation of any type, primarily liquid. It is usually the amount that is measured by a rain gauge. Precipitation composed of liquid water drops of more than 0.5 mm in diameter, falling in relatively straight, but not necessarily vertical, paths.

Rain gauge
Instrument for measuring the depth of water from precipitation that is assumed to be distributed over a horizontal, impervious surface and not subject to evaporation and measured during a given time interval. Measurement is done in hundredths of inches(0.01").

Reconnaissance Aircraft
This is an aircraft, which flies directly into the eye of a hurricane to make a preliminary survey to gain information about a hurricane using advanced meteorological instruments.

Saffir-Simpson Hurricane Wind Scale
A scale relating a hurricane's winds to the possible damage it is capable of inflicting and it was first introduced in 1971 by Herbert Saffir and Robert Simpson.

Satellite
Any object that orbits a celestial body, such as a moon. However, the term is often used in reference to the manufactured objects that orbit the earth, either in geostationary or a polar manner. Some information that is gathered by weather satellites, such as GOES9, includes upper air, temperatures and humidity, recording the temperatures of cloud tops, land, and ocean, monitoring the movement of clouds top determines upper level wind speeds, tracing the movement of water vapour, monitoring the sun and solar activity, and relaying data from weather instruments around the world.

Satellite Images
Images taken by weather satellite that reveal information, such as the flow of water vapour, the movement of frontal systems, and the development of a tropical system.

Shower
Precipitation from a cumuliform cloud. Characterized by the suddenness of beginning and ending, by the rapid change in intensity, and usually by a rapid change in the condition of the sky. The solid or liquid water particles are usually bigger than the corresponding elements in other types of precipitation and usually lasts less than an hour in duration.

Storm
An individual low pressure disturbance, complete with winds, clouds, and precipitation. Wind with a speed between 56 and 63 knots (64 and 72 mph); Beaufort scale number 11.

Storm Surge
This is the mound or rise in ocean water drawn up by the low pressure below a hurricane; it causes enormous waves and widespread damage if the hurricane reaches land.

Storm tide
The actual level of sea water resulting from the astronomic tide combined with the storm surge.

Swells
Ocean waves that have travelled out of their generating area. Swells characteristically exhibits a more regular and longer period and has a flatter wave crests than waves within their fetch.

Temperature
In thermodynamics, the integrating factor of the differential equation referred to as the first law of thermodynamics, in statistical mechanics, a measure of translational molecular kinetic energy (with three degrees of freedom). In general, the degree of hotness or coldness of a body as measured on some definite temperature scale by means of any of various types of thermometers.

Thunderstorm
A local storm produced by cumulonimbus clouds and always accompanied by lightning and thunder.

Tornado
The name given to a very strong and damaging whirlwind with a clearly visible dark, snake-like funnel extending from a cumulonimbus cloud to the ground. The track of a tornado at the ground level is rarely very wide, but buildings, trees, and crops may be totally devastated.

Tropics
The region of the earth located between the tropic of Cancer, at 23.5 degrees North Latitude, and the Tropic of Capricorn, at 23.5 degrees South latitude. It encompasses the equatorial region, an area of high temperatures and considerable precipitation during part of the year.

Tropical depression
A mass of thunderstorms and clouds generally with a cyclonic wind circulation between 20 and 34 knots.

Tropical disturbance
An organized mass of thunderstorms with a slight cyclonic wind circulation of less than 20 knots. It is a moving area of thunderstorms, which maintains its identity for 24 hours or more.

Tropical storm
A storm that forms over warm waters, with spinning winds between 40 and 73 miles per hour.

Tropical Wave
An inverted, migratory wave-like disturbance or trough in the tropical region that moves from east to west, generally creating only a shift in winds and rain. The low level convergence and associated convective weather occur on the eastern side of the wave axis. Normally it moves slower than the atmospheric current in which it is embedded and is considered a weak trough of low pressure. Tropical waves occasionally intensify into tropical cyclones. They are also called Easterly Waves.

Tropical Storm Watch
A tropical Storm Watch is issued when tropical storm conditions, including winds from 39 to 73 mph (35 to 64 knots) pose a possible threat to a specified coastal area within 36 hours.

Tropical Storm Warning
A tropical storm warning is issued when tropical storm conditions, including winds from 39 to 73 mph (35 to 64 knots) are expected in a specified coastal area within 24 hours or less.

Typhoon
The name given in the Western Pacific and particularly in the China Sea to violent tropical storms or cyclones with maximum sustained winds of 74 miles per hour or higher. This same tropical cyclone is known as a hurricane in the eastern North Pacific and North Atlantic Ocean, and as a cyclone in the Indian Ocean.

Weather
The state of the atmosphere, mainly with respect to its effects upon life and human activities. As distinguished from climate, weather consists of the short-term (minutes to months) variations of the atmosphere.

Willy Willies

A colloquial Australian term for a violent tropical storm or cyclone affecting the coast of northern Australia.

Wind

Air in motion relative to the surface of the earth. Almost exclusively used to denote the horizontal component.

Wind direction

The direction from which the wind is blowing, measured in points of the compass or in azimuth degrees.

Wind Shear

The rate of the wind speed or direction change with distance. Vertical wind shear is the rate of change of the wind with respect to altitude. Horizontal wind shear is the rate of change on a horizontal plane. Directional shear is a frequent change in direction within a short distance, which can also occur vertically or horizontally.

World Meteorological Organization (WMO)

This is the governing sub-body for meteorology within The United Nations made up of 185 member states and territories. It succeeded the International Meteorological Organization, which was founded in 1873. It is the United Nations system's authoritative voice on the state and behaviour of the Earth's atmosphere, its interaction with the oceans, the climate it produces and the resulting distribution of water resources.

Printed in the United States
by Baker & Taylor Publisher Services